the Mad keen Fisherman's Road Trip

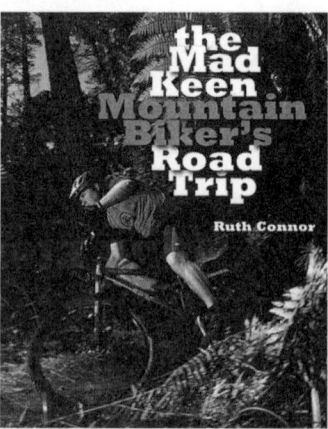

the Mad Keen Fisherman's Road Trip

36 trips to New Zealand's best salt- and freshwater fishing spots

John Eichelsheim

RANDOM HOUSE
NEW ZEALAND

A catalogue record for this book is available from the National Library of New Zealand

A RANDOM HOUSE BOOK
published by
Random House New Zealand
18 Poland Road, Glenfield, Auckland, New Zealand
www.randomhouse.co.nz

Random House International
Random House
20 Vauxhall Bridge Road
London, SW1V 2SA
United Kingdom

Random House Australia (Pty) Ltd
20 Alfred Street, Milsons Point, Sydney,
New South Wales 2061, Australia

Random House South Africa Pty Ltd
Isle of Houghton
Corner Boundary Road and Carse O'Gowrie
Houghton 2198, South Africa

Random House Publishers India Private Ltd
301 World Trade Tower, Hotel Intercontinental Grand Complex,
Barakhamba Lane, New Delhi 110 001, India

First published 2007

ISBN 978 1 86941 906 6

Maps and icons: Deborah Hinde
Cover and text design: Nick Turzynski, redinc., Auckland
Cover illustration: Corbis
Printed in China by Everbest Printing Co Ltd

Acknowledgements

This book was largely written in a blur of early mornings, usually in the quiet, pre-dawn hours before my family awoke.

Nonetheless, it is to my wife Megan and daughter Mila that I'd like to dedicate *The Mad Keen Fisherman's Road Trip*. Because, though they may have slept on while I wrote, my little family still had to put up with my increasingly sleep-deprived and grumpy disposition. To their credit and my extreme gratitude, neither of them complained . . . much.

As Random House's deadline rapidly approached, I certainly began to wonder what on earth possessed me to agree to write my first book 'in my spare time' while also working flat out to survive my first year as a freelance writer. It seemed my every waking hour was spent in my cramped home office staring at a computer screen.

But when the corrected proofs came back to me, I'll admit to feeling a certain sense of accomplishment, along with a great deal of respect for my copy editor, Bronwyn Sell, who did a fantastic job of culling out the dross. Bronwyn was also remarkably tolerant of the many quirks of my writing style and I thank her for her sympathetic handling of the manuscript and her unfailing rigour in checking details — memory is not always reliable, especially mine, and anyway, things change with time.

I'd also like to thank my editor, Sarah Ell — always upbeat and supportive — and also Tim Porter, my old boss at Fairfax Magazines. It was Tim who set Sarah onto me, and once she got hold she wasn't letting go.

Finally, I'd like to acknowledge the many fishing friends and acquaintances whose company I've enjoyed over the years. I shared road trips with many of them and it's possible they'll recognise some of the places described in this book. They've all contributed to it in some way, along with colleagues, friends and fellow fishos who supplied current information on locations I haven't visited in a while. Thanks.

Contents

Foreword

New Zealand is an angler's paradise. The keen Kiwi fisho has so many options, so many places to go and such a variety of fishing to enjoy, much of it in spectacular surroundings.

When Random House invited me to compile this book, based on an extended angling road trip or a series of fishing weekends, I thought, 'Great — I've done thousands of those.'

I've been a mad-keen angler from birth — I love any sort of fishing, saltwater or fresh. It has shaped my life, at various times determining where I lived and guiding my career choices. But even after 30-plus years of fishing, travelling and writing about fishing, when I started this book I quickly realised I'd barely scratched the surface of what's available in New Zealand.

On the other hand, in that time I've managed to see a lot of the country and sample plenty of fishing as part of my job, which has at various times included fishing writer, magazine editor and freelance marine journalist. I've seen more of this country's fishing than most.

And that was just during the week. On weekends my friends and I went fishing — a sort of busman's holiday. Fishing weekends were my life!

Family responsibilities came to me late but once my daughter was born I found days on the road (and on the water) suddenly curtailed. It came as a slight surprise to me to learn that fishing wasn't everybody's idea of the best way to spend a weekend. Nowadays I have to work my fishing around activities the rest of the family enjoys.

That's the basis for this book, really. It's about places to go fishing but it's also about the other things a family or couple might enjoy while they're there. So the majority of entries in this little guide are not too far off the beaten track and offer a range of non-fishing activities. OK, there are a couple of exceptions — I couldn't resist reliving a few of my old days as a mad-keen single angler — but I guess that helps justify the 'keen' in the book's title.

But even the locations with the most 'other' things to do — Rotorua, for instance — were still selected primarily because they offered great fishing. The reader will find plenty of angling action to enjoy at each of the locations chosen for this book and much else besides.

The selection is also personal; they're places I can recommend from firsthand experience. I've visited them all and fished most of them, though it would be dishonest to claim I've fished every one recently — there simply hasn't been time.

For that reason I'm grateful to other keen fishers who helped me out here and there, and to various other sources for current information on accommodation, eating out, activities and facilities. The entries are as accurate and current as I could make them, though by no means comprehensive.

The internet also proved an extremely useful resource. I have listed a number of handy sites with each entry, which should help the reader plan a weekend getaway. Hopefully you'll find places in this book your family will enjoy visiting, which means your chances of spending some of the time fishing are much improved!

Maui's fish

New Zealand contains a lifetime's worth of fishing opportunities. In fact, one could spend a whole lifetime just exploring the North Island without ever visiting the South Island or vice versa.

The North Island's coastal geography encompasses rugged West Coast beaches, headlands, harbours, islands and bays; rocky shorelines, large, deep harbours, gulfs and extensive island complexes. Inland lie numerous lakes and rivers, including New Zealand's largest examples: Lake Taupo and the Waikato River.

The North Island's fiery heart is full of volcanoes and thermal wonders. It's also home to trout — lots of them. The introduced rainbow trout is king and the Taupo–Rotorua region has some of the best trout fishing in the world.

Elsewhere, wilderness rivers rush through steep valleys in bush-clad mountain ranges, challenging the adventurous and fit angler, while other waters offer more accessible fishing, often right in town.

The ocean is the North Islander's playground, especially in the north where the weather is milder and sea conditions generally more benign. The island's huge diversity and length of coastline, its numerous islands and many sheltered harbours offer the sea angler an abundance of angling choice. New Zealand has one of the world's highest rates of per capita boat ownership and most of those boats are engaged in fishing for fun at some point in their lives. Shore fishing is popular and effective.

A fisher's canoe

Its Maori inhabitants variously call the South Island of New Zealand Te Wai Pounamu, Te Waka o Maui and Te Waka o Aoraki.

The first roughly translates as 'greenstone waters' but it's the last two that appeal to the fisherman in me.

'Te waka' means 'the canoe' and everyone knows fishers use canoes. Indeed, the great Polynesian hero Maui is said to have fished the North Island — Te Ika a Maui, 'the great fish of Maui' — from the Pacific Ocean using the South Island as his waka. (The third name refers to a god called Aoraki who once mispronounced a karakia or prayer, turning him, his waka and his brothers into stone, thus creating Mt Cook.)

Fittingly, the South Island remains a great place from which to fish; it's rivers and lakes are home to trophy trout and its rugged coasts offer a variety and abundance of marine life.

Best of all, for a North Islander such as me a fishing safari to the South Island is a total break with the familiar: different scenery, different fish species and a different way of life. It's almost like travelling to another country except that the language is the same, almost — those Southlanders sound a bit strange!

The biggest challenge in planning a fishing road trip to the South Island is the sheer over-abundance of excellent fishing opportunities. For someone who can't help but peer over every highway bridge to glimpse the river below, the South Island quickly induces a crick in the neck. There are so many rivers, most of them full of fishy potential that a bridge-peerer soon finds himself in need of a neck brace.

It would take a lifetime of weekends and more to truly explore the South Island's fishing. Like most people, I don't have that kind of time so for this book I've picked out a few reasonably accessible, family-friendly locations where I've enjoyed good fishing in the past. For the more adventurous, a bit of exploring in virtually any direction from the places mentioned in these pages will put the keen angler onto yet more great fishing.

Living in New Zealand can be such a trial!

John Eichelsheim

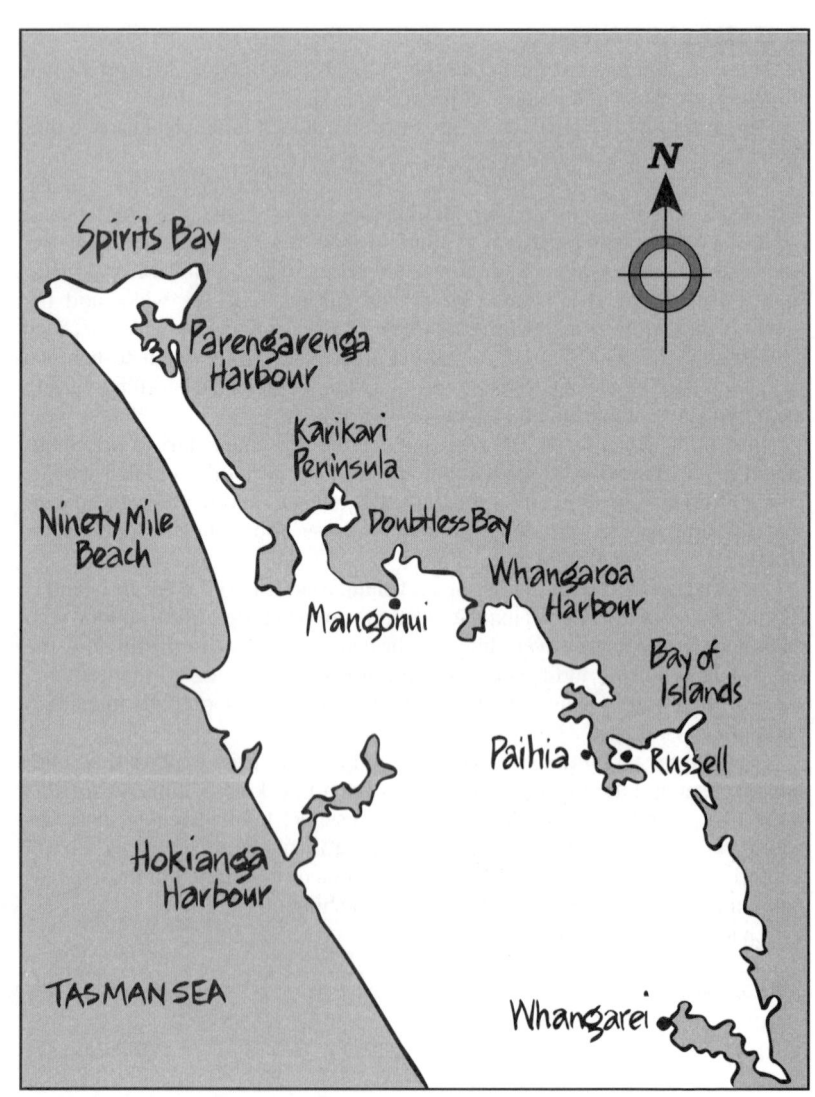

the Far North

The Far North is a narrow land flanked by mighty oceans, magnificent beaches, sweeping bays and spectacular harbours. Bordered on the west by the Tasman Sea and the east by the South Pacific Ocean, this loosely defined region stretches from a line somewhere just south of the Bay of Islands across to the Hokianga Harbour, and northwards to spectacular Cape Reinga where sea and ocean meet.

The Far North has great spiritual significance for Maori, who believe the souls of the dead leave New Zealand's shores at Cape Reinga, leaping from the branches of a sacred pohutukawa on their way to legendary Hawaiki.

The Far North is also a fisher's paradise and for this reason, as well as geographical tidiness, it's a sensible place to start this book.

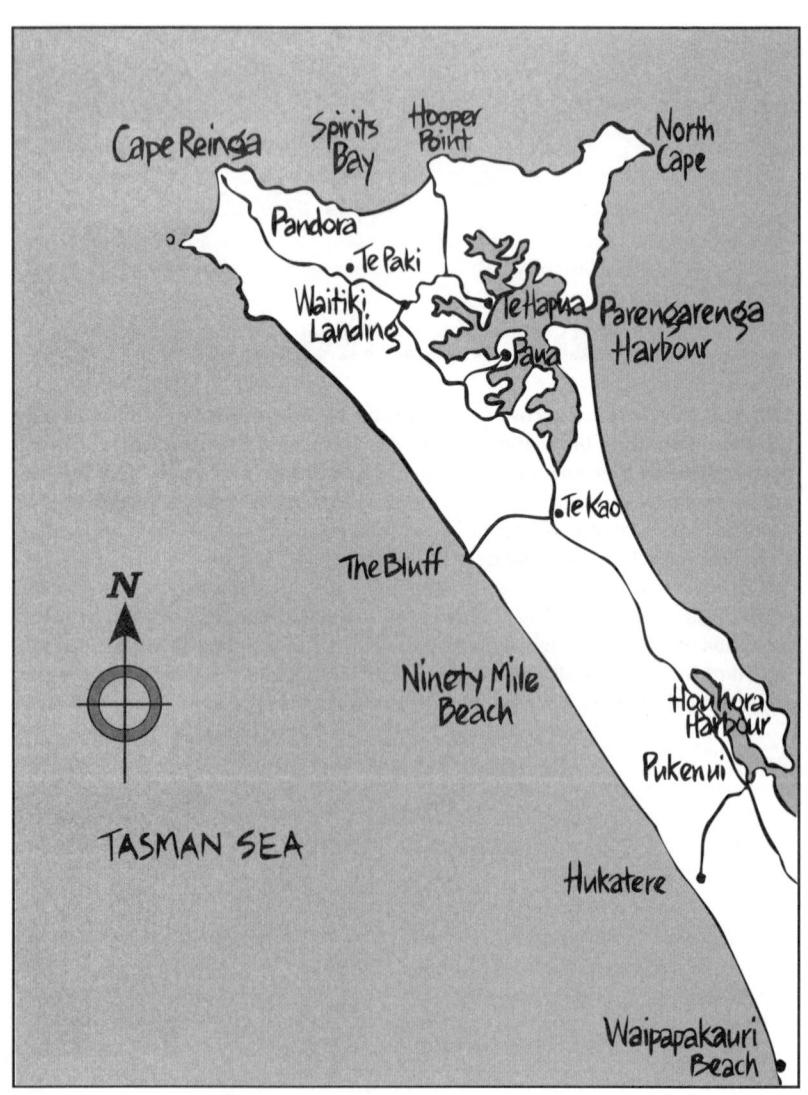

1

Spirits Bay and Parengarenga Harbour

Whether one believes in Maori tradition or not, there is something eerie about Spirits Bay, especially at night. At times the play of moonlight and shadow on the steep slopes of Maunga Piko, the mountain that defines the eastern end of the bay, and the almost constant keening of the wind in the cabbage trees and kanuka, can turn your mind towards things spiritual.

Fortunately, for me at least, the bay's often-spectacular fishing is a foolproof distraction. Spirits Bay, Kapowairua in Maori, is at the end of the road. It's as far north as you can drive in the North Island — a smidgen higher than the spot where State Highway 1 ends at Cape Reinga, though there's not much in it.

From Auckland it's a seven-hour drive on State Highway 1 to Waitiki Landing then another 20 minutes or so to the campground at Spirits Bay. I always like to make a Spirits Bay weekend a long one by adding a day or two to make the drive worthwhile.

From the turn-off at Waitiki Landing a gravel road winds down through kanuka scrub to a Department of Conservation campground at the bottom of the valley, directly behind the sand dunes.

Facilities are rudimentary — long-drop toilets and piped fresh water — but camp fees are minimal. Honesty boxes are scattered around the campground, which extends well away from the beach and under the canopy of large kanuka trees and the occasional pohutukawa. Every couple of days a DOC ranger drops by to collect camp fees — more regularly during summer holidays, when the camp can be very crowded. But go in August or September and sometimes you have the whole magnificent bay to yourself.

 The fishing — Spirits Bay

Spirits offers the fisher plenty of choice. The golden sand beach sweeps for several kilometres westward, slowly bending northwest towards Pandora, a small beach separated from Spirits by a rocky headland. There's good surf fishing all along its length with rock fishing at either end, though the walk along the entire beach to Pandora takes two or three hours.

Surf fishers do best at dusk and dawn. The ability to read a beach is an advantage, of course, but the beach at Spirits drops away fairly steeply so gutters and sandbanks are not often apparent.

Sheltered from the swell by Pananehe Island, the campground end of the beach is sometimes fishable when big seas render everywhere else too difficult or too dangerous. The island is popular with rock fishers. Jutting out into the bay from the beach opposite the campground, it's accessible on foot at low tide but is cut off from the beach for several hours either side of high tide.

Fishing from the end or off the sides can be good, particularly for kahawai and trevally. Snapper are not uncommon, especially at change of light, while large sharks can make a nuisance of themselves at times. Big kingfish are caught here too, though it's not as famous for kingfish as some of the ledges on the mainland.

Rocky platforms facing on the bay's eastern side can provide excellent fishing. The best spots require a tramp over the hills to skirt deep gutters, though it's possible to reach the best-known platform, Rod Holders, at low tide by wading across the gutters.

The best fishing is right on the eastern point — Hooper Point — and on other, unnamed promontories further around, but access on foot requires a steep climb over the ridge and down precarious goat tracks. In any sort of swell, Hooper becomes too dangerous to fish.

Rod Holders, named for the concrete rodholders set into cracks in the rocks by club anglers in the 1970s, is best known for its kingfish. Large specimens cruise past the ledge and past Buck's Ledge a bit further around. They can be targeted with kahawai livebaits, poppers and jigs.

Baitfishing on the bottom will turn up snapper (especially in winter), sharks and trevally. Kahawai are common and even skipjack tuna have been taken from the rocks here.

Spirits Bay is usually considered a shore-fishing destination. With direct access to the beach blocked by sand dunes, launching boats of any size is impractical. However, the lagoon formed behind the sand dunes, home to mullet, flounder and native fish, sometimes carves a channel out to the sea. It's also the source of the bay's notorious mosquitoes. Dinghies and inflatables can be launched in the creek, floated down to the beach and dragged over the sand to the sea.

Boat fishing can be exceptionally good. A reef in the middle of the bay within easy reach of small boats can produce excellent snapper and kingfish and the full range of other northern species. In summer, large schools of skipjack tuna sometimes enter the bay, providing great sport and a welcome source of bait.

Camping at Spirits Bay is an enjoyable experience when the weather's good. But you need to be well organised, with your own cooking equipment, light and ice. Alternatively, Waitiki Landing offers comfortable accommodation, meals, fuel and groceries. It's only 18 km from Spirits Bay and strategically positioned to explore other areas, including Parengarenga Harbour.

 ## The fishing — Parengarenga

Parengarenga Harbour is New Zealand's northernmost harbour and also its most pristine. White sand and a huge expanse of clear, fishable water make it an attractive destination for anglers. It has a tricky entrance so boaties need to take care if they wish to leave the harbour to explore the coast up towards North Cape. Often the bar breaks all the way across, making it totally unworkable, and care should be exercised if there's any sort of swell. One of the beauties of Parengarenga Harbour is that it's fishable when much of the rest of the coast is not. Sometimes, when Spirits Bay, Tapotupotu and other land-based fishing spots are out due to wind or swell, it's still possible to wet a line at Parengarenga.

There are two access points: off State Highway 1 at Paua Road, which will take you down to Paua Wharf, a very basic campground and rough boat ramp; or by turning right at Waitiki Landing and following the signs to Te Hapua. Like Paua, Te Hapua has a wharf.

While neither of them looks particularly impressive, both can offer superb fishing for snapper, kingfish, trevally, rays and sharks. In general, wharf fishing is better on a rising tide but, since both wharves access deep channels, they can be fished at all stages of the tide. Dusk and dawn are good times to try your luck.

Boat fishing inside the harbour can be excellent. Small boats and kayaks are suitable, though they should stay well clear of strong, treacherous tidal currents in the area around the harbour entrance.

The gate to the boat ramp at Paua is locked but keys are available from Te

Kao Store, 09 409 8866, for a small fee.

Larger boats can explore the harbour. There's good snapper fishing on the flats and into the mangroves on a rising tide, plenty of kingfish on the edges of the channels and fantastic john dory fishing almost everywhere in spring.

 ## Things to do

A weekend isn't just about fishing. But Spirits Bay and Parengarenga Harbour are quite a way off the beaten track so the range of non-fishing activities isn't extensive. However, from a base at Waitiki Landing or the campgrounds at Spirits Bay or Paua it's an easy hop across the peninsula to Ninety Mile Beach.

Spirits Bay offers gorgeous walks and as much beach as anyone could wish for, and there are other magnificent beaches within 30 minutes' drive.

If camping isn't your thing, consider basing yourself at the harbour town of Houhora, 30-odd kilometres to the south. Houhora offers a range of accommodation options, from hotel and motel beds to lodge and homestay accommodation. There are also shops, takeaways and restaurants in town. It's an excellent base from which to explore both coasts.

Houhora has excellent fishing in its own right, inside the sheltered harbour and outside, either up the coast towards Henderson Bay or down towards the Karikari Peninsula. The wharf is a popular fishing spot with visitors and locals — fishing livebaits on the bottom on a rising tide produces kingfish in summer and john dory in winter. Kahawai, snapper and trevally are available year-round. Good boat ramps by the wharf and down the harbour at the Big Game Fishing Club can accommodate trailer boats of any size.

 ## Accommodation

Campgrounds at Kapowairua (DOC), Tapotupotu (DOC), Paua and Houhora (Wagener Park, 09 409 8564); cabin accommodation at Waitiki Landing and motels, B&Bs and holiday homes in Houhora. For more details, check out www.accommodationinnewzealand.co.nz.

Boat ramps

Paua (key from Te Kao Store), Houhora Wharf and Houhora Big Game Fishing Club. Launching for dinghies and inflatables at Spirits Bay and Tapotupotu.

Ninety Mile Beach

No guide to fishing the Far North would be complete without the Ninety. Extending 60 km from Scott Point in the north to Ahipara Bay in the south, it is New Zealand's second-longest (after Ripiro) beach.

Access to this vast expanse of sand can be gained at Ahipara and Waipapakauri in the south, Hukatere via Raio in the middle and The Bluff via Te Kao in the north. To reach Ahipara turn off State Highway 1 at Kaitaia. Raio and Te Kao are on the main road north from Awanui.

The beach is designated a highway and all the normal rules of the road apply, including the speed limit. It can be driven its full length but a rising tide steadily reduces the width of driveable beach.

Driving on the beach can be dangerous at any tide; rogue waves known as sweepers can swamp unwary vehicles, and streams, logs, soft sand and other dangers can trap inexperienced drivers. Stick to the edge of the damp sand and stay far enough away from the water's edge to avoid sweepers.

 The fishing

Ninety Mile Beach is famous for its surfcasting. Every year New Zealand's largest fishing contest is held there, attracting thousands of keen anglers from New Zealand and overseas. Snapper is the species of choice among Ninety Mile Beach anglers but the surf also yields kahawai, trevally, parore (black snapper), sharks and rays, along with the occasional kingfish.

Beach fishing is a specialised skill and the most successful anglers on the Ninety have honed their craft over years of fishing the gutters and holes along its length. However, visitors can enjoy good success simply by using their eyes and choosing fishing spots carefully.

To fish the beach properly, drive along it looking for gutters and holes formed by the surf. Usually these areas are betrayed by gaps in the surf break, indicating deeper water just offshore. Cast into the calmer areas.

Reading a beach is an acquired skill but newcomers can try fishing at The Bluff, where beach knowledge is less important. The Bluff is a rocky outcrop two-thirds of the way up the beach, the only such feature along its entire length. It attracts a lot of fish into a small area and can be excellent for trevally and snapper.

It's possible to fish from the rocks of The Bluff in calm conditions or from the beach on either side. Trevally grow large here and parore sometimes snaffle every bait, especially if tuatua is used. But when the snapper are on, The Bluff can be fantastic.

Baits for the Ninety include the usual fish baits of pilchard and mullet. Squid is good and octopus is popular with snapper specialists, since it attracts fewer kahawai, sharks and rays. Probably the most popular is tuatua, the main food source for all the fish that patrol the beach. Tuatua are easy to find all along the beach at low tide. Gathering bait usually takes just a few minutes.

In general, fish-flesh baits tend to attract kahawai, sharks, snapper and rays. Squid and octopus are good snapper bait and tuatua is attractive to everything except sharks.

Boat fishing takes a back seat to surfcasting on this coast but locals regularly launch into the surf at Shipwreck Bay, just south of Ahipara. It's possible to launch quite large craft with a tractor at Shipwreck in good conditions but local knowledge is important and the surf can be treacherous.

Locals and visitors occasionally launch off the beach at The Bluff. A tractor or capable four-wheel drive is essential to negotiate the sandy track through the dunes from where the road from Te Kao ends. The Bluff offers some shelter on each side, with the northern side the safer option. Conditions must be near perfect for safe launching and boaties need to be aware of changing conditions — if the swell picks up it can be extremely difficult to retrieve boats off the beach.

 **Things to do**

Like most of the Far North hotspots featured here, the Ninety is close to a variety of fishing and other outdoor activities. The isthmus is narrow so it's an easy drive to east coast beaches for a change of scenery or if the wind is blowing too hard from the west. If it's good coffee you want, Houhora isn't far away or else take the road to Awanui or Kaitaia. Kaitaia also has its fair share of interesting attractions, including antique shops and museums.

A drive up the Ninety is worth it just for the experience but give yourself a few hours to do it justice. Visitors can also catch one of the many tours that pass through the area, running up to Cape Reinga, including quad bike and sand buggy tours.

Accommodation

Campgrounds at The Park, Waipapakauri and Kaitaia; baches/beach houses, backpackers, hotel, motel, B&Bs at Ahipara and in Kaitaia and Awanui; lodge at Te Kao; and numerous farmstays and alternative accommodation. The Park at Waipapakauri, 09 406 7298, has a bar, restaurant, comfortable and well-priced rooms, cabins and a campground. There are even boat-washing and fish-cleaning facilities.

For a comprehensive guide to options, check out www.tourism.net.nz/region/northland/accommodation.

Boat ramps

Beach launching at Shipwreck Bay, Waipapakauri and The Bluff. There's a boat ramp for the east coast at Awanui.

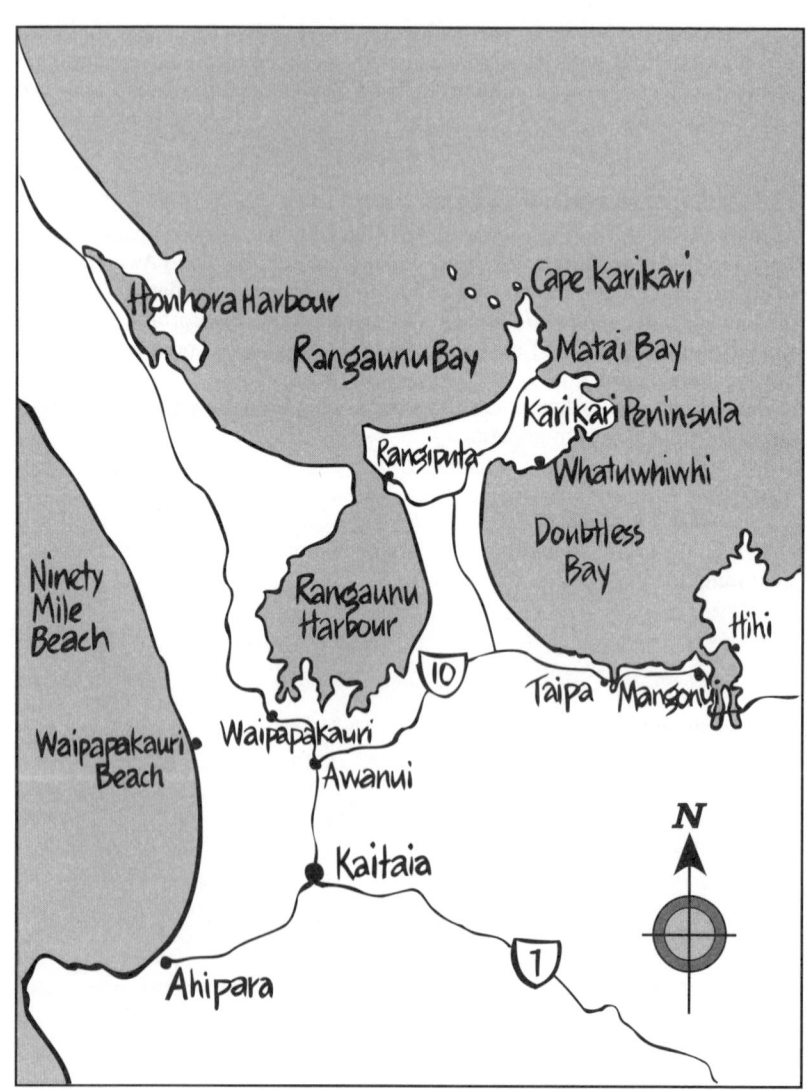

Mangonui, Doubtless Bay and Karikari Peninsula

Mangonui holds a special place in my heart. For several halcyon years in the late 1970s and early 1980s, I travelled there each summer with a group of friends from our homes in Wellington. We would stay for several weeks and fish almost exclusively for kingfish from the wharf that juts into the harbour.

While we can't claim to have discovered the exceptional kingfishing, the techniques we used and our success rate were a revelation for local and visiting anglers alike. As the years went by, Mangonui Wharf fishers became more and more switched on, the wharf became more crowded and, inevitably I suppose, the catch rate began to drop off.

Although just a shadow of its former glory, Mangonui, like Houhora, still has the occasional good run of kingfish into the harbour during summer and autumn. And when the fish are in, the wharf turns on fantastic fishing.

About four hours' drive north of Auckland, Mangonui is a pretty little town right on the edge of the harbour. Like the harbour itself, the town is small, though it has spread along the road north with new beachfront developments at Coopers Beach and Cable Bay.

The town features a character-filled pub, restaurants, takeaways, craft shops, a petrol station and grocery stores. There's also the famous Mangonui Fish Shop, built on stilts over the water, which serves up fish and chips that are regularly judged the best in New Zealand. Sitting beside the harbour enjoying a feed of fresh fish or delicious seafood is part of the Far North experience.

Mangonui is no longer on the main road, State Highway 10, as a few years ago the town was bypassed. This reduced traffic through the narrow harbourside road, making it safer for pedestrians, but the nature of the town has changed. Some larger service businesses have migrated up to Coopers Beach on the main drag, leaving the town to more tourist-orientated boutique shops.

The fishing

Boat fishers are spoiled for choice. There's good fishing inside Mangonui Harbour for snapper, kahawai, john dory and kingfish. Baits of piper, pilchard and skipjack produce snapper and some huge rays, while live jack mackerel fished on the bottom will turn up kingfish and john dory.

Outside the harbour, Doubtless Bay offers a huge expanse of water with excellent fishing for all northern species, especially around reef complexes scattered through the bay. The best known are Albert Reef and Fairway Reef, both well out in the bay, but there are smaller areas of foul ground within easy reach of small boats on a good day.

At the northern end of the bay, Karikari Peninsula offers excellent fishing. Its rugged, indented coast is studded with rocks and foul ground, making it a haven for snapper and other reef species. The points are a sure bet for kingfish while the blue water laps against the peninsula in summer, bringing tuna and marlin close to the rocks and into Doubtless Bay.

At the other end of the bay, Berghan Point is an obvious landmark. The rocky coastline all the way out to the point produces good snapper fishing in close, when school fish are common out in the bay. At times large schools of kingfish foam on the surface and jigging can be fantastic.

The land-based fisher has plenty of choice too. While the wharf is hard to go past when the kingfish are on, there are several other good spots around the harbour to target kingis and other species. Live bait is the key to kingfish success, though fresh piper is almost as good, and the best kingfishing is invariably on the rising tide.

Even if you intend to fish elsewhere, catch your live bait at the wharf. A few live mackerel in a bucket of seawater will survive transportation and storage, provided the water is changed regularly.

Livebaits are easiest to catch early in the morning before the sun comes up. At times the water out in the channel foams with thousands of mackerel feeding under the wharf lights before dawn.

As the light gets stronger they move into the shelter of the wharf's piles and become increasingly difficult to catch. They may be impossible to snare in the middle of the day.

Bait flies or sabikis work best. Sweeten them with small baits of squid if bait fishing is tough.

Livebaits can be fished from the wharf or transported elsewhere. To catch kingfish, fish livies on the bottom. A 7/0 hook on a short trace of around a metre and a six-ounce (170 g) sinker above a swivel should do the trick. From the wharf, 15 kg line or heavier is mandatory for kingfish; 10 kg is fine if fishing from a boat.

Other spots to try include the small wharf at Mill Bay. This produces a few kingfish at times and some nice snapper to cut baits cast well out. John dory is almost a certainty here. It's usually less crowded too.

The rocks at the harbour entrance on the western side are an easy climb through bush and scrub from the road end at Rangikapiti Pa. Once at water level you have the option of fishing out into the bay or into the harbour. Currents can be strong and the bottom is very foul, especially fishing into the harbour, but snapper, kahawai and kingfish are taken consistently. Try spinning for kahawai and kingfish.

Kahawai can be taken from numerous points and bays around the harbour, with snapper accessible wherever a channel is in casting distance from the shore. The bridge over State Highway 10 to the south is a good place to catch bait and also produces kingfish at the top of the tide.

Beach fishing from Coopers Beach, Cable Bay and further round at Tokerau Beach and on the other side of Karikari at Puheke can be productive; scallops are sometimes washed up on the beaches after a big blow. The small rocky points between beaches at the western end of Doubtless Bay are worth fishing too.

Things to do

Aside from the craft shops, good coffee and a pub full of character, Mangonui offers superb beaches with safe swimming and is strategically positioned within easy driving of many of the North's famous attractions. Karikari Peninsula is not far away and a drive to Hokianga Harbour and Waipoua Forest makes an interesting day trip.

Mangonui is on the bus route to Cape Reinga and Ninety Mile Beach. Visitors can book a range of trips, activities and charters at Coopers Beach. Fishing and sailing charters are available out of Mangonui, the harbour and bay are ideal for kayaking and there's good golfing at a number of courses nearby — Carrington on the Karikari Peninsula, with its spectacular views of Doubtless Bay and attached resort, is undoubtedly the pick of the bunch.

Aside from the fish shop, there are several interesting cafes and a couple of half-decent restaurants in Mangonui and Coopers Beach. Kaitaia is only 30 minutes away if you're looking for a pub meal or a change of scenery.

Accommodation

Campgrounds at Hihi in Mangonui Harbour, Whatuwhiwhi on the northern side of Doubtless Bay and the beautiful Matai Bay on the Karikari Peninsula (sadly, campgrounds at Taipa and Coopers Beach have given way to housing developments); baches, beach houses, B&Bs, motels, lodges, apartments and homestays in Mangonui, Mill Bay, Coopers Beach, Cable Bay and Tokerau; luxury resort accommodation at Taipa and at Carrington on the Karikari Peninsula.

Boat ramps

The launching ramp at Mill Bay in Mangonui Harbour will cope with trailer boats of most sizes. It's an all-tide ramp and the safest launching spot in the region. There are other good ramps up at Taipa and Hihi and dinghy launching is possible at a number of places in Mangonui and off the beaches. On the Karikari Peninsula, there is beach launching at Matai Bay, Whatuwhiwhi and Tokerau.

Whangaroa Harbour

Whangaroa Harbour is as historic as it is spectacular. Arguably Northland's most beautiful harbour, Whangaroa — 'long harbour' in Maori — was much fought over before and after European contact. The first European ships arrived in the early 19th century. In 1809 the ship *Boyd* was burned and its crew massacred in revenge for ill treatment of a local chief. This kept Europeans away until 1819, when the first ship arrived to load kauri.

The first permanent European settlers arrived in 1840 and by 1875 there was a thriving boat-building industry pioneered by Lane and Brown at Totara North, as well as whaling, fishing and copper mining. Almost enclosed by a narrow rock-walled entrance, Whangaroa is dominated by high volcanic breccia peaks that contrast with undulating countryside, and low sedimentary islands adjacent to high rocky ones such as Peach Island.

The harbour is an excellent deep-water anchorage and has been home for many years to a small commercial fishing, crayfishing and recreational game-fishing fleet. In the summer months Whangaroa is one of a number of important northern ports where gamefishing is king.

Aside from Kaeo, up the river a wee way from the harbour proper, the main settlements are at Whangaroa on the eastern side of the harbour and Totara North on the western side. Both offer basic services including fuel for trailer boats and launches, general supplies, foodstuffs, a pub and accommodation.

The gamefishing fleet and Whangaroa Big Gamefish Club are based in Whangaroa. The clubrooms are a good place to eat, as is the historic pub opposite. As well as providing fuel facilities, Whangaroa's wharves are the pick-up and drop-off points for various cruises, gamefish charters and other water activities. They're also a good place to wet a line and home to large schools of yellowtail, which make excellent live bait for the john dory and kingfish that also frequent the harbour.

Like most northern wharves, those at Whangaroa produce their fair share of good-sized kingfish for skilled and patient anglers.

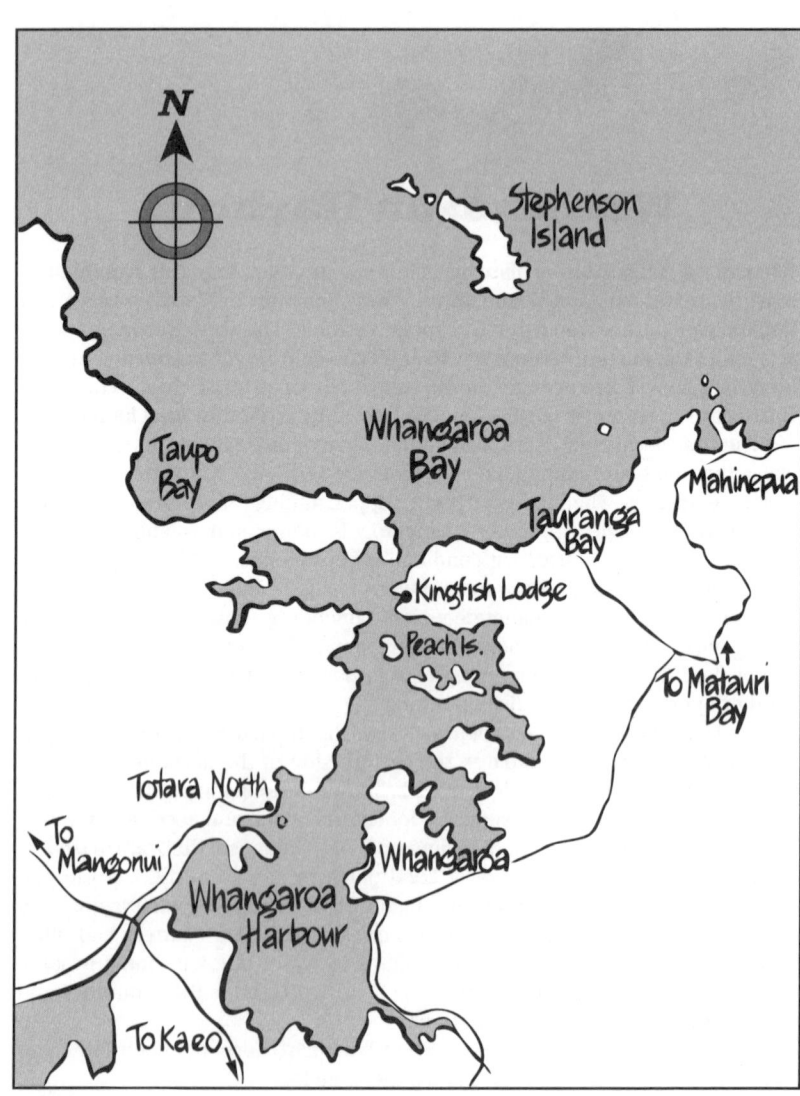

The fishing

Whangaroa is blessed with superb fishing, inside and outside the harbour. In places the harbour is deep, and swift currents are a feature near the narrow entrance. Snapper are present year-round, with the most consistent catches in summer. Trevally is a common catch in winter, along with kahawai.

Kingfish move in and out of the harbour with the tides. Land-based fishers do well from the rocky points near the entrance, accessible only by boat, and from wharves and other promontories. Boat anglers can target similar spots with livebaits or lures. John dory is a welcome bycatch.

Snapper fishing is best in the channels when the tide is running, though some big fish are taken in shallow water up on the mudflats, especially at night. Some of the better-known spots include the Haystack, Kingfish Point, the pipi beds at Peach Island and Waihi Point (Honeymoon Cottage). This last is especially well suited to small boats.

Outside the heads there's good fishing in every direction. Snapper can be targeted close to shore around the extensive reef systems east and west of the entrance, or out at Stephenson Island, which dominates Whangaroa Bay.

Stephenson is a few nautical miles from the entrance but offers a variety of fishing for all the common species. Northwest of Stephenson there is plenty of foul ground, rising to 30 m from 50 m, offering spectacular fishing at times. Deeper spots produce good hapuku fishing and kingfish are always a possibility. During the season, boats troll for marlin, which are sometimes hooked inside Stephenson, ranging up and down the coast and particularly down towards the Cavalli Islands. Much of the trolling water is within reach of trailer boats launched from Whangaroa, Taupo Bay and Tauranga Bay.

Striped, black and blue marlin are taken, as well as yellowfin, skipjack and albacore tuna and various game sharks. Charter boats and much else besides, including accommodation, can be booked at the Boyd Gallery and General Store at Whangaroa.

 # Things to do

Whangaroa is on the main tourist route north. From Kaeo you can join tour buses to Cape Reinga and Ninety Mile Beach and there are plenty of other activities available including harbour cruises, line fishing charters and of course gamefishing, in season. Kaeo has a golf course and there's another, highly exclusive, course at Kauri Cliffs, Matauri Bay, overlooking the Cavalli Islands. It's a magnificent setting, complete with luxury lodge for the well heeled.

Beaches at Te Ngaire, Matauri Bay, Tauranga Bay and Taupo Bay are first-class — typical east coast Northland with blue sea, moderate surf and golden sand fringed with pohutukawa. Some beaches have campgrounds and most offer a variety of other accommodation.

Walkers have plenty of bush and coastal tracks to choose from, including Puketi Forest and walks on the coastal loop and Mahinepua Peninsula. A popular choice is the track to the harbour's Western Arm (also known as Pekapeka Bay), starting at Totara North.

There's excellent trout fishing on the Waipapa River in Puketi Forest, as well as an interesting bush walk beside the river.

Houseboat holidays on Whangaroa might be a good way to combine fishing with cruising and sightseeing. There's also kayak hire and excellent diving, including dives on the wreck of the Greenpeace boat *Rainbow Warrior* at Matauri Bay.

Accommodation

Campgrounds at Whangaroa, Taupo Bay and Matauri Bay; a DOC hut at the Western Arm that must be booked in advance; baches, beach houses, B&Bs, motels, lodges, apartments and homestays in Whangaroa, Totara North, Taupo Bay, Matauri Bay, Mahinapua, Te Ngaire, Taupo Bay and many other settlements around the harbour and on the coast; luxury resort accommodation at Kauri Cliffs in Matauri Bay and Kingfish Lodge on Whangaroa Harbour, accessible only by private boat or water taxi.

Boat ramps

Whangaroa, Taupo Bay, Totara North; beach launching Tauranga Bay.

Hokianga Harbour

No matter which way you come — from the north via State Highway 1 through Awanui and the Mangamuka Gorge, from the Bay of Islands via Kaikohe or from the south on State Highway 12 through Dargaville and the Waipoua Forest — the Hokianga is an impressive sight.

One of the country's largest harbours, its deeply indented shoreline, labyrinthine inlets and mangrove-filled upper reaches empty into the Tasman Sea through a narrow entrance at Opononi, where the currents are fierce. Opposite Opononi village, towering dunes of golden sand dominate the northern side of the harbour. They are the Hokianga's trademark.

Long a popular holiday destination, Hokianga Harbour offers good fishing in its relatively sheltered, though swiftly flowing, waters and superb fishing for a variety of species outside. In addition there's Northland's best trout fishing in the rivers and streams feeding the harbour and draining the Waipoua Forest, whose tall trees shade the trout streams, ensuring cool water year-round. Around the harbour a number of isolated settlements occupy headlands and bays. On the northern side the principal one is Kohukohu, linked to Rawene on the southern side by vehicular ferry. The northern settlements face the water, linked by narrow and often rudimentary metal roads. The rugged countryside is backed by native bush and scrub, one of the wildest areas of Northland.

Rawene is well up the harbour, positioned at the end of a peninsula on a minor road, like so many other small settlements on the Hokianga. Out towards the heads, back on the main road, Opononi and Omapere are the largest settlements, one merging into the other as holiday houses, baches and permanent dwellings spread along the waterfront.

Opononi and Omapere are well endowed with accommodation and offer basic supplies. You can get petrol and frozen bait in the area and a cold beer at one of several pubs. The closest town of any size is Kaikohe, some 60-odd kilometres distant, which also has a domestic airport.

If you're contemplating crossing the notorious Hokianga bar, try to cross in

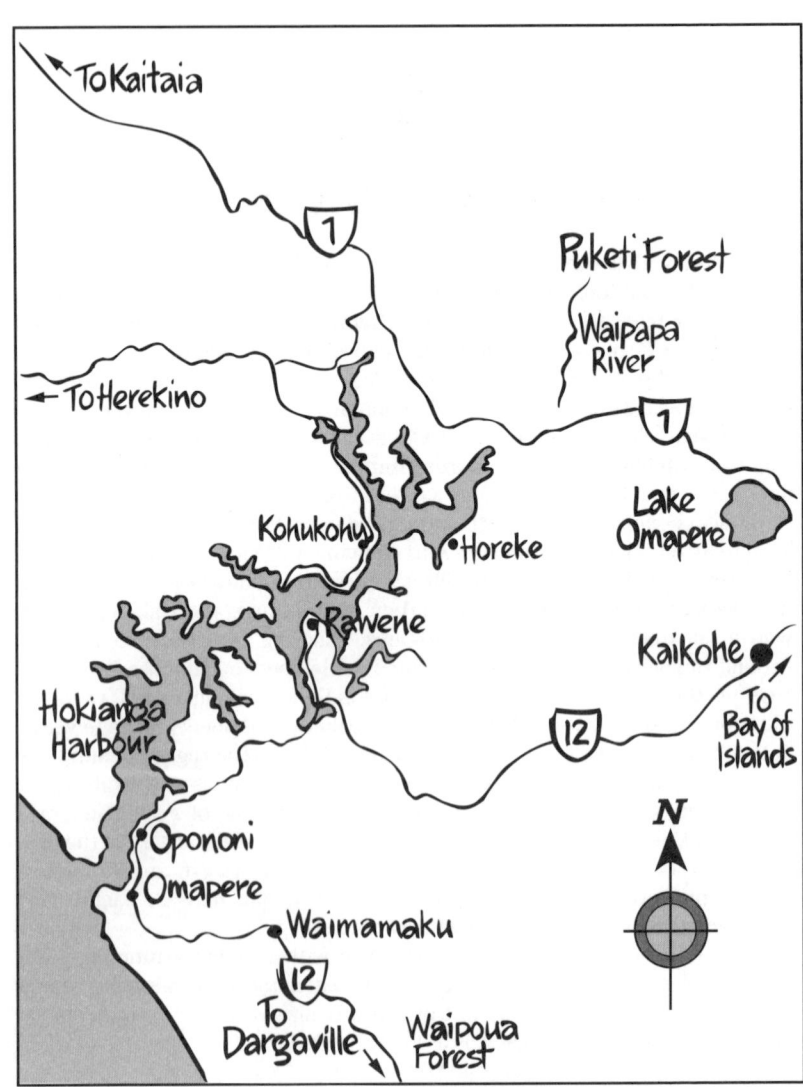

the company of local boats or better still take an experienced local with you. Boats need to be seaworthy and powerful enough to meet the challenges of this highly dangerous, unpredictable bar. A breakdown could be fatal.

The local Coastguard does an excellent job and visiting boaties are urged to get in contact before attempting a bar crossing. The local sportfishing club is a useful resource and a great place to meet local anglers.

The fishing

There's good fishing throughout the harbour but the most consistent is close to the heads. The upper harbour produces good snapper and trevally at times, often right up in the mangroves, as well as flounder and some very big sharks in spring and early summer. Closer to the heads the water tends to be clearer and the fishing is more consistent. In general, fishing is best an hour or two either side of high tide. Strong currents make plenty of lead mandatory in most locations. The points on both sides of the harbour are good options. Anchor on the edge of the channel in 20–25 metres and fish with long traces for snapper, trevally, kahawai and the occasional gurnard.

Much of this fishing is accessible to small boats and it's usually possible to find sheltered water on one side of the harbour or the other. Watch out for strong currents though; wind against tide can put up some steep and nasty seas, even inside the harbour.

Close inside South Head there are a couple of reefy spots fishable in good conditions that turn on some spectacular fishing for kingis at times. Livebaits are the way to go — catch them inside the harbour early in the morning or from the jetty at Omapere — or use piper, sunk deep and slowly retrieved. Trolled Rapalas also work well.

Shore-fishing options are limited but a boat does allow access to North Head and some good beach fishing, though the rip is fierce. Shore anglers experience some success on the south side too, fishing into the harbour channels or from the rocks inside South Head.

Outside the harbour there's good bottom fishing over the sand — look out for fish on the sounder, then drift or anchor over the concentrations — and over isolated areas of foul ground up and down the coast. Deeper areas of reef produce hapuku in season as well as snapper and kingfish. Twenty nautical miles out, on the edge of the shelf, some locals fish in 300 m of water or more for big bass, hapuku and bluenose.

In summer, spectacular marlin fishing is accessible from the Hokianga in settled conditions. Marlin run past the harbour in waves or pulses — if anglers are lucky enough to intercept such a pulse, multiple-fish days are not unusual. Most marlin fishing takes place a few nautical miles off the coast in water between 50 and 100 m deep.

 **Things to do**

From a base at Omapere there are plenty of activities to keep you occupied if fishing's not on the agenda. There's a small golf course at Rawene and sand-board riding on the huge dune face at North Head. Organised sand-board riding tours leave by boat from Opononi each day — check out the information centre for schedule details.

Waipoua Forest is just down the road. Waipoua is the largest remaining tract of native forest in Northland and one of the last bastions of New Zealand's giant kauri tree.

The drive through the forest is interesting enough but visitors will be rewarded by taking the time to stop and walk the short access tracks to some of the forest's more famous trees — Tane Mahuta and Te Matua Ngahere are must-sees.

For the more adventurous and well equipped, longer forest walks are available, offering the chance to see and hear some of New Zealand's rarest birds, including the elusive kokako. A trip to the Waipoua Visitor Centre is also worthwhile. Along with information about tracks, walks and scenic attractions, it has historical displays and natural history information. Camping is available.

 Accommodation

Campgrounds at Rawene and Opononi; baches, beach houses, motels and homestays in Opononi, Omapere, Rawene and Kohukohu; cabins at Omapere, Opononi and Waipoua.

 Boat ramps

Two concrete boat ramps, one at Opononi and one at Omapere, next to the jetty, are suitable for trailer boats of all sizes and workable in all but low spring tides.

Bay of Islands

The Bay of Islands is possibly New Zealand's premier summer watersports playground. Visited by boaties and holidaymakers from all over New Zealand and beyond, its complex of beautiful bays, secluded coves, rocky headlands, islands and beaches is so vast that you can always find somewhere in the bay to yourself, even in peak season.

And while the waters of the bay can be accessed from any number of settlements scattered around its shores, two towns in particular — Paihia and Russell — are the focus for the bulk of visitors. Each is worthy of a visit in its own right.

The town of Paihia is nestled beside the ocean across the water from Russell. It's adjacent to and merges with the historic settlement of Waitangi, where in 1840 New Zealand's founding document, the Treaty of Waitangi, was signed by northern Maori chiefs and representatives of the British crown.

The Bay of Islands was one of the first parts of New Zealand to be permanently settled by Europeans, who had a presence here from the earliest years of the 19th century. Historic buildings such as the Stone Store and Kemp House at Kerikeri, as well as old churches and other buildings, bear testament to the region's early European history, while the marae complex at Waitangi is among the country's largest and most important.

Paihia is better geared than most New Zealand towns to cater to the needs of visitors. A thriving tourist destination, it is dominated by motels, hotels, apartments, timeshares, backpackers and campgrounds to suit every budget and taste. Dozens of restaurants, cafes and small eateries line the waterfront and the streets of the village, and the town has a full complement of services, shops and supermarkets.

Getting to Paihia is straightforward enough. From the south, turn off State Highway 1 at Kawakawa and take State Highway 11, which heads out to the coast past the port of Opua. The road loops back alongside the Waitangi River to rejoin State Highway 1 at Puketona. The road is narrow and winding in

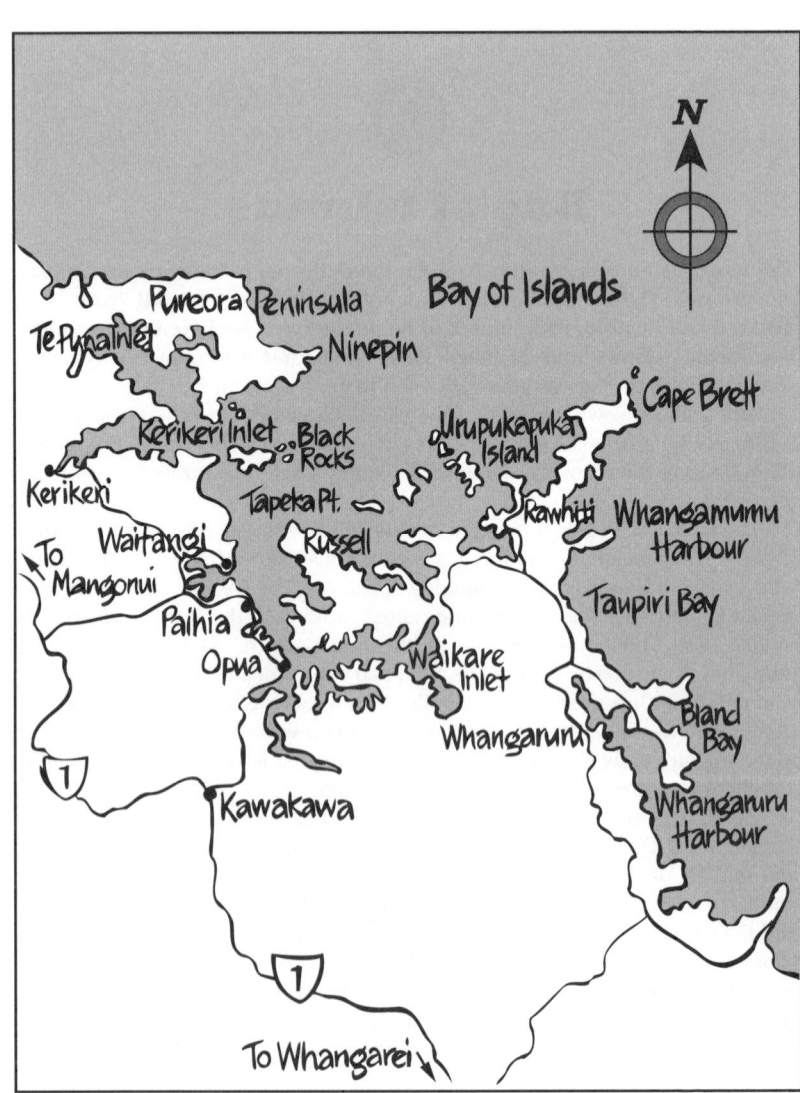

places but scenic enough, especially once the waters of the bay come into view at the top of the hill above Opua. Turn right to go to the port of Opua, its wharf, vehicular ferry to Russell, sailboat charter base, marina and associated marine precinct, or keep going to Paihia.

From Paihia it's possible to book any number of sightseeing trips, water activities, fishing, diving and dolphin charters, kayaking, helicopter rides, scenic flights, parapenting — you name it, Paihia's got it. The town is also on the tourist bus route north to Cape Reinga and Ninety Mile Beach, via Mangonui.

The township of Russell lies across the water from Paihia, wrapped around a picturesque bay. Butting up against a steeply shelving pebble beach, its wharf and moorings are protected from northerly and easterly storms, always the most destructive on this part of the coast.

If possible, Russell is even more historically significant than Paihia and Waitangi. Used as a whaling base from the late 18th century, Kororareka, to use its original Maori name, was home to New Zealand's first Europeans — beachcombers and deserters who made a poor living on the beach or as slaves of the local Maori.

By the 1820s Russell was known as the hellhole of the Pacific, notorious for its grog shops, brothels and general filthiness. At any one time there could have been up to 20 ships anchored in the bay — American, British, French, even Russian.

When Russell became New Zealand's first capital in 1840 it turned almost respectable, attracting 'serious' settlers and churchmen — including the French Catholic Mission which built Pompallier House, a must-see on the Russell foreshore.

But by 1844 the loss of revenue from the dwindling whaling industry, increasing official scrutiny of local chief Hone Heke's land sales, and friction between Maori and European settlers, became too much for Heke. He sacked the town, famously chopped down the flagpole (for the first time — he chopped it down twice more in the ensuing year) and, with his ally Kawiti, set the north alight in what was to be the first phase of the New Zealand Wars, a series of protracted, bitter and bloody conflicts between Maori and Pakeha that lasted almost 50 years.

Russell's picturesque and sleepy appearance today belies its turbulent early history but the proof is there, in the church graveyard, the museum, Pompallier and other historic buildings.

The fishing — Paihia

As the gateway to the Bay of Islands, Paihia is a great spot for the visiting angler. One of the beauties of the Bay of Islands is that it's almost always possible to find sheltered water somewhere. This makes it ideal for small craft happy to potter around in the sheltered waters of the upper reaches of the bay's many arms. There's good fishing year-round for a variety of species, even well up into the Waikare and Kerikeri inlets. During summer school snapper are plentiful, as are kahawai and other species. Large sharks are a feature of the upper harbour in spring and early summer, giving birth in the warm, sheltered waters.

Larger boats have the whole bay to play in. Once again, sheltered water is usually easy enough to find behind one or another of the bay's numerous islands. In good weather, the deep reefs and broken rubble of the middle sections of the bay, Cape Brett, Piercy Island and the Ninepin are accessible to trailer boats.

The fishing around the headlands and over deep foul can be excellent for snapper, kingfish, tarakihi, kahawai and a lot more besides. September through to December is big snapper time in the bay, when the fish aggregate to spawn. Often called the 'schooling season', it's a time that most boat fishers are able to find snapper, some well over 10 kg. The 'middle ground' in 30–35 m and close to Red Head and Roberton Island are favoured big-fish spots during the snapper run. Deeper rocks wider out produce good-sized hapuku to those anglers knowledgeable and keen enough to seek them out.

In summer tuna and marlin frequent the bay, which is why it's the spiritual home of big-game fishing in New Zealand, and has been since gamefishing was put on the map in the 1920s by American author Zane Grey. Skipjack tuna often penetrate deep into the bay, especially in autumn, providing great light-tackle sport for small boat anglers and a welcome supply of fresh snapper bait.

Shore fishers are rather less lucky, though there's some reasonable angling from the rocks at Waitangi below the golf course, but only in calm conditions. The wharf at Opua produces john dory and snapper at times, along with kahawai and the occasional kingfish, but it can be crowded and is often busy with boats and ships.

Shellfish can be gathered at Te Haumi beach at low tide and flounder can be netted in most of the bays in the region. Trout fishers can find reasonable fishing in the Waitangi River, which also holds tench and rudd, the Kerikeri

River, Waipapa Stream and Tirohanga River, all within easy reach of Paihia. Lake Manuwai, an irrigation lake just north of Kerikeri, holds a good population of rainbow trout, which can be targeted from a rowboat or from the shore.

 ## The fishing — Russell and the outer Bay of Islands

Like Paihia, Russell is well positioned for the visiting angler wanting to explore the Bay of Islands. In fact, when the wind blows from the north or east, as it often does in summer, Russell is a much better place to be. The peninsula shelters the shoreline along the Russell side, while around Tapeka Point, a notoriously rough stretch of water, it's usually possible to find shelter in among the islands.

Fishing can be excellent quite close to Russell. Even the inside of Russell Bay can produce consistent snapper fishing, particularly close to the rocks at either end. Tapeka Point and reefs slightly offshore and further out in the channel also produce good fish, especially during the schooling season.

Further afield, larger boats can access the islands out to Cape Brett. There's excellent fishing for all species as well as diving for scallops and crayfish. If the long haul up to the cape doesn't appeal or your boat is a bit on the small side, tow it up to Rawhiti and launch from the concrete ramp by the store or from the beach opposite the old school. From there you're within spitting distance of some of the bay's best fishing, without the need to cover large tracts of open water.

Land-based anglers have a lot more scope on this side too. The rocks at either end of Long Beach are worth a shot, particularly after a storm, and there's good rock fishing at Tapeka Point.

On the road out to Rawhiti there are numerous opportunities for land-based anglers, or you can walk over the hill to Whangamumu Harbour. Although, like Whangamumu, they're a fair way from Russell by road, Elliot Bay and Taupiri Bay offer excellent beach and rock fishing.

If all this sounds much too strenuous, a walk out onto the 'island' at the Pompallier end of Russell Bay at low tide can produce some surprisingly good snapper fishing, especially in autumn. And there's always the wharf. On winter nights it's a trevally hotspot and, though busy during the day, especially in summer, it can turn up snapper, john dory, kahawai and kingfish for the persistent angler, along with any number of sprats for the kids.

Things to do

Paihia and Russell are the ultimate destinations for fishers with non-fishing dependants, companions and partners. There's so much to do that I certainly don't have room here to list all the possibilities.

While Paihia probably has the most to offer, Russell tags on to most of the major activities and has a few that are unique. There are booking offices on both sides of the water so you're unlikely to miss out either way.

Popular activities include bay cruises, high-speed rides to the Hole in the Rock at Piercy Island and dolphin discovery tours, all of which pick up and drop off at both Paihia and Russell.

Russell has a large charter fishing fleet, as does Paihia; clients can be picked up from either port. There's day-sailing, sailing charters and tuition, parasailing, parapenting, kayaking, water skiing, motorboat hire, bottom fishing, gamefishing, diving — anything you can imagine on, in or under the water.

Facilities in both towns are excellent, though Paihia has the only full-sized supermarket (near Waitangi). Numerous restaurants and bars ensure the winer and diner is well looked after, while Paihia has a selection of nightspots popular with the young. Overseas tourism is important for the Bay of Islands and Paihia in particular is quite a cosmopolitan place. The town feels more resort-like than Russell.

Russell's nightlife is confined to its restaurants, the Swordfish Club — well worth a visit — the Duke of Marlborough Hotel on the waterfront and the Russell Tavern. It's still largely the preserve of locals, supplemented in summer by well-to-do part-time residents — mostly New Zealanders but increasingly Americans or Europeans — who occupy flash holiday houses at Long Beach, Tapeka and Flagstaff Hill.

 Accommodation

Virtually every taste and budget is catered for. Options include campgrounds, budget and backpacker accommodation, B&Bs, boutique and heritage hotels, charter boats and cruises, baches and beach houses, homestays, farmstays, lodges, hotels, motels, eco- and nature resorts, exclusive luxury accommodation, time-share, self-catering, apartments — the list goes on. Paihia has a greater number and range than Russell, but both are well served.

the Mad Keen Fisherman's Road Trip

For a comprehensive list check out www.tourism.net.nz and select Bay of Islands or www.bay-of-islands.co.nz/accomm.

Boat ramps

There are launching facilities for trailer boats at Waitangi, just inside the river mouth on hard sand. A concrete club ramp is also available for a small fee. Over the hill at Opua, a large concrete boat ramp in the marina will accommodate the largest trailer boat. Small boats can be launched from the beaches and into stream mouths here and there at high tide.

Other ramps at Paihia (small boats only), Te Haumi (small boats) and Rawhiti. Moorings are available for hire, as are marina berths at Opua.

Russell has a reasonable concrete ramp at the far end of the beach, with another at Tapeka, suitable for small craft. It's also possible to launch quite large trailer boats into the calm waters of Matauwhi Bay from half-tide upwards, though a tractor or four-wheel-drive is recommended.

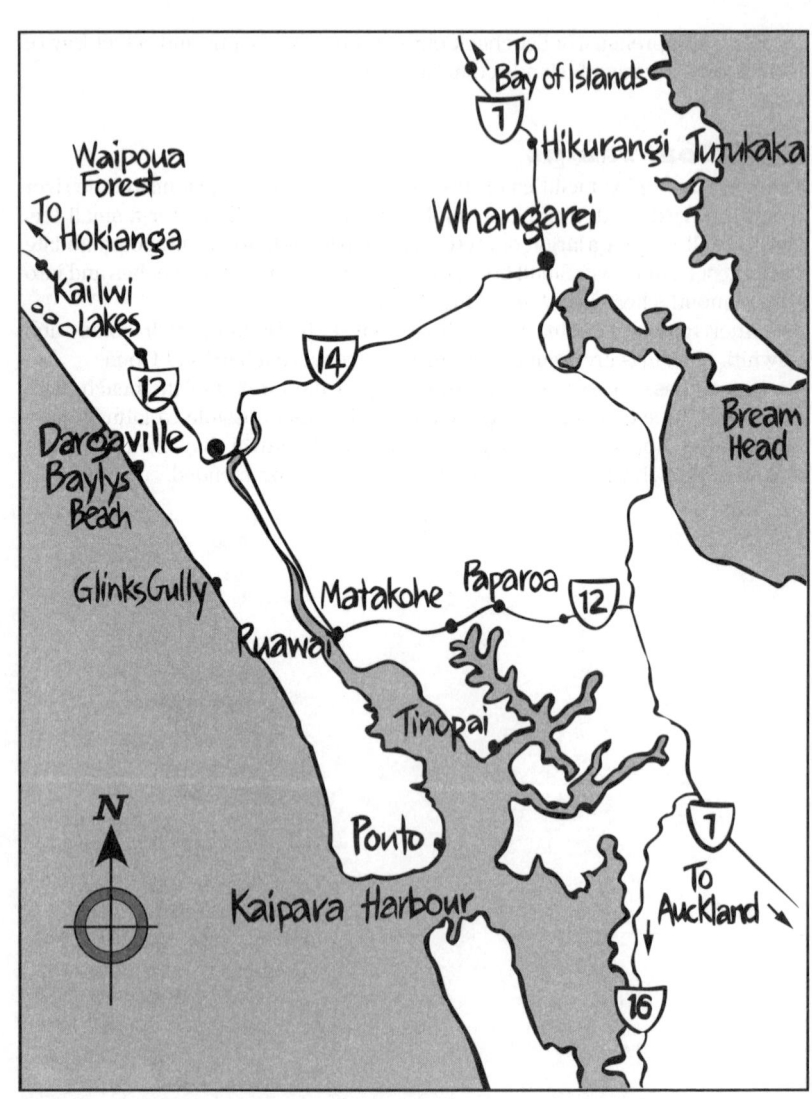

the Mid-North

For three very enjoyable years in the early 1980s I lived and worked at Whangarei. For a Wellington boy who'd grown up on the hard fishing and often cold, windy and miserable weather of the capital, it felt like paradise.

For me Whangarei and environs was a marine wonderland of warm, blue, fish-filled water. I was captivated by its beautiful harbour, awestruck by the magnificent coastline and constantly amazed at the variety and quality of the fishing available.

Where I lived, beside the harbour at Whangarei Heads, opportunity was always knocking for a mad-keen angler who also enjoyed diving and water-skiing. The locals thought the Wellington boys were crazy to water-ski in winter, but Northland winters felt like summer to us.

I retain a fondness for the mid-North and visit regularly. From my Auckland home it's an ideal destination for a fishing weekend.

Quite possibly there are official boundaries demarcating the region but I have never looked into it too closely. Somewhere on State Highway 1 heading north you pass a sign that says, 'Welcome to Northland'. That's good enough for me — it means I'm out of Auckland.

In reality the topography and, most importantly, the fishing changes little between the mid- and far North. What's more striking is the difference between the west coast, with its mighty surf beaches and massive, shallow harbours, and the east, dominated by volcanic headlands, rocky shores, islands, coves and golden beaches. The mid-North, like most of the rest of New Zealand, is divided between east and west and that's how I'll divide my weekend getaways.

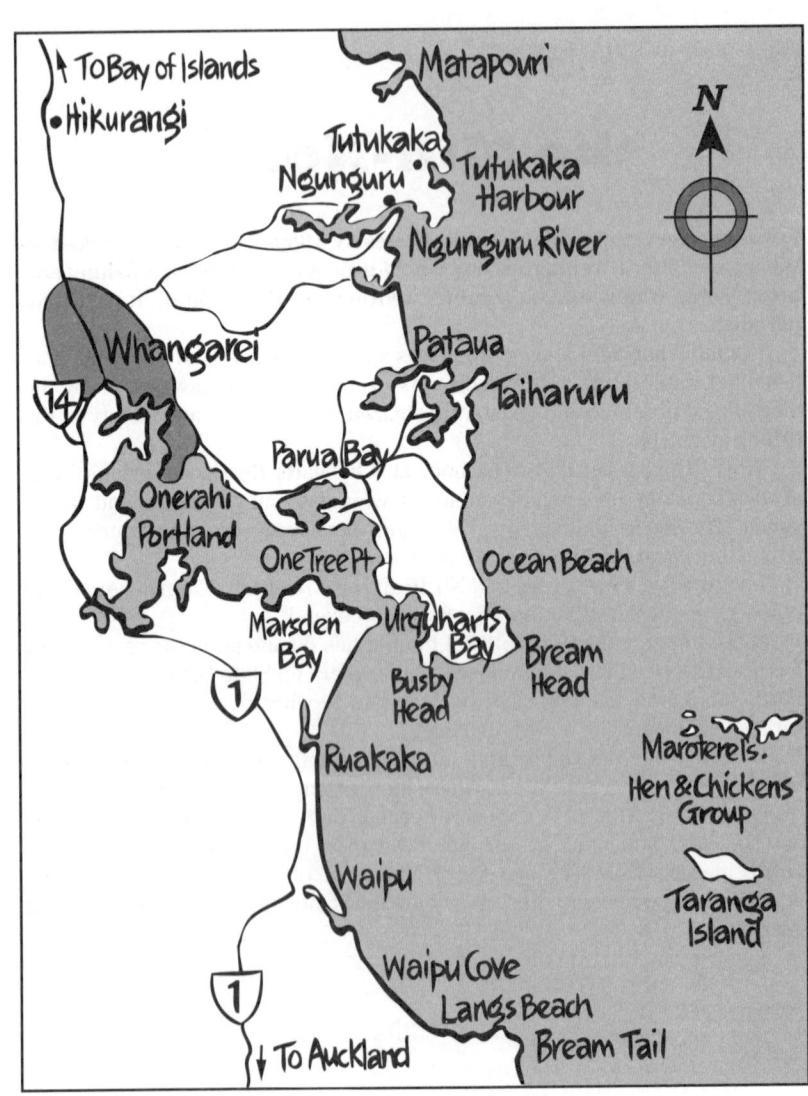

7

Whangarei, Tutukaka and beyond

Just a couple of hours up State Highway 1 from Auckland, Whangarei is Northland's premier city. Fast growing, modern and vibrant, it is wrapped around the upper reaches of Whangarei Harbour and straddles the banks of the Hatea River.

Beach suburbs have slowly spread around the harbour and out to the Heads, some 30-plus kilometres from the city centre. Most of these harbourside settlements on the northern side — Waikaraka, Parua Bay, McLeod Bay, Whangarei Heads, Reotahi Bay and Urquharts Bay — backed by the imposing bulk of Whangarei's trademark basalt chimneys and volcanic peaks, retain a distinct character. These days, holiday houses at the Heads are becoming rare, steadily replaced by substantial permanent dwellings, the residents of which commute into town each day on the now-sealed road.

Takahiwai and Marsden Bay on the southern side are somewhat different in flavour — their focus is as much on the magnificent ocean beach stretching down past Ruakaka to Waipu as it is on Whangarei Harbour. Many of the residents work at Marsden Point refinery. The impressive new Marsden Cove marina and canal complex is changing the whole flavour of the district and will soon be lined with palatial dwellings, jetties and million-dollar launches.

Whangarei's port is the largest and most important in Northland, while the refinery at Marsden Point is the only such plant in New Zealand.

A short drive over the hill from Whangarei lie the seaside settlements of Ngunguru and Tutukaka. Though both are an easy commute from town, they retain a beachside holiday character. Ngunguru is nestled beside an estuary while Tutukaka, home to a large big-game fishing and sport-diving charter fleet, overlooks a beautiful harbour.

Between Ngunguru and The Old Woman at Whangarei Heads, a series of relatively remote beaches, rocky coves, headlands and small estuaries, including Pataua and Taiharuru, offer a variety of fishing and diving opportunities. It's a relatively little-visited stretch of coast with spectacular scenery and excellent fishing.

South of Whangarei Harbour the long stretch of beach curves around Bream Bay to Waipu, Waipu Cove, Langs Beach and ultimately Bream Tail, where sand gives way to high volcanic rock bluffs once more.

The fishing

Whangarei offers so much to the visiting angler. Accommodation's a snip — there are dozens of choices to fit every budget — and the area is so diverse that every sort of fishing is possible.

Boaties can pick and choose. During summer there's excellent fishing inside the sheltered waters of Whangarei Harbour for snapper, trevally, kahawai and kingfish, as well as excellent diving and dredging for scallops. Pipis and cockles abound on the harbour's sandbanks, especially Snake Bank near the entrance.

Near the Heads, snapper tend to be bigger, though the rip in the channel is fearsome and can catch small-boat owners unawares. Around the channel's marker buoys, schools of kingfish take up residence in summer. The fish vary in size from 'rats' of a few kilos to bruisers of 20 kg-plus. Poppers or baits of fresh piper are the go and the new-style soft plastic baits should also prove irresistible.

In the harbour's deeper holes, large bronze whaler sharks gather to breed in early summer, along with large numbers of smaller, more manageable school sharks. These can provide good sport and more than a few surprises for boat fishers, as do the many XOS stingrays that frequent the harbour.

Outside the Heads there's excellent straylining around the headlands and on up the coast for snapper and other inshore species. Kingfish are common and kahawai often school not far offshore. Three Mile Reef, just out from the harbour entrance yet inshore enough to be easily accessible to small boats, is a consistent producer year-round.

Bream Islands off Ocean Beach can produce a variety of species and more than a few big snapper, as do the Hen and Chickens Islands a few nautical miles offshore. In summer anywhere wide of the Heads can produce marlin and other gamefish, while the Hen and Chicks are a known yellowfin tuna hotspot.

Tutukaka is the gateway to the Poor Knights Islands, now a no-take marine reserve. While just a shadow of its former self, the gamefishing charter fleet at Tutukaka still works these waters, though bottom-fishing charters are mostly a thing of the past. Dive charters are now the mainstay of the town but the work is highly seasonal.

Tutukaka is, however, an excellent starting point for small-boat gamefishers wanting to access the deep, blue water that sweeps close inshore along this part of the coast. It also has excellent marina facilities for visiting boats so it's a popular staging point for launches and yachts heading north or south.

Ngunguru and the smaller estuaries to the south are really only suitable for trailer boats; the entrances to Taiharuru and Pataua are dangerous in all but the calmest conditions. Nevertheless, local and visiting small-boat anglers regularly shoot the narrow entrances to access excellent fishing offshore and up and down the coast.

To the south, Bream Bay has scallop beds and isolated reefs scattered over the sand. Some are close inshore, just behind the surf line, providing good fishing when the snapper are in.

Opposite the old power station at Marsden Point, the hot water outlet half a mile offshore, no longer pumping, is still a magnet for all sorts of fish.

Sail Rock, out in the middle of Bream Bay, also acts as a reference point for schooling fish. Kingfish are always present and snapper can usually be found somewhere in the vicinity. Bream Tail and its associated reef structures offer good fishing as well as crayfishing.

Land-based anglers are similarly well served. The Heads area offers hundreds of fishing opportunities — from small wharves and jetties, all of which produce kingfish, john dory, snapper and other species, to headlands, channel edges and points.

Busby Head is popular with anglers seeking big kingfish while Home Point inside the harbour produces its share of big snapper (and crayfish). The small jetties on the northern side of the harbour can fish well but Marsden Point Wharf on the southern side is in a league of its own. Jutting out into deep water with plenty of current, it is home to school snapper and kingfish in summer and john dory and large trevally in winter, with big snapper, rays and sharks possible year-round. The new timber wharf just up-harbour is off limits to anglers but there's good fishing off the rock wall at times.

Up the coast towards Whangaruru, there are so many ledges, points, coves and beaches, the shore-based angler is spoilt for choice — take a look at a chart of the area and you'll quickly see what I mean.

The coast between Whangarei Heads and Cape Brett offers some of the best rock fishing in the country, though a small boat or inflatable is useful to access some of the more remote possies.

Freshwater fishers can try their luck at the city's water supply dam at Whau Valley, in some of the region's larger streams (check the Northland part of Fish and Game's website for details, www.fishandgame.org.nz) or in the newly created irrigation lake inland from Waipu, recently stocked with brown and rainbow trout.

 # Things to do

A visitor to Whangarei has plenty to choose from. As a good-sized city of 50,000 residents, Whangarei has all of the facilities one would expect: shops, restaurants, theatres, art galleries, museums, parks, recreational facilities and more. As well, there are a number of unique attractions for visitors, including the Clapham Clock Museum, papermaking and much more.

A visit to the marine reserve at the Poor Knights Islands is recommended and there are some superb gardens to visit for the botanically minded. Whangarei Heads offers several interesting walks of varying difficulty, as well as beaches, coves and coastal scenery.

The east coast is blessed with superb beaches; Ocean Beach, Ruakaka, Whananaki, Whale Bay and Waipu Cove are particularly popular with locals and visitors. Whangarei is also strategically positioned for easy day trips to the Kaipara Harbour and Kauri Coast to the west.

With so many beaches and harbours close by, the Whangarei region is a water sports heaven, offering sailing, surfing, sea-kayaking, boating, water-skiing and swimming, as well as fishing. The busy Town Basin plays host to a large fleet of international yachties who spend the summer in New Zealand to avoid the hurricane season in the tropical Pacific Ocean. There are always a few interesting yachts to ogle and the influx of foreign visitors in summer gives Whangarei a cosmopolitan atmosphere.

For a comprehensive guide on things to do in Whangarei, check out www.whangarei.co.nz. Another handy website is www.whangarei-nz.org.nz.

The information centre just off the main road as you enter the city on State Highway 1 from the south can help out with accommodation and activities. The cafe on site is excellent too and kids will enjoy playing in the gardens.

Accommodation

Whangarei can accommodate every budget and virtually any taste. There's accommodation ranging from the most exclusive beachfront with total privacy to a range of budget options including excellent campgrounds, backpacker lodges and budget motel/cabin accommodation. In between is the full range of hotel, motel, homestay and rental accommodation.

With so much coastline, the Whangarei region boasts more than its fair share of beautifully positioned waterfront accommodation. Start your search at www.holidayguide.co.nz.

Boat ramps

Although plentiful, the quality of boat ramps in the region varies widely. Many are small and suitable only for small to medium trailer boats. Many people launch off the sand, either off ocean beaches in calm weather or, more commonly, into harbours and rivers. Boat ramps are provided all over the harbour, varying in size and quality, as well as at Tutukaka, Ngunguru, Marsden Point (large and well appointed), Marsden Cove (two) and Ruakaka. Beach launching is common in the harbour and at Waipu Cove. North of the city, there's a concrete ramp at Oakura but it's often slippery and most people launch off the beach, and small ramps both sides of Bland Bay north of Whangaruru Harbour, but no formed ramps at Helena and Teal Bays Mimiwhangata or Whananaki. Boats can be launched into the Whananaki River but the bar is sometimes treacherous. Small boats can also launch into the Matapouri River.

Tutukaka has a good concrete boat ramp and there's one at Pataua South, suitable for small boats only. Pataua North and Taiharuru are sand-launching only and tide dependent. The Pataua bar can be dangerous.

In Whangarei Harbour, small boats can launch near the heads at Urquharts and Little Munro bays as well as at Reotahi, which has a concrete ramp; bigger boats should use the excellent concrete ramp complex at Parua Bay further up the harbour. There are also good concrete ramps at Onerahi and Marsden Point, and into the new marina complex/canal development at Marsden Cove, Ruakaka. Waipu Cove and Langs Beach offer beach launching only — tractors are recommended. Trailer boats can also launch into the Waipu River but the river bar is passable only at high tide in good conditions.

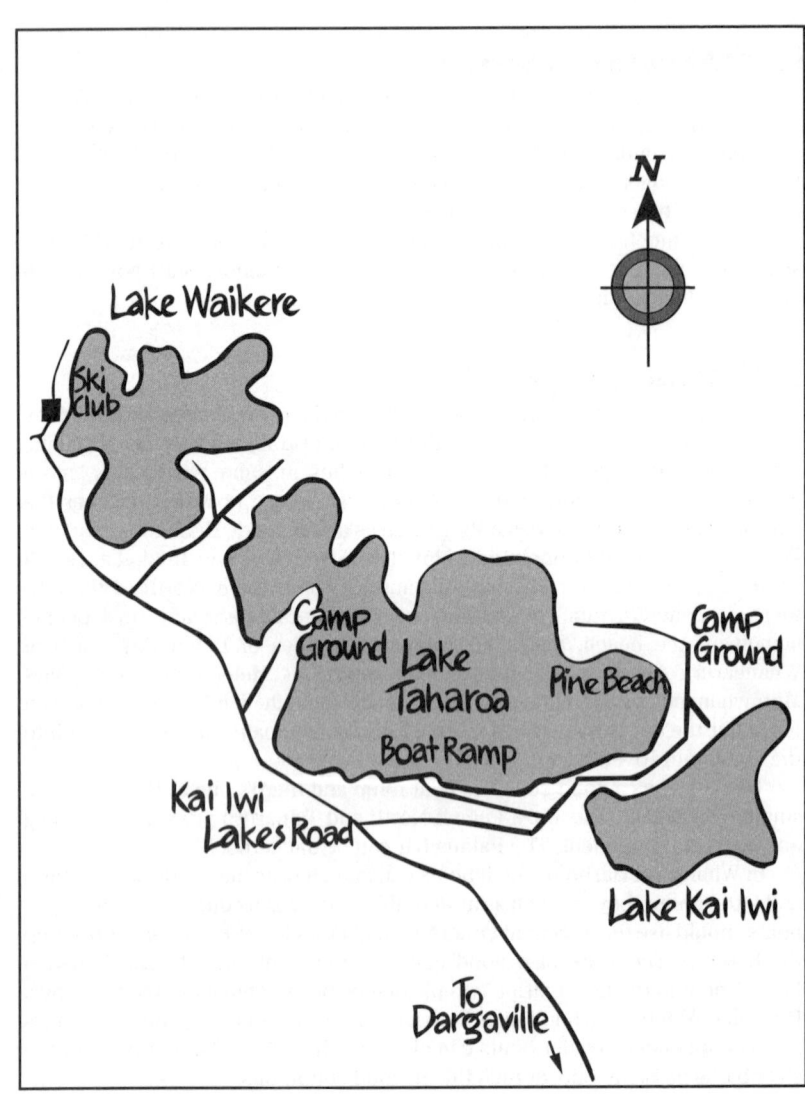

8

Kai Iwi Lakes and the Kauri Coast

My first visit to Kai Iwi Lakes was quite disorienting. Although I'd been told about them, when I drove over the hill and caught my first glimpse of the lakes, impossibly clear, blue and surrounded by dark green exotic forest, I couldn't believe my eyes. They looked completely out of place among the flat kumara fields and dry dune country north of Dargaville. The spectacular view simply didn't match my conception of Northland — Rotorua, perhaps, but not somewhere north of muddy old Kaipara Harbour.

Kai Iwi Lakes are a Northland secret, only loosely kept, but nonetheless little known outside the region. They're the largest and deepest of a string of sand dune lakes found up and down the west coast of the North Island. Most are relatively small and shallow but a few, like those at Kai Iwi and Lake Ototoa, closer to Auckland at Kaipara's South Head, are extensive bodies of water supporting excellent trout fisheries. For Northland freshwater anglers, Kai Iwi offers the best trout fishing for hundreds of kilometres.

Kai Iwi consists of three lakes, 35 km north of Dargaville, accessed from Kai Iwi Lakes Road, off Omamari Road. Covering 305 ha, they are nestled in the 538 ha Taharoa Reserve, of which 60 ha is in pine plantation. The lakes are well signposted, with the turn-off into Omamari Road just north of Dargaville on State Highway 12. Alternatively, continue on the main road until just south of the village of Maropiu and turn left.

The largest lake is Taharoa. At 40 m deep in the middle, it's also the deepest and the most important for trout anglers. Just to the northwest, the much smaller Lake Waikere holds fewer trout but they're often larger. However, this lake is home to the local water-skiing club so trout fishers face competition for space and solitude.

Lake Kai Iwi is the smallest and shallowest of the three. No longer stocked with trout, it still held the odd large specimen last time I visited, in winter 2005, relics from historic releases that have grown large and fat. These fish will certainly disappear soon, if they haven't already — rainbow trout seldom live longer than five years — but the lake once held the system's largest fish.

As well as attracting water-skiers and trout fishers, Kai Iwi Lakes has always been popular with Northlanders as a family holiday destination. In earlier times the lakes were permanently occupied by local Maori who valued them for their clear, fresh water and abundant populations of eel and dwarf inanga, a small native fish and now an important trout food. The name 'Kai Iwi' loosely translates as 'food for the people'.

Nestled behind the sand dunes, the lakes are sheltered from the region's incessant westerly winds. It's only a short 2.5 km walk through farmland and dunes to Ripiro Beach, and campers regularly trek over the dune track to the ocean to swim, fish and collect abundant tuatua. Toheroa are also present, though they have been off-limits in recent times in an attempt to halt the precipitous decline of New Zealand's most famous bivalve.

Popular Aranga and Omamari beaches are just a few kilometres to the north and south respectively, with Baylys Beach a few kilometres further south again.

The fishing

Kai Iwi Lakes are stocked with rainbow trout, which grow as big as 4 kg, though the average fish is closer to 1 kg. They feed on native fish and koura (freshwater crayfish), as well as insects and the introduced pest fishes gambusia (mosquito fish) and rudd in the lakes' margins. Growth rates are good, with year-old fish regularly reaching 2 kg.

In winter flyfishers have the edge. Most winter fishing is done from shore using fast-sinking lines and streamer flies. Anywhere the shore drops off quickly into deep water is favoured by wading anglers, though there are several places where it's possible to fish to sighted trout with a floating line. The lakes' margins are typified by rushes and expanses of firm white-sand shallows where fish can occasionally be seen cruising.

A foot track gives access to the portion of Lake Taharoa's shoreline not accessible by road, so anglers have plenty of choice, but some of the best fishing is close to the campgrounds.

Lake Waikere, despite competition from water-skiers in summer, is well worth fishing. Occasionally, 4 kg fish have been taken here and the lake gives up more 2 kg fish than much larger Taharoa. Flyfishing from shore is possible, though many of the smaller bays are choked with reeds. Ski Club Cove is popular with wading anglers, as is Deepwater Point, where wading is not always needed. Both these locations offer drop-offs into deep water close to shore. Flyfishers can also fish the lakes from a boat or float tube.

Most boat fishing involves trolling using monofilament, high-speed, high-density flylines, or leadlines. Boat fishing accounts for most of the fishing in the lakes and is popular with holidaying families in summer. During the warmer months deep trolling is the most effective technique, since the lakes' surface water temperature often climbs well above levels comfortable for trout, sending them deep. Trollers concentrate on the drop-offs, circling the lake following contour lines. A depth sounder is an advantage.

In summer flyfishers still get a look-in at night, wading deep and fishing the edges of the deepest drop-offs with fast sinking lines and luminescent or dark-bodied streamer flies. During the day boat fishers enjoy the most consistent fishing, however. Other techniques that take fish include spinning and jigging. Although the lakes are managed and stocked to ensure optimum trout growth, over-harvesting can affect trout numbers so visitors should consider catch and release, especially if visiting for a longer period of time. Minimum size is 30 cm and there is a maximum daily bag limit of three fish per person. A current Fish and Game trout fishing licence is required. Kai Iwi trout are good eating, particularly the larger specimens that feed on koura, the consumption of which gives them beautiful pink flesh.

For sea fishers, Ripiro Beach is one of the country's longest, offering excellent beach fishing for surfcasters, kontiki and kite fishers when conditions allow. There's good snapper fishing inside the Kaipara and Hokianga harbours, with even better fishing outside. Gamefish can be taken in season by boats launching off the beaches or crossing the Kaipara and Hokianga bars. Local advice is recommended. The Bay of Islands is only one and a half hours' drive away if visitors want a break from freshwater pastimes.

Things to do

Like most lakes, Kai Iwi attracts visitors for a variety of reasons. During summer the clear waters warm sufficiently to make swimming a pleasure, and water-skiing, sailboarding and yachting are year-round pastimes. Campers enjoy the superb surroundings, swimming, fishing and other water sports, with the added bonus of a wonderful surf beach a brisk walk away over the dunes. The reserve has an extensive network of walking tracks, which also take in Shag Lake at the northern edge. This shallow dune lake is an important refuge for rare birds, including the dabchick. As well as walking, mountain biking is popular in the domain.

The famous sights and sounds of Waipoua Forest are a scenic drive of 20-odd kilometres north along State Highway 12 (see the entry for Hokianga Harbour). Hokianga's beach and harbour attractions are only an hour or so from the lakes, and the beaches nearer Dargaville are popular destinations year-round.

Dargaville and Ruawai are centres for the region's thriving kumara industry, as well as being historical settlements with roots in kauri milling and gum digging. There are several excellent museums celebrating the region's past.

Other activities easily accessed from a base at the lakes include forest tours, horse treks, guided coastal and nature walks, mountain biking, gamefishing (Hokianga or Bay of Islands), beach fishing and cultural tours taking in sights with significance to Maori people. Dargaville's website, www.dargaville.co.nz, lists all these activities and more, or check out the information centre at 69 Normanby Street on the way through Dargaville, 09 439 8360.

Accommodation

Two sheltered council-run campgrounds on the shores of Lake Taharoa offer basic facilities — one is under the pines at the spectacular white-sand Pine Beach at the eastern end of the lake, the other is near The Promenade, where Taharoa narrows. Both get crowded in summer. Further campsites are available in Trounson Kauri Park at Donnellys Crossing, at Baylys Beach and in Dargaville, which also has a range of hotel and motel accommodation.

If a luxury weekend is more to your taste, Waipoua Lodge, 30 minutes' drive from the lakes, offers five-star facilities, awesome forest views, outstanding cuisine and a range of activities. See www.waipoualodge.co.nz.

Other popular alternatives include beach and lake cottages sleeping between four and 10 guests. These self-contained baches are fully equipped and reasonably priced. A few are close to the lakes, with others on the coast at Omamari (see www.holidayhomes.co.nz). There are also a few farmstays and homestays around.

 **Boat ramps**

There's a concrete boat ramp at Lake Taharoa and another at Lake Waikere. A five-knot speed restriction is in force for Lake Taharoa except in marked areas and ski lanes, and motorised craft are banned on Lake Kai Iwi.

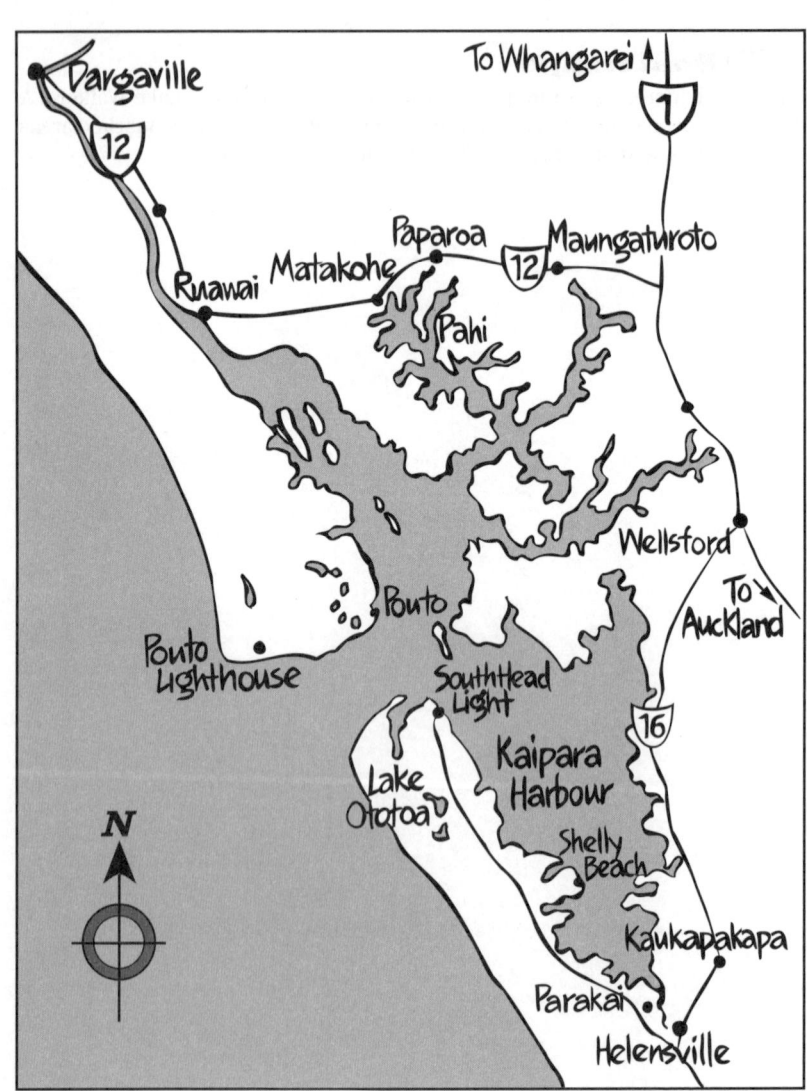

9

Kaipara Harbour

The mighty Kaipara Harbour is so large it dominates the mid-North region. Mostly shallow and rather muddy, it consists of several arms, each a drowned river valley. At the head of each, as is the pattern in Northland, lies a town positioned at what was once the limit of waterborne navigation.

At the northern end on the muddy Wairoa River lie the towns of Ruawai and Dargaville, as far upstream as the timber scows could easily sail on the tide. At the harbour's southern end, nearly 60 km away and within spitting distance of Auckland, is Helensville, an important rural service centre and one-time timber town on the Kaipara River. The fishing town of Port Albert is on the Oruawharo River. Maungaturoto — these days too far upstream to reach by boat — straddles the Otamatea River, while Pahi and Matakohe lie beside the tidal reaches of the Arapaoa River.

During the 19th and early 20th centuries, the harbour and its rivers underwent massive change as the region's mighty native forests were clear-felled and burnt, exposing Northland's unstable soils. Huge quantities of silt choked the rivers and irrevocably altered the character of the harbour, covering much of its white-sand bottom in mud, smothering eel grass and shellfish beds and affecting the abundance and variety of fish species. To this day the rivers and harbour are silt-laden as erosion continues apace.

Today the Kaipara Harbour is typified by huge areas of tidal mudflats, extensive sandbanks bisected by swift-flowing tidal channels, and muddy saltmarsh- and mangrove-lined margins. With all that mud and the treacherous tides, navigation can be tricky, especially since water clarity is generally poor.

If all of this is sounding a little uninspiring from a fishing point of view, the visiting angler shouldn't worry — with an area of 520 sq km, the Kaipara Harbour is one of the largest in the world. Boasting more than 3200 km of shoreline and all that water, there's plenty of good fishing for boat anglers inside the harbour, as well as excellent beach and offshore fishing outside the heads.

The Kaipara is easy to reach but its vastness means you need to choose which part of it you wish to visit. In the south, Helensville, Woodhill Forest, the west coast beaches and the sand dune lakes and lagoons of Kaipara's South Head are within easy reach of day-trippers from Auckland. Simply head on up the northwestern motorway and continue north on State Highway 16. For South Head, turn left at the junction signposted 'Parakai'; for Helensville, continue on State Highway 16 for another kilometre or two.

State Highway 16 skirts the eastern side of the Kaipara, passing through small towns on its shores before joining State Highway 1 at Wellsford. For Port Albert, take State Highway 1 from Auckland and turn off at Wellsford.

Dargaville and the northern Wairoa region are reached via State Highway 1, then State Highway 12. The turn-off at the base of the Brynderwyn Hills is well signposted. State Highway 12 is a pleasant, interesting drive that passes through the regionally important towns of Maungaturoto, Paparoa and Matakohe. The drive from Auckland to Dargaville takes about two and a half hours.

 The fishing

Fishing inside the harbour is varied, though to the casual observer the vast expanse of shallow water looks uniform. Pipis, cockles and mussels are abundant throughout the harbour while scallops are common in sandy areas along the channel edges. Fish move through the harbour channels with the tide, spreading onto the sandbanks and mudflats to feed as the water rises. They also move well up the rivers, which are salty many kilometres inland.

Not surprisingly, flatfish — flounder and sole — are abundant, with yellowbellies the most common catch. Flatfish support a considerable commercial industry within the harbour.

Mullet is another species supporting a commercial fishery inside the harbour. Like flounder, they are often netted well up mangrove-lined creeks. They are delicious smoked and make excellent bait for all west coast species.

During winter, gurnard, kahawai and trevally are the dominant species inside the harbour; in summer snapper take over, joined by kingfish, with trevally becoming less common. Parore, sharks and rays are present year-round, but an influx of large sharks occurs every year in spring and early summer as they seek warm, shallow water in which to give birth. Sixty years ago there was an important shark-catching industry in the Kaipara.

The Kaipara empties into the Tasman Sea through a 4 km wide entrance. With so much water trying to exit through such a narrow gap, tidal currents are ferocious and the entrance is a dangerous place. Like all west coast harbours, there is a sand bar upon which the ocean waves break, often in a solid line. Breakers can extend many kilometres out to sea.

The Kaipara bar is worse than most, with no clear channels through to the open sea. The harbour is no longer used by ocean-going craft. Pleasure boats and smaller commercial craft still cross the bar regularly but the process can be nerve-wracking. Most boats are forced to run northwards, parallel to the beach, for several kilometres, dodging breakers as they go, before finally turning left and heading out into the open sea.

Many local pleasure boats cross the bar to chase tuna and marlin. For many it's a 30 km run just to reach the harbour entrance before heading out to sea so plenty of fuel must be carried. To safely negotiate the entrance, local knowledge is essential.

The area close to North Head inside the harbour entrance is called 'The Graveyard' — the final resting place of many ships and smaller craft. The deepest part of the harbour, it offers the best and most consistent fishing in the Kaipara. Currents are fierce so plenty of lead is required to get baits to the bottom — up to a kilo at times. The Graveyard yields big snapper, kingfish, school and bronze whaler sharks, kahawai, trevally and incidental species. Fishing is best during the warmer months but big snapper can be caught all year.

Several charter boats working from Dargaville/Ruawai or Helensville offer fishing excursions to the Graveyard, Pouto Point and heads areas when conditions allow. This is a safer and probably more productive option for visiting anglers.

Away from the heads, boat fishers concentrate on the channel edges. In summer snapper fishing can be excellent though the average fish size is small. School snapper can be caught almost anywhere while sharks are always a possibility and often a nuisance. In the upper reaches of the harbour's arms, small boats and dinghies can safely fish with every chance of bringing home a feed. Long traces, plenty of weight and oily baits are the order of the day.

Land-based fishers have fewer options than boat fishers but the Kaipara still offers a range of opportunities. To the south the wharf at Shelly Beach reaches right into the main channel where gurnard and kahawai can be caught. The odd snapper is taken as well.

Further up the peninsula at South Head, the lagoon is an excellent surfcasting spot. Fish off the beach into the harbour or lagoon, or trek/drive around and fish into the Tasman Sea. Access is by foot or mountain bike via tracks in Woodhill Forest, or by driving along the beach in a four-wheel-drive convoy at low tide from the Rimmers Road access point. The beach and South Head area is a favourite with kite fishers, who take some exceptional catches.

Like South Head, North Head offers excellent shore-based fishing. There's road access to Pouto and surfcasters can fish anywhere either side of the township. Scattered around the harbour are a number of other land-based spots well worth a look. The wharf at Tinopai can produce a few surprises on the incoming tide, as can the wharf at Port Albert. In a few places it's possible to fish into a channel from shore and such possies are worth exploring. If you can reach the channel you can reach the fish.

 ## Things to do

The Kaipara district is largely rural in nature. Consequently, most activities have a country bent. Dargaville and many of the other towns around the harbour were important ports in the heyday of the timber trade in the late 19th and early 20th centuries — so you're never far away from reminders of the importance of the kauri tree.

Dargaville is an excellent base from which to explore the upper Wairoa, Kauri Coast and greater Kaipara region. The town has plenty of attractions of its own, including an excellent museum and art gallery and a mill that crafts paper from rice grass growing wild beside the Wairoa River.

From Dargaville, most of the region's other attractions are an easy drive away. Activities include bush and coastal walks, parks, forests, beaches, trout fishing (see the Kai Iwi Lakes entry), scenic and adventure tours, quad-bike rides, beach buggy hire, golf, sailing and more. See www.dargaville.co.nz or stop in at the Information Centre at 69 Normanby Street, 09 439 8360.

At Matakohe, 45 km south of Dargaville, there's the excellent Kauri Museum, one of the standard stopovers for tour buses but well worth a look all the same. Inside are displays of kauri gum, antique kauri furniture, restored timber milling machinery, including New Zealand's oldest tractor, a working steam-driven sawmill and several replica buildings from the 1860s and '70s.

The small towns of Matakohe and Paparoa, like much of the rest of the district, were settled by Europeans in the early 1860s. Timber milling and kauri gum extraction were soon replaced by pastoral farming.

Paparoa is today a quiet village with a pub, a few shops and a couple of eateries but it was once a thriving shipping and boat-building centre servicing the Kaipara Harbour. Its village green is a nice place for a picnic lunch.

Helensville, at the southern end of the harbour just 40 minutes from Auckland, was named one of New Zealand's top 10 small towns by *North and South* magazine. With a growing population and a progressive community, it's an interesting mix of new development and heritage buildings. Well endowed with shopping, facilities, accommodation and restaurants, the town benefits from its proximity to downtown Auckland, Albany and Kumeu.

Attractions range from peaceful garden visits to gliding and skydiving. Visitors can enjoy museums or horse trekking along stunning beaches. There are cruises, natural hot pools at Parakai, golf, walks, trout fishing at Lake Ototoa and a great deal more. See www.helensville.co.nz.

Accommodation

The district surrounding the Kaipara is so large there are hundreds of accommodation options in dozens of towns, villages and small settlements around the harbour. Most bigger towns and villages offer hotel and motel accommodation. Dargaville has homestay, backpacker, B&B, lodge, cabin and camping options, as well as hotels, motels and hostels. There's a comprehensive list of contacts at www.dargaville.co.nz.

There are also campgrounds at Baylys Beach and Glinks Gully on the coast west of Dargaville, Pouto and Kellys Bay at North Head, Matakohe (with cabins), Pahi on the Kaipara near Paparoa, and at Paparoa itself. Many of these places also offer holiday homes for rent, motels, hotels and B&Bs. Helensville offers a similar range of accommodation options. See www.helensville.co.nz.

Boat ramps

There is boat access to the Kaipara at Ruawai, Tinopai, Pahi and Kellys Bay. Quality varies and some ramps are tide-dependent. An excellent all-tide concrete ramp at Port Arthur gives access to the eastern end of the harbour and there's another all-tide ramp at Stables Landing. The southern end of the harbour can be accessed from ramps at Helensville and Parakai, or further round towards South Head at Shelly Bay, which boasts a good concrete public ramp.

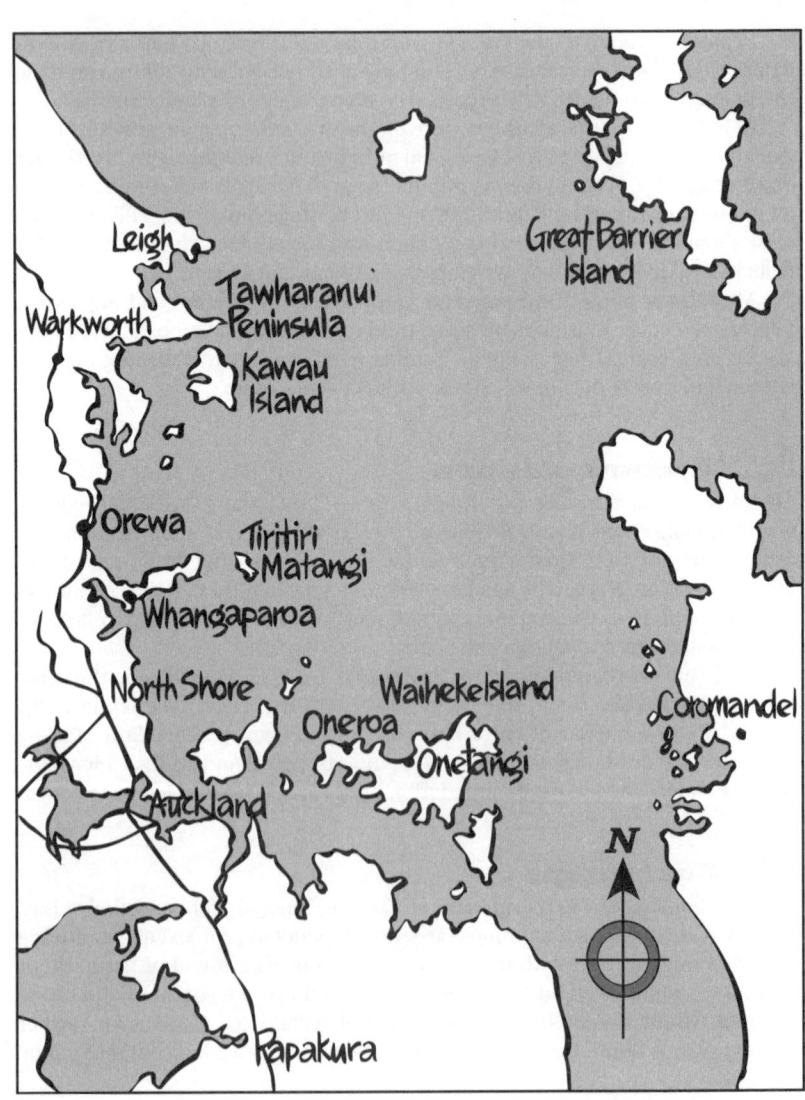

Auckland and the Hauraki Gulf

About here things become a little tricky . . . Auckland, New Zealand's largest city by far and home to nearly a third of the country's people, is seldom considered as a destination for a fishing weekend, especially by Aucklanders. Yet the islands of the Hauraki Gulf and outlying areas to the north and south of the city offer everything one could want in a fishing weekend getaway. Visitors who want to spend a weekend fishing could do worse than base themselves and the family in Auckland City.

Auckland is a maritime city surrounded by water. Located on a narrow isthmus between the Waitemata and Manukau harbours, it embraces the sea on every side. Auckland is also a city of fishers. The angler is never far from the sea and the city is exceptionally well-geared to an angler's needs: tackle and bait are universally available and a well-developed boating and charter infrastructure means getting out on the water is a snip.

Shore fishers can take their pick of productive positions around both harbours and beyond, including wharves and inner city locations, which turn up some surprising catches at times. The keen locals fishing under the Harbour Bridge on a summer evening are not there simply for the view.

Nevertheless, for the purpose of this guide — a road trip and a collection of weekend getaways — we'll concentrate on locations away from Auckland city itself, although a boat is a prerequisite to get to some of them.

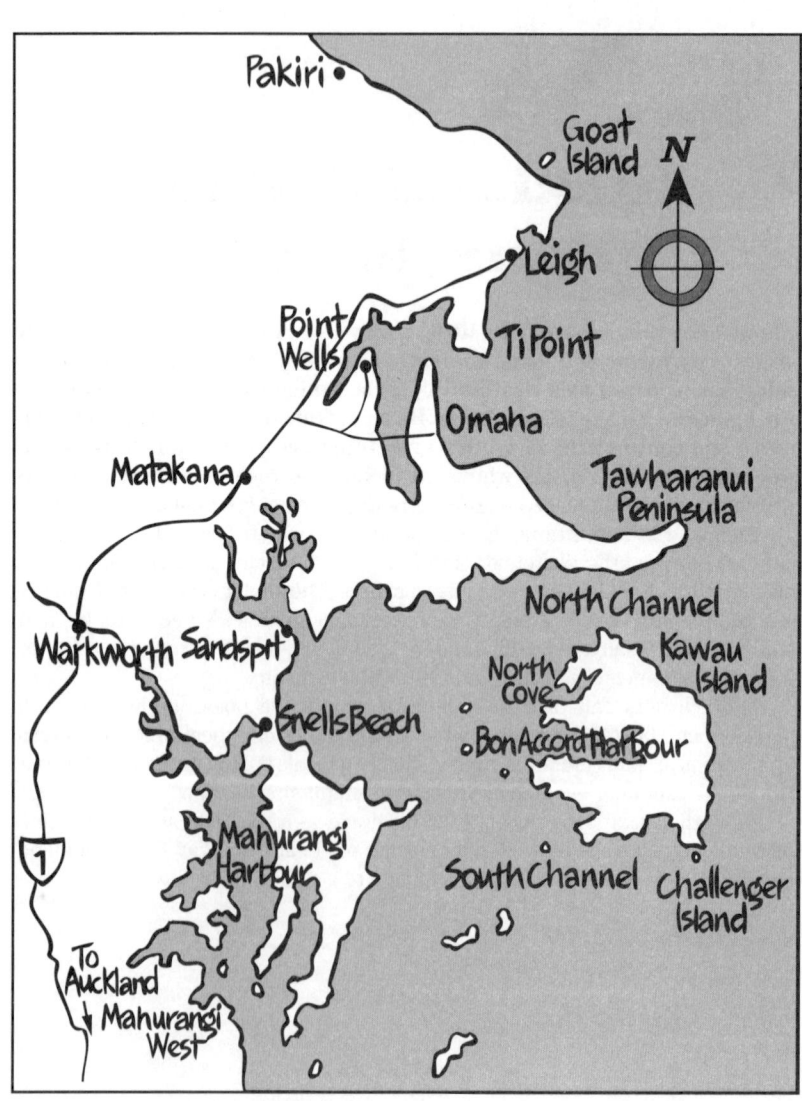

10

Kawau Island, Omaha and environs

Only 90 minutes' drive from Auckland's Sky Tower, the string of beautiful bays, coves and harbours of Kawau and Omaha bays, as well as Kawau Island, are immensely popular with visitors. Any Friday afternoon, especially in summer, State Highway 1 north of Auckland slows to a crawl as thousands of Aucklanders stream north to take up residence in holiday homes and other accommodation on the coast. Once at Warkworth, the majority spreads out, taking various scenic routes to the peninsulas, bays and beaches of the area.

Some take the ferry from Sandspit to Kawau Island, also a popular destination for boaties leaving from Auckland, but most settle down for the weekend in places such as Mahurangi West, Snells Beach, Sandspit, Takatu, Tawharanui, Omaha, Point Wells, Whangateau, Ti Point, Leigh and Pakiri Beach further north.

This area has seen a lot of development in recent years, with some of the sleepy beachside settlements transforming into full-blown commuter towns, many of whose inhabitants travel to and from Auckland each day. Nonetheless, there's no escaping the beach flavour of most places, and some settlements retain more of their holiday character than others.

One of the side effects of massive growth has been the huge improvement in the region's facilities and services — a visitor to the area need not go short of anything. There's excellent shopping, a huge range of recreation options and plenty of accommodation at stunning seaside locations.

Bush-covered Kawau Island is the largest island in this part of the Hauraki Gulf. Accessible only by boat, it has no roads but boasts dozens of safe anchorages, including magnificent, nearly landlocked Bon Accord Harbour. Bon Accord runs roughly west to east, almost splitting the island in two. It is home to most of the island's many holiday homes, as well as Mansion House

Bay with its wharf, gardens and historic mansion, once owned by Governor George Grey, a yacht club and much else besides. The harbour offers shelter from the prevailing winds and smooth water at all times so it's a haven for visiting boaties.

Other visitors must take the ferry. A regular ferry service between Sandspit and the island runs daily, dropping visitors at Mansion House Bay and several other wharves scattered around the island.

The fishing

This is a large area so the fishing is fairly diverse, though, like the rest of the Hauraki Gulf, snapper is king. Other common species include the usual northern cast of kingfish, kahawai and trevally, with summer visitors including the odd school of skipjack tuna, frigate mackerel, sharks (including makos), and the occasional marlin wide of Kawau Island and Cape Rodney.

Mahurangi, Sandspit and Whangateau harbours offer sheltered estuary fishing for school snapper, flatfish and other species; Mahurangi is by far the biggest of the three with the best fishing. Mussel farms always produce a feed of snapper on the rising tide and there are good-sized kingfish patrolling the harbour entrance and the islands nearby.

Bon Accord Harbour offers similar opportunities but boat traffic can be heavy, especially at weekends.

Kawau Bay is mostly shallow but fishes well in summer to boats drifting over the sand or fishing under birds feeding on baitfish pushed to the surface by water-based predators. Scallops, the focus of many visiting boaties and divers in the season, are common throughout.

Rocky shorelines to the north and south fish well, including both sides of the North Channel between Tawharanui Peninsula and Kawau Island, as does the eastern side of Kawau. Maori Rock in the channel is popular year-round and produces large snapper and kingfish at times. The current is strong so fish the tides and use plenty of lead where necessary.

The islands and reefs of Kawau Bay and south to Mahurangi offer good fishing, as do the sandy areas between. There's such a diversity of fish habitat and so many islands and bays, there's always somewhere to fish regardless of the weather.

Outside Kawau Island are a number of reefs and shoal areas rising out of relatively deep water. The best known is Flat Rock, famous for its spectacular snapper fishing. At times it consistently produces big snapper and kingfish but it's not easy to fish. Success demands careful boat positioning and the right bait — whole jack mackerel are the weakness of Flat Rock's large snapper.

Omaha Bay is also shallow but bounded by rocky coasts north and south. Tawharanui Peninsula and its marine reserve dominate the bay's southern side; Leigh Harbour and Cape Rodney define its northern extent.

Omaha Bay fishes well in summer for school snapper in close, on the sand and over scattered areas of reef close to shore. Ti Point and the entrance to Whangateau Harbour can be good places to catch kingfish, while Leigh Reef and some of the deeper pins around Cape Rodney are reliable producers of bigger snapper, kingfish and other species. Towards the end of warm summers Omaha Bay sometimes sees an influx of frigate mackerel. These small tuna are often mistaken for baby skipjack — taken on light tackle, they're excellent sport and make equally good snapper bait, fresh or frozen.

Shore fishers will find fewer opportunities than those with boats but there are still plenty of likely spots from which to cast a line. Surfcasters can choose between the expanse of Pakiri Beach and the less daunting tip of Omaha Beach. Both produce fish, with Omaha best on an outgoing tide.

Where Takatu Peninsula merges into Omaha Bay, an extensive area of rock and foul is a good location to fish floating baits from the rocks for snapper or livebaits for kingfish. Shore fishers also enjoy success at the southern side of the entrance to Sandspit Harbour.

Mahurangi West, on the southern side of Mahurangi Harbour, accessed through the regional park at the end of Mahurangi West Road off State Highway 1, produces good-sized snapper at times, kingfish and kahawai. It's best fished either side of low tide.

Although many of the anglers visiting Kawau and its environs travel by boat from Auckland, one of the beauties of the area is its easy access for small boats.

Well served by launching ramps and safe harbours, the bays and islands offer shelter from wind and sea, making them a small boat haven. The fact that the area also consistently offers exceptional fishing is a real bonus.

 Things to do

While it's only an hour from Auckland, one of the beauties of the area is that you really feel you've left the city behind. That doesn't mean you've left all the city's amenities behind as well — Warkworth has everything a small town could offer and many of the growing beach settlements are well endowed with shopping and other attractions. Warkworth District Museum is definitely worth a visit.

Cafes, restaurants and vineyards are a feature, with Matakana the centre of New Zealand's fastest-growing wine region. Tastings, tours and wonderful dining are offered by a number of vineyards; there are garden centres to visit; interesting walks, river and harbour cruises; day excursions to Kawau Island and all of the usual water-based activities one would expect in a coastal region.

Beaches are varied and too numerous to list, from open ocean surf beaches at Pakiri to sheltered sandy coves and safe swimming beaches in Kawau Bay. Kayakers and sailboarders can have a ball exploring dozens of islands and reefs, bays, coves and estuaries, most relatively protected from the worst of the weather, while Kawau Island offers some of the best anchorages in the gulf for the cruising set.

Goat Island and Tawharanui marine reserves offer interesting snorkelling and diving, with Goat Island perhaps the best shallow-water dive in New Zealand when the water is clear. The fish life is spectacular. Guided dive tours and gear hire are available at Goat Island Reserve and from dedicated dive shops on the road to the reserve.

Tawharanui Marine Reserve is part of the larger regional park, which boasts excellent coastal walks and interesting birdlife.

Accommodation

Accommodation options on Kawau Island centre around private beach houses, some palatial, many of which are available for weekend hire or longer periods. Start by looking at www.bookabach.co.nz and www.holidayhouses.co.nz. There is also limited lodge accommodation.

Back on the mainland, visitors have any number of accommodation options, from farmstays to beach houses, campgrounds and luxury retreats. All of the region's villages and seaside settlements offer accommodation, including motels, with boutique hotels and B&Bs increasingly popular with weekend visitors.

The Kowhai Coast website, www.warkworth-information.co.nz, has links to accommodation options for the greater region.

 **Boat ramps**

There are boat ramps at most of the bays, though many are only workable through part of the tide. Locals often launch off the beaches. Mahurangi Harbour has two concrete boat ramps and there is a natural sand boat ramp at Sandspit suitable for the largest trailer boats. Omaha has a decent concrete ramp and there's another at Leigh beside the commercial wharf, though the winding access road is a challenge for bigger boats.

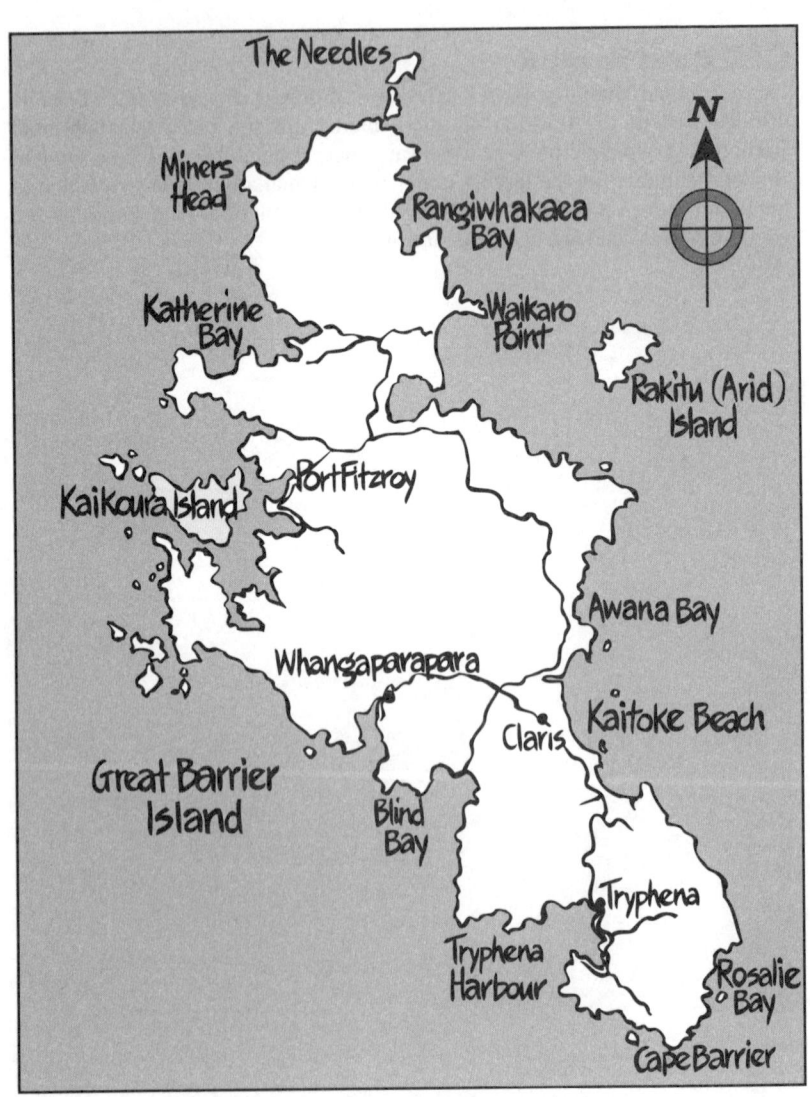

Great Barrier Island

Visiting Great Barrier Island is like travelling back in time to a New Zealand all of us sort of remember but none of us have actually experienced. Isolation and geography, as well as the islanders' self-conscious desire to maintain a relaxed, alternative lifestyle, make Great Barrier — called Aotea by Maori — one of New Zealand's more interesting destinations.

A little over 50 nautical miles (88 km) by sea from Auckland, Great Barrier is the largest island in the Hauraki Gulf and the fourth-largest landmass in New Zealand. About 700 permanent residents occupy the island's 285 sq km, so overcrowding is not an issue. More than 60 per cent of the island is administered by the Department of Conservation; its forests and wetlands are free of many of the animal pests of the mainland and are home to a number of rare and endangered native plants and animals.

Great Barrier is a high island with a rugged interior. Mt Hobson — Hirakimata — rises to 621 m and is the highest point in Aotea's mountainous spine. Like most of the gulf islands, Great Barrier is volcanic in origin, its soaring bluffs, rock chimneys and black basalt cliffs indicating its geological connection to Coromandel Peninsula and Whangarei Heads. It's warmer and drier than the mainland, especially in winter, and its waters are home to a stunning range of sea life, including many unusual species and tropical visitors.

Numerous archaeological sites survive on the island, evidence of its long Maori history. When Europeans arrived they found a rich bounty of resources to exploit: migrating whales were hunted for their meat and oil; copper, gold, and silver ore were mined from the island's rocks; the huge kauri trees which covered the Barrier were felled for their timber and then raided for their valuable gum; other trees were logged for the firewood trade. Relics of all these exploitative industries can be seen today, including impressive timber dams once used to drive kauri logs down the Kaiarara River.

The island's western side is a succession of magnificent fiord-like bays —

actually drowned river valleys — which provide superb anchorages in all weather. The island's principal settlements, Port Fitzroy, Whangaparapara, Okupu and Tryphena, are on this side.

The eastern side features magnificent sandy beaches and rocky coves. The island's airstrip is at Claris, next to a large area of wetlands, connected to the other settlements by a mostly unsealed road.

There's no public transport on the island but cars, taxis and bicycles are available for hire. There is also no reticulated power, water or sewerage, no banks, ATMs or street lighting. Shopping is limited to essential goods from a few general stores scattered about the island and cellphone coverage is limited. Needless to say, permanent residents are independent and self-sufficient types — to a certain degree visitors should be too.

For Auckland's cruising yachties and launch owners, Great Barrier has always been the 'great escape'. Its innumerable safe, sheltered and beautiful anchorages make it a haven in all seasons — the traditional holiday and long-weekend destination for Auckland boaties.

In good weather the island is accessible to trailer boats too, though they need to have the range and seakeeping ability to cross a fairly large expanse of open ocean. From Leigh, smaller boats can make the journey in two hops, so to speak, crossing first to Little Barrier Island (no landing allowed), then on to Great Barrier.

Most visitors come by ferry or air from Auckland. Both services are regular and reasonably priced. The fast-ferry ride takes a couple of hours but it operates only in summer and on most public holidays. The Sea-Link ferry operates year-round and can carry vehicles. It takes four and a half hours for the crossing — longer in bad weather. Flights take about 30 minutes. See www.greatbarriertravel.co.nz.

There's plenty of accommodation on the island, ranging from budget backpacker to luxury lodge, but bookings are advised on holiday weekends and during the peak months of summer.

 The fishing

In a word: fantastic! Great Barrier has some of the best fishing in the Hauraki Gulf. Its size and geographical position ensure a multitude of habitats with fishing to match.

The western side gets the most attention from visiting anglers and locals. Its indented coast and numerous bays, coves, islands and harbours provide plenty of sheltered water in most conditions. Big snapper can be taken only a few minutes from popular anchorages at Port Fitzroy.

The southeastern end of the island at Cape Barrier experiences strong currents — care is advised — but once the cape is rounded, the coast and Rosalie Bay offer excellent fishing and shelter from westerly winds.

The island's eastern side faces the Pacific Ocean and is generally rougher. The fishing can be fantastic though, from boats or off the rocks. Arid Island (Rakitu) lies a kilometre or so offshore and offers a safe anchorage in a nearly enclosed bay for a couple of boats. There's good fishing around the island and its associated reef structures.

At the northern end of the Barrier, the Needles (Aiguilles Island) are spectacular to look at and — at times — to fish. Usually surrounded by schools of surface-feeding maomao, trevally, parore and kahawai, the Needles are home to some huge kingfish and plenty of big snapper.

Further round, Miners Head and the reef just offshore produce consistent snapper fishing and a few hapuku. Most of the deeper pins off the island's northern and eastern sides are worth prospecting for hapuku, which are often taken in less than 50 m here.

In summer yellowfin tuna and marlin can be targeted to the north and east of the Barrier, sometimes coming right in close to the island to feed around the Needles.

As well as fish, Great Barrier offers bountiful scallops, crayfish and even paua, though, as seems to be the case for most northern paua, many are undersized. Beaches yield pipi, cockles and tuatua, and mussels and oysters carpet the rocks. Mussel farming is important to the island economy and the mussel farms offer anglers consistently good fishing in sheltered water.

Shore fishers can enjoy some of the best rock and beach fishing anywhere. Access is not always easy but tours with local guides can put visitors onto some of the less-accessible rock ledges. As always, local knowledge is priceless.

Night fishing off Medlands, Kaitoke, Awana or Palmers Beach can turn up some real surprises, including XOS sharks, and a feed of kahawai is almost guaranteed during the day.

In 2006 Conservation Minister Chris Carter approved a DOC proposal for a huge marine reserve on the eastern side of Great Barrier Island, despite opposition from many Barrier residents, Auckland boaties and fishers and tangata whenua. At the time of writing, the 50,000 ha reserve, which would take in the whole of the northeastern end of Great Barrier Island, the Needles and Arid Island, was awaiting final approval and gazetting.

When gazetted, the reserve will be the largest in New Zealand, effectively excluding a quarter of Great Barrier's coastline to fishing, as well as a huge area extending 12 nautical miles out to sea.

Things to do

Activities on Great Barrier revolve around the island's natural attractions. All of the usual beach fun can be enjoyed, though you'll be disappointed if some of the more mechanised and glamorous water sports are your thing — parapenting, water-skiing, jetskiing. Instead, surfing is king, along with fishing and quieter pursuits more in keeping with the island's unspoiled and laid-back nature.

Kayaking is popular, with guided kayak tours available; there are excellent dive tours and gear hire facilities; horse riding, tramping and ATV tours. A network of DOC-administered coastal and mountain tracks criss-cross the island. For details and maps, contact the DOC office at Port Fitzroy, 09 429 0044.

A variety of coach and four-wheel-drive tours are available, most of which take in the island's four interesting museums. There are two vineyards on Great Barrier, a nine-hole golf course at Claris, and numerous art and craft shops, studios and exhibitions.

Getting around Great Barrier is never easy unless you bring your own car but hire bicycles are particularly popular in summer. Otherwise, taxis or hire cars are the way to go. Distances between settlements are considerable — Port Fitzroy to Claris is 35 km, for instance, and only some roads are sealed.

Eating out on the Barrier is limited, especially in winter when many operators close down. Tryphena has the greatest scope, with five establishments offering meals, but bookings are essential. Claris has three restaurants including a Thai eatery; Whangaparapara has Great Barrier Lodge and Port Fitzroy has The Boat Club. A burger bar operates just up from Fitzroy Wharf in summer.

The information and travel office in the Stonewall shopping complex at Tryphena has details on all the island's facilities and activities.

Accommodation

Accommodation options on Great Barrier include luxury and boutique, lodge and backpacker-style, B&B and self-contained. Camping is also possible at several DOC campgrounds as well as three private establishments. There's even a DOC hut available free of charge at Kaiarara on a first-come, first-served basis. At the other end of the spectrum, Earthsong Lodge overlooking Tryphena Harbour is the island's only five-star accommodation.

Recommended Great Barrier Island websites are www.greatbarriernz.com, www.thebarrier.co.nz and www.greatbarrierisland.co.nz.

 Boat ramps

Locals launch into harbours or over beaches. Hire boats are available on the island but many visitors either come by boat or take their own on the car ferry.

Diesel and petrol fuel is available at Port Fitzroy and Whangaparapara; trailer boats can refuel at Claris, Port Fitzroy and Mulberry Grove at Tryphena.

Numerous anchorages are available for visiting boaties, most of whom choose to anchor in one of the island's hundreds of sheltered coves and bays. The many safe, quiet anchorages close to Port Fitzroy are particularly popular.

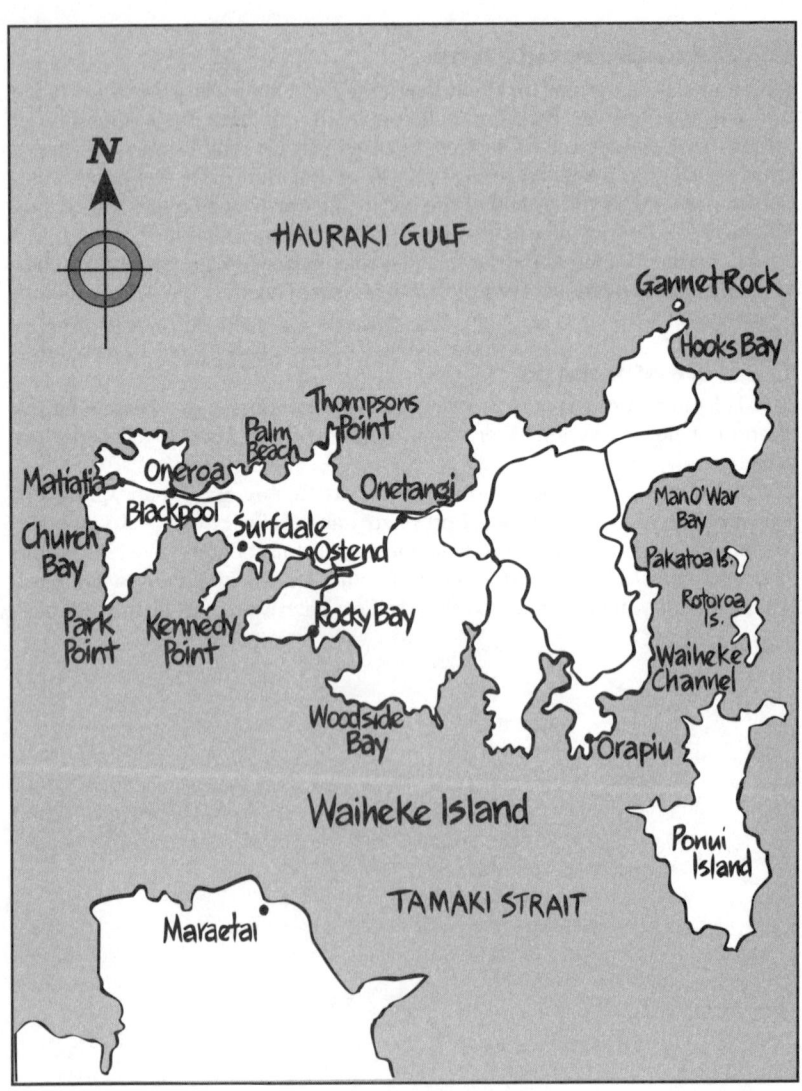

Waiheke Island

The second-largest island in the Hauraki Gulf after Great Barrier, Waiheke has a completely different character by virtue of its proximity to Auckland City. Despite its physical and administrative position as an adjunct to Auckland, Waiheke Island has managed to maintain an alternative, artsy flavour much valued by residents and visitors alike.

Waiheke Island, like Great Barrier, qualifies as a fishing destination because of its size, diversity and relative isolation. Like Great Barrier, Waiheke is accessible only by boat or plane — or by helicopter, and plenty of them buzz in to park beside the island's multimillion-dollar homes each evening.

Grandiose architectural wonders of the very rich aside, most of Waiheke's 8000 residents live in small villages concentrated at the island's western end. Ferries dock at Matiatia, close to the main settlements of Oneroa and Blackpool. Immediately to the east of these are Palm Beach, Surfdale, and Ostend, while a little further east lies Onetangi. Much of the eastern end of the island is privately owned farmland.

Waiheke was settled by Maori around AD 1200 and was home to several different groups over the years. Visitors to the island can explore pa sites and other archaeological evidence of the long years of Maori occupation.

Oneroa is part of a longer Maori name meaning 'long beach of weeping sands', and marks the place where in the 1820s Hongi Hika's musket-wielding Nga Puhi massacred local Ngati Maru in a great battle on the shore.

European settlement began with whalers and sealers before the first permanent residents began clearing forest in the 1850s. For most of its European history Waiheke's farms supplied foodstuffs to nearby Auckland.

Waiheke Island is a delightful mix of beaches, vineyards, olive groves, native forest and farmland. With an area of 93 sq km, the island is 19.3 km long, varying in width from just a few hundred metres to 9.65 km at its widest point. Its 135.5 km of coastline includes 40 km of beaches, most offering safe swimming. Waiheke's climate tends to be warmer and drier than Auckland's, just 17.7 km away, with higher sunshine hours, making it ideal for vineyards.

Although many of the island's inhabitants commute to Auckland to work each day, a good proportion stay put to pursue artistic and other 'alternative' pastimes. Always a popular weekend and holiday getaway, Waiheke Island has recently boomed as a tourist destination with a range of accommodation, restaurants and activities to match.

There are good roads on the island. Most residents have their own vehicles and there is a car ferry service to and from the mainland. Cars, motorcycles and pushbikes are available for hire.

From Auckland's downtown ferry terminal at the bottom of Queen Street, Matiatia is approximately 40 minutes by fast ferry. That's just long enough to buy a beer from the onboard bar and relax with local commuters heading home on a Friday night. The trip is always interesting as the ferry runs down the busy Waitemata Harbour out into the Hauraki Gulf, passing other islands on the way.

Other visitors make their own way to the island in private craft. It's a popular overnight stopover for visiting boaties, many of whom anchor in one of the island's many lovely bays, often without venturing ashore. During holidays and weekends trailer boats by the hundreds visit Waiheke to fish and enjoy its beaches. Any of the more popular beaches will be crowded with boats just offshore on fine summer weekends.

The fishing

Waiheke Island has plenty to offer the visiting angler. Although boat fishers tend to visit its surrounding waters without going ashore, excellent shore fishing rewards weekend visitors staying on the island. Waiheke is also home to a number of fishing charter businesses offering day trips from Matiatia.

Anyone with access to a small boat on the island is almost guaranteed a feed of snapper during the summer months. Keen boaties can bring their boats across to the island on the Sea Link ferry, a popular option, especially during holidays. Good launching ramps at Matiatia, Sandy Beach, Kennedy Point, Orapiu and Rocky Bay cater to the needs of locals but parking can be a problem in summer when there are a lot of visitors.

In general, the western end and southern (mainland) side of Waiheke provide good channel fishing for snapper in areas of strong tidal streams. The bottom is generally soft sediment with patches of reef extending from the island's headlands. There are a few deeper holes and scattered patches of reef in the channels which are always worth fishing, as well as deep bays, some lined with mangroves, and the island's only marine reserve.

The northern (ocean) side and eastern end, usually known as 'The Bottom End' provide different and more varied fishing for shore-based and boat anglers alike. The Bottom End includes a series of picturesque bays beside the swiftly flowing Waiheke Channel that runs between Waiheke Island and Ponui, Rotoroa, Pakatoa and Shag islands. There are plenty of protected anchorages either side of the channel for overnighting boaties.

This area is well known for its excellent snapper fishing and an abundance of big kingfish in summer and autumn. Hooks Bay produces plenty of juicy scallops, as do many other bays around the island, while the deep holes off Thumb Point are consistently good places to take large snapper. Gannet Rock, not far from Thumb Point, is famous for XOS snapper and some extremely large kingfish. The deeper holes in this general area are one of the few places close to Auckland where anglers can realistically target tarakihi.

Around the back of Waiheke, facing the Coromandel Peninsula, the water is more oceanic in nature, tending to be clearer and more affected by ocean swells. Fish such as koheru, blue maomao, red moki and other ocean reef species are common on this side, which offers a variety of reef and sandy bottom habitats. Rock fishers can choose from dozens of headlands adjoining deep water where snapper and kingfish can be caught. Boat fishers can fish the rocks and reefs close to the island or seek out schooling fish under work-ups of birds or look for concentrations of snapper showing on their sounders over the sand. Drift fishing is popular and productive across the sand wide of the island or further out into the Firth of Thames.

Things to do

The great attraction of Waiheke Island is that it combines outstanding fishing with a wonderful mix of cultural, gastronomic and outdoor activities. While close to Auckland, its island nature ensures a total break from urban living. And if matters in the city become too pressing, a 40-minute ferry ride will return you to downtown.

Vineyard tours are a popular attraction on Waiheke. Many weekend visitors combine other activities with visits to some of the island's wonderful wineries, most of which have superb dining facilities. But the island's vibrant artistic and cultural life also attracts visitors — Waiheke is famous for its art galleries, museums, artists' studios and sculptures, many of which are exhibited outdoors to complement the island's stunning maritime scenery, as well as its popular weekend craft markets.

A selection of wonderful beaches draws locals and visitors alike, summer and winter, with safe swimming and golden sand. Sea-kayaking, sailing and windsurfing are just some of the possibilities on Waiheke. A range of coastal walks caters to all levels of fitness and guided or unguided tours take in all of the island's sights.

The Stony Batter gun emplacements at the northwestern extremity of the island were built during World War II to guard the Hauraki Gulf against invasion. Its complex of more than 1.3 km of underground tunnels, gun emplacements, an engine room, command post and associated militaria draw thousands of visitors each year.

There is so much to see and do on Waiheke that people visit time and time again. And with so much to occupy non-fishers, there's every chance partners and family won't miss the keen angler who takes time out to pursue his or her favourite pastime, making it an excellent destination for the considerate fisher! The website www.waihekenz.com is a good place to start looking for activities on Waiheke Island. Fullers Cruises' offices and the information kiosk on the waterfront in downtown Auckland also have masses of information about what to do and where to stay on Waiheke and other Hauraki Gulf islands.

Accommodation

There's plenty of choice on Waiheke Island, though it tends towards the boutique and more expensive — beach houses, top-quality B&Bs and luxury retreats — as befits a fashionable weekend getaway for busy Aucklanders with money to spend. There are, however, several budget accommodation options, including waterfront lodges and a range of backpackers' hostels costing as little as $22 per person per night. Visitors should consider where on the island they want to stay, especially if they don't have transport, since accommodation, while concentrated at the western end, is scattered the length and breadth of the island. Check out www.waihekenz.com, www.gotowaiheke.co.nz and www.waiheke.co.nz for accommodation options.

 **Boat ramps**

Concrete boat ramps at Matiatia Bay, Sandy Beach, Kennedy Bay, Orapiu and Rocky Bay service local boaties as well as visitors. Beach launching is possible at the western end of Oneroa Beach and at Onetangi Beach, but a four-wheel-drive or tractor is recommended.

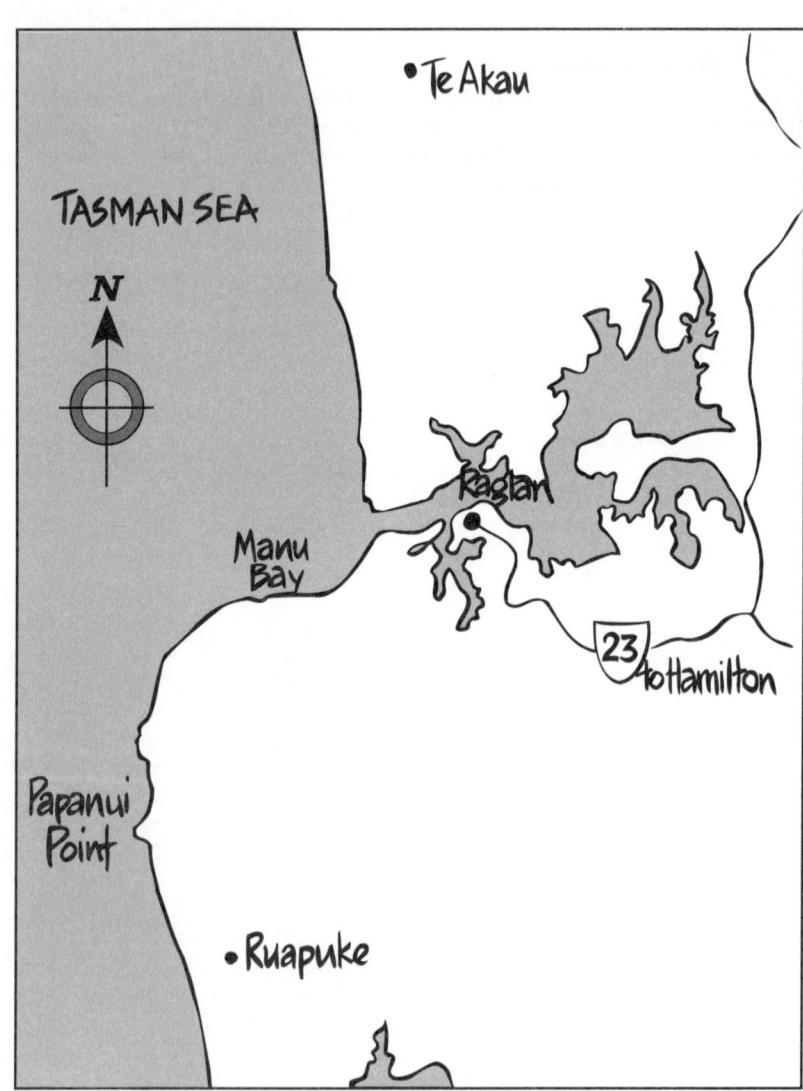

Raglan

Raglan is one of New Zealand's quintessential seaside towns. The village is on the southern side of Raglan Harbour, about 50 km west of Hamilton. It's a popular holiday spot and is probably best known for its surfing.

Raglan has about 4000 permanent inhabitants, many of whom are attracted to the town's relaxed and slightly alternative lifestyle and its lively cafe and live music scene. The area boasts breathtaking panoramic views of the Tasman Sea and has a rich and colourful history. Maori settled here in the 11th century and European settlers started buying land here in the 1850s when the town was called Whaingaroa, a name still used locally.

If the weather won't behave or the fishing's off, there are worse places to kick back and enjoy a quiet drink or a good meal. You can sit on the front terrace of the Harbour View Hotel on the main street and admire the palm trees and the backdrop of Mt Karioi, a majestic dormant volcano that overlooks the coastal town.

 ## The fishing

Although surfing dominates the town, fishing is a popular and productive pastime and many surfies are also keen anglers. The harbour offers safe fishing for kids, from the bridge over the harbour and the wharf. Baitfish, yellow-eyed mullet and kahawai are the main catches but snapper are regularly taken.

There is some small-boat fishing for snapper and kahawai inside the harbour but strong tidal currents can be dangerous and local knowledge is important. Flounder are netted or speared in the harbour's upper reaches. Surfcasters enjoy good kahawai fishing inside the harbour at Putoetoe Point right next to the campground, and at the harbour entrance. Strong rips make these spots easiest to fish an hour or so either side of slack tide.

Outside the harbour, several good locations await the shore-based angler. The closest is Manu Bay, loved by the surfing fraternity for its world-famous left-hand break. When the sea is too calm to surf it's ideal for fishing. A lot of trevally and snapper are caught from the beach to the right of the rocks and boat ramp.

Twenty minutes' drive further south along a narrow gravel road is Papanui Point, a rocky peninsula accessed by crossing a paddock and negotiating a steep track down the cliff. The fishing can be excellent for big snapper and kingfish. The water around the point is deep and the swell can be dangerous but in good conditions Papanui Point is one of the best land-based spots on the west coast of the North Island.

Two kilometres south of Papanui Point, Ruapuke Beach offers good beach fishing, particularly at night. The beach isn't suitable for swimming due to a fierce undertow, though the stream-side campground in the valley behind the beach is popular with holidaymakers.

North of the harbour there's good beach fishing but access is only by boat. After crossing the harbour, you have to walk a couple of kilometres up the beach. Mussel Rocks is popular with surfcasters and boaties.

Boat fishers often negotiate the Raglan bar to fish outside the harbour. It's a treacherous stretch of water and should only be attempted in good conditions. Enlisting the help of an experienced local is advisable for first-timers. Even on good days the bar can cut up badly. Slack tide is the best time to cross, preferably at high tide, so a 12-hour day at sea is quite normal.

The other option is launch at the boat club ramp at Manu Bay, which is protected by a rock breakwater. This ramp is really only suitable for boats up to 6 m and is unworkable in any sort of swell. And if there are surfers in the water, forget about launching here. Boaties using this ramp need to keep a close eye on conditions while out fishing; if the swell gets up it can become extremely difficult to retrieve your boat. If the swell appears to be building, cut your losses and make a run for the ramp before it's too late.

Once outside, boaties have a number of options. Like most of the west coast, Raglan can fish well over the sand at any time — simply look out for fish signs on the sounder or drift-fish in a particular depth range according to what's recently been fishing well.

A few areas of structure, notably Bar Reef and Jackson's Reef, attract fish at times and can provide superb fishing when they're on. Jackson's is a good spot for kingfish. Boaties also enjoy success close to shore to both the north and south of the harbour when the snapper are in.

During summer many of the bigger boats target marlin and tuna. There's excellent gamefishing off Raglan, though billfish are not always present. There can be exceptional fishing one day and nothing the next.

Most of the fishing takes place in water more than 60 m deep, which is many kilometres offshore, so boats need to be well founded and must carry sufficient fuel for a long day on the water. Suitable safety gear is mandatory and a call to Raglan Coastguard on entering and exiting the harbour (or Manu Bay) is advisable.

Things to do

Surfing is the first activity that springs to mind but is not everyone's cup of tea. If you're not into surfing you'll still enjoy watching the action on the pumping breaks that have hosted many international surfing championships. If you do wish to give it a go, surfboards, boogie boards, wetsuits and flippers can be rented year-round, and there's a local surfing school on beautiful Ngarunui Beach. A surfing and spa retreat at Whale Bay is dedicated to women surfers.

Other activities around Raglan include guided kayaking tours on the harbour and an 18-hole golf course with an honesty box (try to avoid hitting the sheep). Horse-riding treks up Mt Karioi will reward you with stunning Tasman Sea views. Take in the coastal town atmosphere by visiting artists' studios, relaxing at a cafe or enjoying harbour views from the eateries on the main street.

The more active visitor can try tramping, kite surfing, blow carting, skydiving, paragliding or mountain biking. There's safe swimming in the harbour and at Manu Bay; less strenuous activities include sunbathing on black-sand beaches, sightseeing and kite flying.

Accommodation

There are many holiday homes for rent and a good selection of motels, campgrounds and other accommodation. Start your search on the internet at www.raglan.net.nz.

 Boat ramps

There is a good boat ramp beside the wharf inside Raglan Harbour suitable for trailer boats of all sizes. Parking can be difficult, however. The only other ramp is at Manu Bay, courtesy of the local boating club.

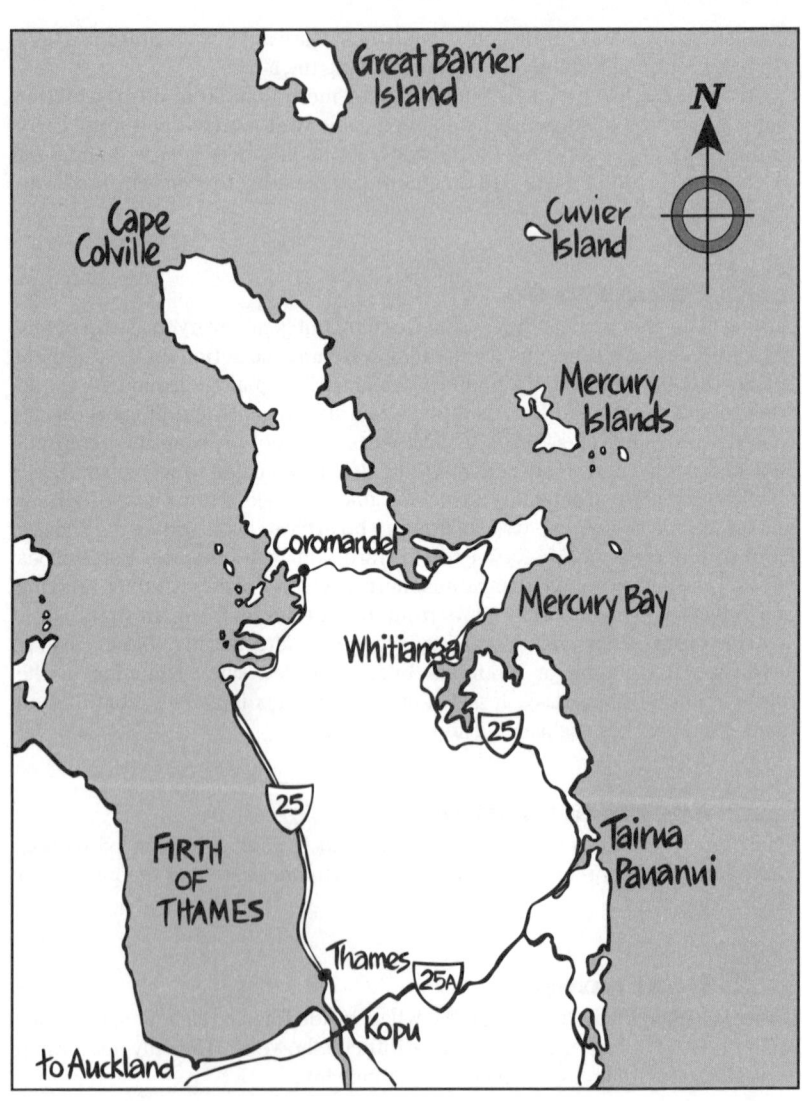

Coromandel Peninsula

Stunningly beautiful Coromandel Peninsula, with most of its east coast beaches no more than two hours' drive from Auckland on a good day, is a regular weekend retreat for thousands escaping the big smoke.

Geologically similar to Northland and Great Barrier Island, the peninsula forms the eastern boundary of the Hauraki Gulf. At the southern end of the Firth of Thames the gulf becomes shallow and silty, thanks to the Waihou River depositing its considerable load of Waikato farmland into the ocean at Thames. The coastline of the Hauraki Plains between Miranda and Thames is all silty margins, saltmarsh and mangroves.

At Thames the character of the coast changes. Travelling north up the western side of State Highway 25, you pass a succession of small rocky bays and silty-sandy beaches. Past Deadmans Point the coast changes again. The sea loses much of its muddy hue and the magnificent harbours and islands around Manaia and historic Coromandel township are reminiscent of Northland and Great Barrier and the rest of the gulf. The northern tip of Coromandel Peninsula remains remote and relatively difficult to get to.

The east coast is where most visitors head. Blessed with beautiful beaches, stunning harbours and magnificent headlands and bays, it's a Mecca for fishers and holidaymakers.

On any Friday evening, all roads to Coromandel are choked with vehicles, many towing boats. The process is reversed on Sunday evenings. In holiday weekends congestion is often severe. Trust me, it's much better to travel to the Coromandel's gorgeous beaches and bush-covered mountains during the week, particularly outside of public holidays.

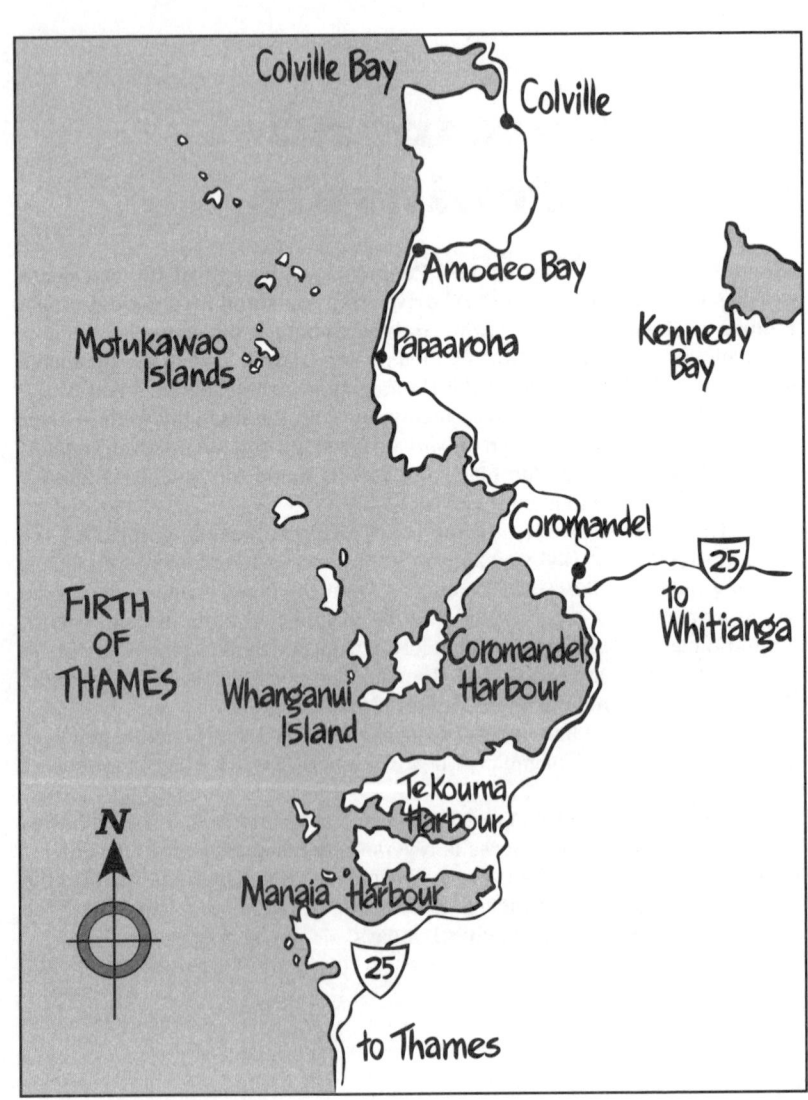

Coromandel, Te Kouma and environs

Magnificent Coromandel Harbour is sheltered by a string of islands that run up the coast almost as far as Colville town. These islands, along with the region's thriving mussel farms, are the main focus for boat fishers.

Coromandel township built its early prosperity on the timber trade, before gold was discovered in 1852. Coromandel's population peaked in the 1890s, declining by the end of World War 1. Tourism and aquaculture (mussel farming) are the region's main industries today.

Clustered around Coromandel are the villages of Manaia and Te Kouma, both with important aquaculture industries. Up the coast, Papaaroha and Amodeo Bay are particular attractions for anglers.

Further north still are Port Jackson and Port Charles, both the domain of the keen, well-organised angler, many of whom set up self-contained fishing camps during the summer. Facilities are non-existent and food and fuel a long, dusty drive away but these two locations are among the most beautiful in New Zealand and offer some of the best fishing in the North Island.

 **The fishing**

The dozens of islands lying just offshore extend north from Deadmans Point up to the Motukawao group opposite Colville Bay. The bottom gradually changes from north to south: Rangipukea Island, outside Te Kouma, is surrounded by a mostly muddy bottom and the rocky shores of the island support a less diverse flora and fauna than the northern group of islands off Amodeo Bay. The water around the more northerly islands is less affected by the silt and mud of the Firth of Thames, so reef species such as maomao and koheru are common. Scallops are also abundant.

Fishing for snapper is good throughout the region. Small-boat anglers, dinghy and kayak fishers enjoy success in the shallow harbours and among the headlands, reefs and holes close to the more accessible islands. The islands further offshore and the pinnacles and reefs in deeper water are best left to bigger boats.

Manaia, Te Kouma and Coromandel harbours contain oyster and mussel farms by the dozen. These are sure-fire fish attractors, exploited by visiting and local anglers. Local charter boats take advantage of mussel harvesting activity to put their clients onto spectacular snapper fishing as the fish gorge themselves on broken mussels, crabs and other debris dislodged when the mussel lines are pulled up and their bounty stripped.

Mussel farms extend well up the coast but are usually located in sheltered water, making them safe destinations for small-boat fishers. By far the best fishing occurs at harvest time — find a working harvester and you're guaranteed great fishing. Don't get too close though. The islands, headlands, reefs and artificial structures of mussel and oyster farms are also the domain of good numbers of kingfish, some very large.

Land-based anglers can take good kingfish on livebaits from any of the points and headlands with deep water close by, and boat anglers can fish livebaits or troll lures around and between the islands, over pins and close to mussel farms. Casting poppers or rigged piper can also be effective.

Kahawai are present year-round and can be taken by a variety of methods. Seeking out working birds in the Firth is worthwhile. In winter large kahawai are usually responsible for work-ups containing masses of diving gannets, shearwaters and often dolphins. Dolphins and kahawai drive baitfish to the surface where diving seabirds take their fill. Underneath, snapper, kingfish and other species join in the carnage. Jigging or baitfishing under and slightly behind the birds can be excellent.

In spring and summer work-ups usually contain fewer gannets, and kahawai are not always the instigators: schools of jack mackerel, sometimes mixed in with smaller kahawai and slimy mackerel, feed on whitebait or anchovies. Terns and small shearwaters mark the feeding activity. They're still worth fishing, especially since the work-ups are often nearly static. Snapper can invariably be found underneath.

For a change of pace, there's wilderness trout fishing on the Kauaeranga River down the road at Thames and over the hill in the Waiwawa River at Coroglen. Rainbow trout numbers are not high but the surroundings are gorgeous.

Things to do

There are plenty of ocean-based activities for non-fishers. There are fishing charters as well as island and harbour cruises, safe swimming in the harbours at high tide or on the east coast at Whangapoua, sailing charters and boat hire.

Hikers can enjoy beautiful bush and coastal walks of varying length and difficulty. Several take you into the peninsula's interior and offer amazing views from the ridge tops and peaks. For the adventurous, Argo eight-wheeler tours are a lot of fun, or try horse riding at White Star Station near Colville.

Cultural attractions include museums, potteries, artists' studios, the unusual Waiau Waterworks and much more. Eating out is fun, with several interesting cafes and restaurants to choose from, as well as hotel bars, takeaways and bakeries.

For a comprehensive guide, see www.coromandeltown.co.nz or visit Coromandel Information Centre, 355 Kapanga Road, Coromandel, 07 866 8598.

 Accommodation

Visitors can choose between backpacker, campground, homestay, B&B and hotel or motel accommodation. Several of Coromandel's atmospheric historic pubs and hotels offer clean rooms at reasonable rates.

Campers have plenty of scope. Private campgrounds at Papaaroha and Amodeo Bay, which also offer caravan and cabin/motel accommodation, are superbly equipped, with excellent boat launching and cleaning facilities, fish cleaning areas, freezer space, boat hire and charter services.

Anglers Lodge at Amodeo Bay is one of my favourites for fishing weekend getaways. DOC also runs a number of basic campsites in the region. Campsites at Kauaeranga, Port Jackson and Fantail Bay are monitored during summer. Facilities are basic and fees modest.

Other options include self-contained bach and cottage accommodation. Check out www.coromandeltown.co.nz for a full list.

 **Boat ramps**

Boat ramps are spread up the coast from Thames; the best are all-tide ramps at Wilsons Bay, Te Kouma and Coromandel. Oamaru Bay, Papaaroha and Amodeo Bay have reasonable boat ramps but they're only usable over the top half of the tide, depending on boat size.

Mercury Bay

Mercury Bay is a lovely stretch of water sheltered from southerly and westerly winds. The gateway to the Mercury Islands, it offers easy boat launching and safe boating inshore with the promise of big fish and great diving among the islands and beyond.

Mercury Bay and the smaller Cooks Bay lie at the seaward end of Whitianga Harbour. The thriving resort of Cooks Beach is tucked into the eastern end of Cooks Bay beside the Purangi Estuary. It's 30 km by road but only a short passenger ferry ride to the historic settlement of Whitianga, a bustling holiday destination. The twin resorts are among the most popular on the peninsula.

Whitianga has plenty of places to stay, eat, drink, shop and generally enjoy the holiday lifestyle, and has a modest marina. Cooks Beach has fewer facilities. The town of Coroglen, home to a trout-fishing stream, lies on the inland reaches of Whitianga Harbour.

Within easy reach of Whitianga are the beach villages of Flaxmill Bay, Hahei, Hot Water Beach and Ferry Landing and, to the north, Kuaotunu, Opito Bay, Whangapoua and Matarangi. Most have accommodation and offer good fishing close by.

 ## The fishing

One of the nicest things about Mercury Bay is the vast scope it offers the keen angler. There's good beach fishing, rock fishing and, in the estuaries, flounder fishing. There are pipis and tuatua in the harbours and on the beaches, crayfish and scallops, and excellent fishing inshore and offshore for all boats large and small.

The dinghy fisher or kayaker can enjoy good success close to Whitianga or Cooks Beach and up and down the coast, while bigger boats can explore the whole of Mercury Bay and the Mercury Islands beyond.

A marine reserve around Centre Island can be a trap for the inexperienced

Mercury Bay

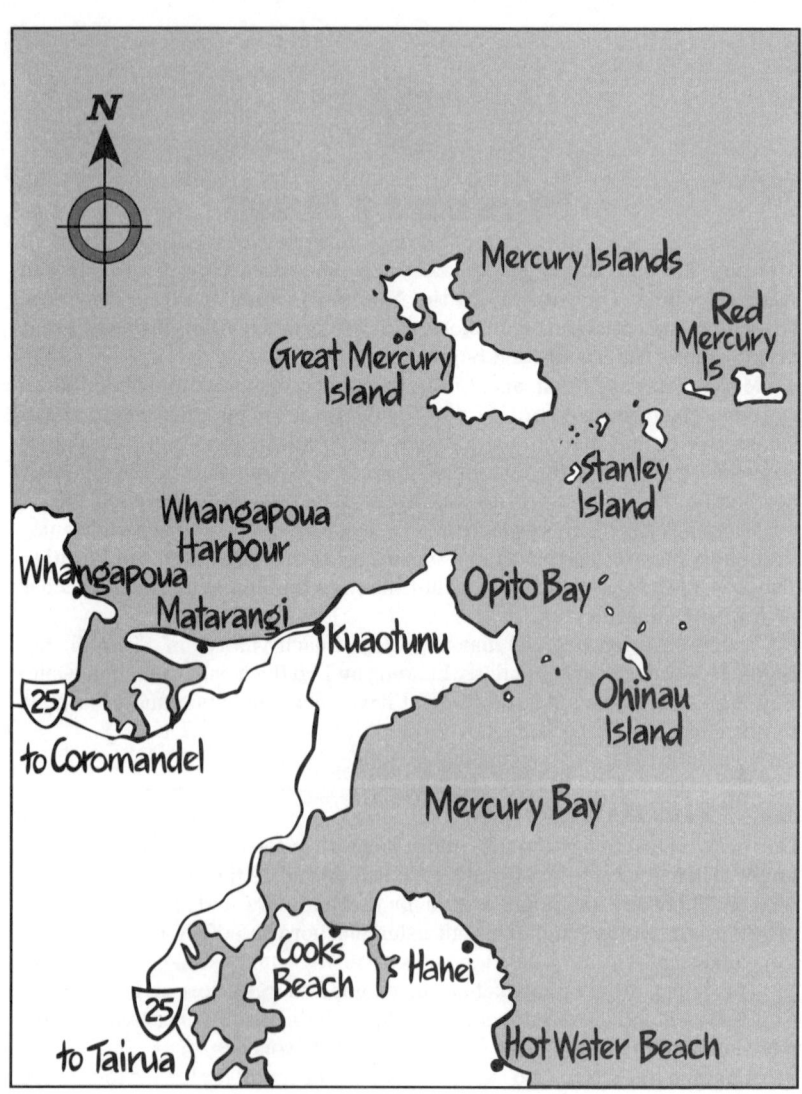

but its boundaries are clearly marked. The eastern side of the reef off the island's northern end, outside the reserve, is a favourite with small boats, producing a variety of species, including kingfish.

Small boats can access much of the inshore coastal fishing in the bay and along the rocky coast on either side. Many launch off the beach or from unformed ramps close to where they intend to fish. This is where kayak fishers, with the supreme portability of their craft, are at an advantage. Larger boats invariably launch from excellent public ramps at Whitianga or Cooks Beach. In summer there can be quite a wait as demand outstrips supply.

With a well-founded trailer boat of 5 m or more, the islands of the Mercury group are within reach. The closest, including Ohinau, are only a few kilometres from the mainland across the Hole in the Wall channel, but a great deal further from Whitianga or Cooks Beach, tucked within Mercury Bay. The outer islands of the group, including Great and Red Mercury, Double and Stanley are further offshore and further still from launching ramps. Boats should carry sufficient fuel and keep an eye on changing weather conditions, since it can be a long, rough passage home, especially between the islands and Needle Rock at the entrance to Mercury Bay proper if the wind gets up.

Fishing around the islands can be superb, summer or winter. Snapper is the most sought-after species but the full complement of northern reef and pelagic species are available. The area is well known for its large kingfish, which can be targeted in summer and autumn using live kahawai or koheru slowly trolled past rocks and headlands or over sunken reefs. Isolated rocks and reef systems in deep water produce small to medium hapuku for those in the know. Early summer is the best time.

In summer gamefish, including various tuna and marlin, frequent the grounds wide of the Mercury Islands, sometimes entering Mercury Bay itself. Skipjack tuna can be taken well into autumn, providing light tackle entertainment and a supply of excellent bait.

The many other islands and rock stacks inside Mercury Bay and close to the coast on either side provide interesting and varied fishing that is more easily accessible to smaller craft. While the Mercury Islands are the goal for many visiting boat fishers, they often drive past excellent fishing much closer to base.

Land-based anglers can usually find somewhere worthwhile to fish, though they may need to travel beyond the confines of Mercury Bay for best results. Many keen land-based anglers use kayaks or inflatable boats to land on and fish inaccessible rocks, bays, headlands and islands.

Even Buffalo Beach, near the entrance to Whitianga Harbour, can turn up good surfcasting at times, though solitude isn't a feature of the fishing experience this close to Whitianga. Further afield, Opito Bay has good surfcasting close to the points either side of the bay and easy scallop diving in the middle, accessible to a snorkeller from the shore. Opito Point, a short walk over the hill at the eastern end of Opito Bay, offers a selection of rock ledges that produce snapper and sometimes kingfish. They fish best when the water has been stirred up by a good easterly storm.

Tokarahu Point, at the eastern end of Whangapoua Bay, can be reached from Opito Bay or Otama. Either way it's around an hour's walk but is worth it for the good kingfish it turns up in summer. Good snapper frequent the area at change of light.

Whitianga is well endowed with fishing and diving charter boats, including self-drive charters, most operating year-round.

Things to do

Whitianga is a thriving community whose population balloons with visitors in summer. Many are regulars and a growing number own holiday homes in the town, Cooks Beach or other coastal villages around the bay. Increasingly, visitors are becoming permanent residents, retiring to the beach or working from home. Consequently, Whitianga is well served with activities of the non-fishing kind, although the sea plays a large role in the recreation of most of the region's residents.

Visitors can wander the Coromandel Ranges, eat at dozens of good restaurants and cafes, enjoy the beautiful coastal scenery from a charter boat, take a walk to Cathedral Cove, visit the marine reserve aboard a glass-bottomed boat, relax in a hot pool dug with their own hands at Hot Water Beach, visit the local wineries or simply relax at the beach.

Diving is popular, as is kayaking, with boats available for hire from Whitianga, Cathedral Cove and elsewhere. There's a surf school at Hot Water Beach, an adventure rope course, a paintball course, banana boats, wind-surfing, bicycle hire, golf, horse riding, sailing and so much more for the adventurous. More gentle pursuits include arts and crafts trails, museums and galleries, shopping, movies, public gardens and scenic tours and flights.

See www.whitianga.co.nz for details, or visit the Information Centre in Albert Street, Whitianga, 07 866 5555.

 Accommodation

As one would expect in such a popular area, Mercury Bay and environs have plenty of accommodation options. Nevertheless, finding a suitable place to stay can be a challenge during peak season and visitors need to be prepared to cast their net beyond the immediate vicinity of Whitianga or Cooks Beach. Many nearby seaside settlements offer accommodation, much of it in the form of holiday houses for rent.

Whitianga, Buffalo Beach and Hahei have numerous motels and lodges for short-stay visitors and good quality B&Bs, farmstays and farm cottages are available throughout the region. A number of lodges cater to seekers of luxury or the eco-minded. Some are located on stunning pieces of real estate, as are many of the region's eight motor camps.

By far and away the most popular accommodation option is rented beach houses, baches or units. Most are let by private arrangement, many to the same families every summer. Have a look at the accommodation section of www.whitianga.co.nz or try www.bluepenguin.co.nz or www.bachcare.co.nz.

Boat ramps

Whitianga has two good ramps that launch into the harbour. The better of the two is by the main wharf. It can be tricky due to tidal flow but it's wide, with a concrete base, and suitable for large trailer boats. The second is further up the harbour off Robinson Road and better suited to smaller boats.

A full-service marina caters to resident and visiting boats. Fuel is available.

Cooks Beach has a good ramp into the estuary and Whangapoua, Matarangi and Hahei all have formed ramps. Most other coastal settlements have boat-launching facilities of some description but a tractor or four-wheel-drive might be needed.

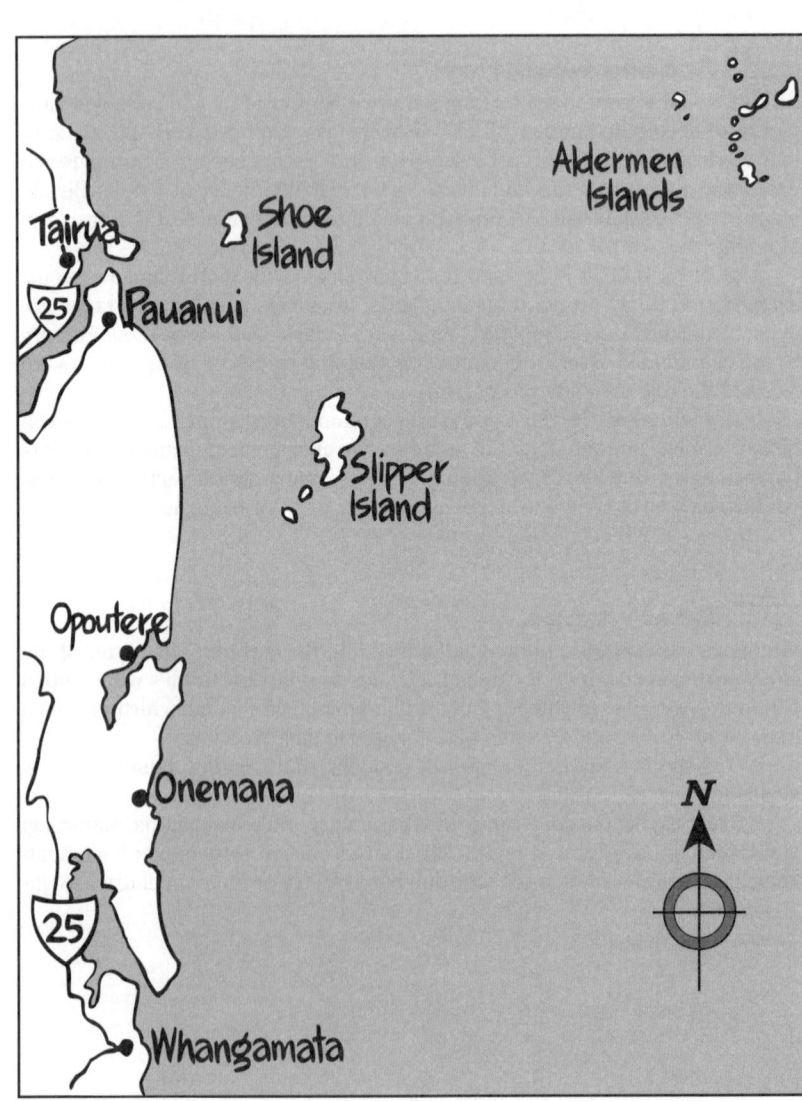

16

Tairua and Pauanui

Tairua Harbour is about halfway up the eastern side of the Coromandel Peninsula. Tairua township is on the northern side of the harbour, one of the Coromandel's finest and most dramatic. On the southern shore lies Pauanui, a large-scale beachside development.

Like much of the rest of the region, gold mining and logging dominated Tairua's early European history. In later years farming became important and today tourism is the biggest earner for the district.

The populations of both towns swell hugely during summer and on any fine weekend as Aucklanders, Hamiltonians, Rotorua-ites and others make the two-hour trek to occupy their holiday homes.

A bridge at the head of the harbour links the twin towns of Tairua and Pauanui, plus there's a regular ferry service. Gorgeous beaches are a feature of the coast to the north and south of the harbour and there's safe swimming for children inside the harbour.

 The fishing

Not far off from the entrance to Tairua Harbour is Shoe Island, with the larger Slipper Island a few miles to the south. Shoe, Slipper and their associated smaller islands, reefs and banks are the focus for many anglers heading out from Tairua and Pauanui. Slipper is also an excellent land-based venue, with anglers' accommodation available and a reputation for mega-snapper off the rocks.

Further offshore, to the northeast on the edge of the continental shelf, lie the Alderman Islands. This complex of steep, craggy volcanic peaks is a magnet for fish of all types — and fishers. During the season, gamefish congregate in the warm blue-water currents sweeping past the islands and there's good fishing year-round for reef species, snapper, kingfish and deep-water inhabitants such as hapuku. Clear water and abundant sea life make the Aldermen Islands a premium dive spot too. A fair way offshore, the islands are the preserve of bigger boats, including well-founded large trailer boats. Many of the flash launches tied up to jetties in Pauanui's canals spend time poking around the Aldermen.

Many of the areas of deeper foul off the Coromandel's east coast offer good tarakihi fishing. From Tairua dozens of such locations are accessible, usually in water at least 40 m deep. Snapper tend to come from reefs in shallower water, though they are caught with tarakihi in some locations.

Kingfish are present year-round but more common inshore in summer. They can be taken around the islands and reefs, in deep water and in the shallows. They are also regular catches for shore-based anglers and even make an appearance inside Tairua Harbour at times.

Land-based options are varied. Fishing for kahawai and the occasional kingfish is easily accessible from Paku Island at the entrance to Tairua Harbour; the rocks at the end of Pauanui Beach offer up school snapper and kingfish; and there's more challenging fishing further along the coast. Many of the best spots involve considerable walking since there's no road access, though many anglers use boats or kayaks. Popular locations up and down the coast include Boat Harbour, Sailors Grave and Pakahina Bay near Opoutere. There's good beach fishing at Opoutere and Ohui, too.

Things to do

As a popular holiday destination, Tairua–Pauanui has plenty to offer visitors. Most of the shops, services, restaurants and casual accommodation are concentrated in Tairua, though Pauanui does have its own marine-oriented commercial hub.

There are plenty of places to eat and a full range of services, including marine engineering and a lot of real estate offices — property sales seems to be the region's biggest business.

Many of the shops fall into the boutique category, but all the basics are available, from a well-stocked supermarket to several smaller grocery and general stores.

A selection of artists' studios, galleries and craft shops should appeal to the culturally minded. Tairua Golf Course is an 18-hole course with reasonable green fees for the visitor.

Visiting anglers can charter a boat from Tairua, take a dive course or hire sea biscuits, water-skis, kayaks and almost any other water sports toy. Surfing is popular, with excellent surf beaches either side of the towns.

Accommodation

Like most Coromandel beach towns, Tairua and Pauanui are dominated by beach houses that are occupied for only part of the year. That leaves a huge pool of quality accommodation empty for most of the year and much of it is available for rent, particularly during the week and in the winter season.

Most beach houses are let privately and many of them are jointly owned, so families come and go right through the year. Finding a suitable beach house to rent shouldn't be too hard if you're flexible about timing. Finding one in the school holidays or during the height of summer is another matter. Try www.tairua.org.nz or www.holidayhomes.co.nz.

Other accommodation includes hotels, motels and lodges, serviced apartments, a couple of motor camps, a camping ground on Slipper Island, plenty of B&Bs and backpacker-style accommodation. See www.tairua.info.

Boat ramps

There's a good public boat ramp at Tairua and another at Pauanui. Many boats are permanently domiciled in the canals at Pauanui.

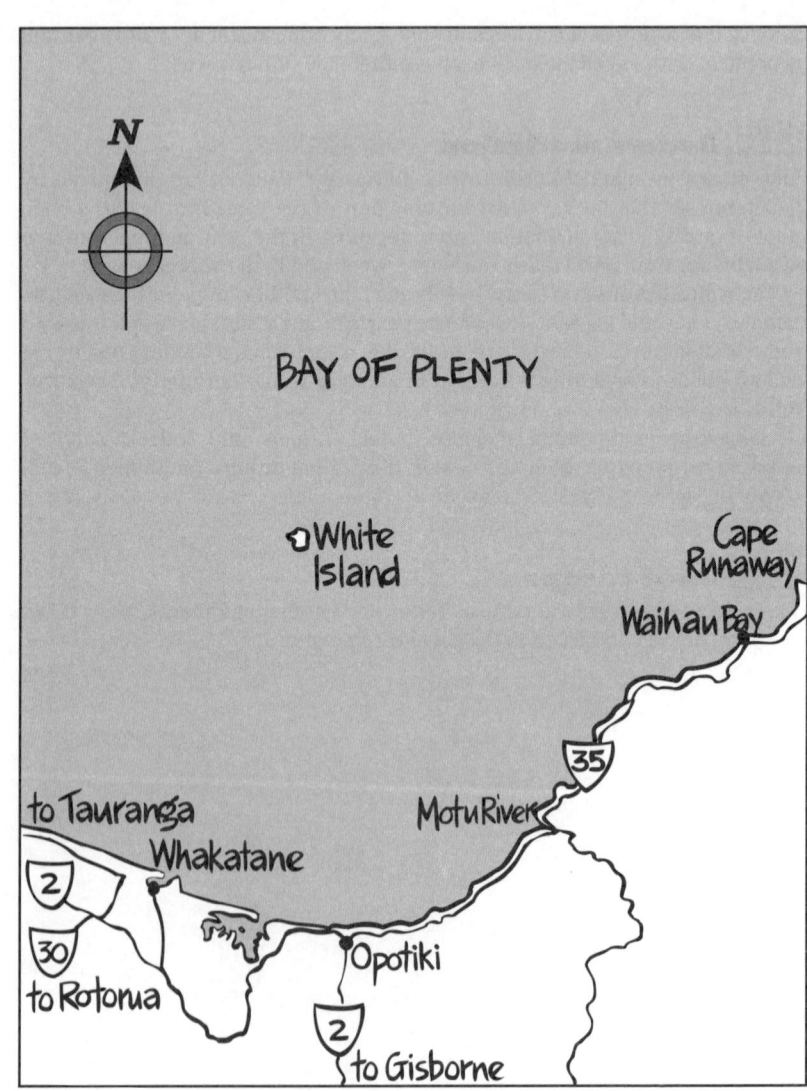

the Eastern Bay of Plenty

The Eastern Bay of Plenty is a fishing heaven that attracts both fish and fishers. With kilometres of sparsely populated coast, it offers a wealth of options for boat and land-based anglers alike.

A wonderful climate attracts visitors and migrants. With some of the highest average temperatures in New Zealand during summer, high sunshine hours and abundant rainfall, the Eastern Bay of Plenty is ideal for horticulture and kiwifruit growing, as well as beach-going.

Magnificent beaches, the brooding active volcano White Island, beautiful harbours, rocky bays, rivers and forests make the Eastern Bay of Plenty an outdoors paradise. In some parts of the region the population trebles over summer.

The huge sweep of the Bay of Plenty dominates the whole region; most of the bay's inhabitants have been fishing at some time and it's a passion for many. Superb fishing is available throughout the Eastern Bay, inshore and offshore. There's also excellent trout fishing in the rivers and lakes inland of the region, some of which are covered in the Rotorua section of this book.

There are a dozen places one could choose for a fishing getaway. I have chosen just two: Whakatane and Waihau Bay.

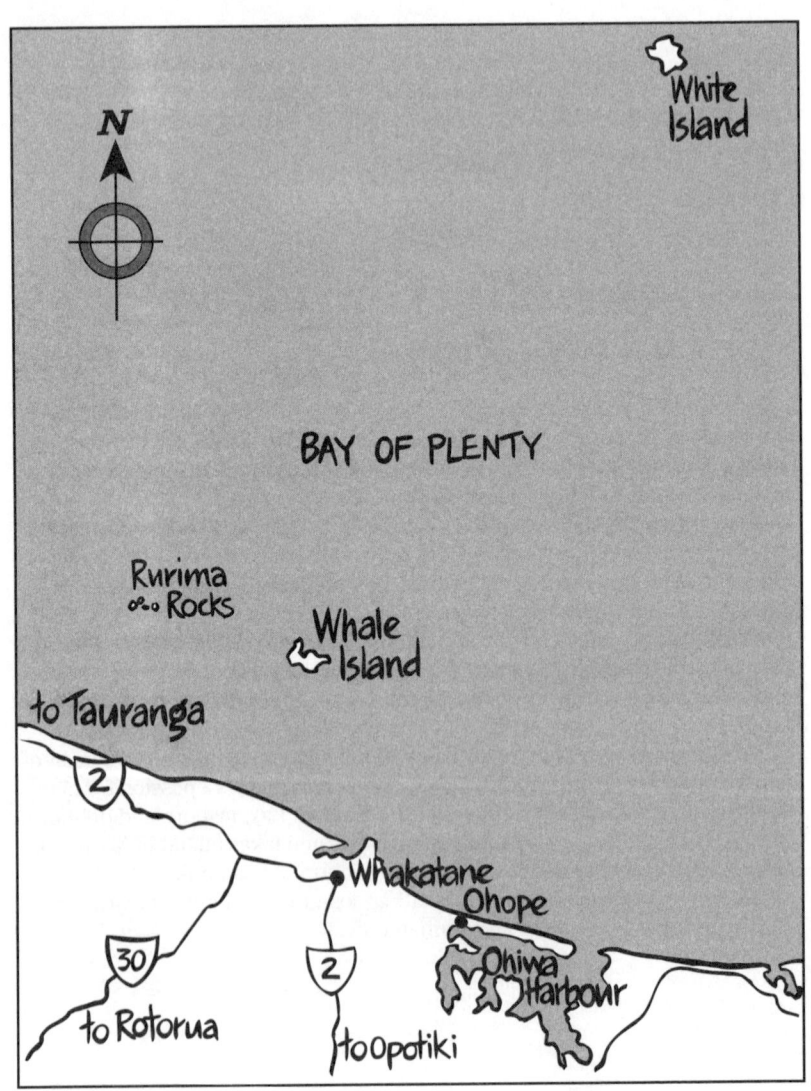

Whakatane

Much of my offshore fishing has been out of Whakatane. For more than 25 years I have enjoyed regular multi-day charters in and around the Bay of Plenty, leaving from the commercial dock beside the Whakatane River.

Whakatane's large charter fleet specialises in overnight and longer fishing trips to White Island, East Cape, Ranfurly Banks and beyond, targeting kingfish, hapuku and bass year-round, with tuna and marlin in summer. I caught my first marlin, first yellowfin and first hapuku from Whakatane charter boats.

Like so many New Zealand towns, Whakatane grew up beside a river with access to the sea. Waterborne navigation was much more important and better developed than overland routes, so patterns of early Maori and European settlement everywhere clustered around harbours and navigable rivers.

Whakatane was settled early in Maori history by a series of migrations, according to oral traditions. It is the site of one of New Zealand's earliest pa — Kaputerangi — and the Eastern Bay of Plenty is now home to Ngati Awa, Tuhoe and Whakatohea iwi.

Breakaway groups left Whakatane over the years to form tribes of their own, including the followers of Puhi, who paddled north to become the Ngapuhi, now the most numerous tribe in Northland.

European settlement began in the 1830s when whalers, sealers and, later, missionaries and traders made their homes here. Today Whakatane is a medium-sized town of 16,000 backing onto a rich and diverse hinterland of farmland, forest and native bush. Forty per cent of the region is protected as a national park.

Several major rivers drain into the Bay of Plenty, including the Rangitaiki, Waioeka and Whakatane. It has excellent air links with the rest of the country, and is three and a half hours by road from Auckland, one and a half hours from Rotorua and slightly less from Tauranga.

The fishing

From Whakatane much of the sea-fishing is concentrated around Whale Island, a few kilometres offshore, and the Rurima Island area to the west. Both these easily located landmarks offer good fishing over an extensive area, producing kingfish, snapper, tarakihi and a range of other species. In summer skipjack and yellowfin tuna are found close by, and striped and black marlin also patrol the reefs and islands.

The sea floor immediately opposite the Whakatane River entrance and west to Matata is mostly mud and sand. It provides excellent gurnard fishing from just behind the breakers to a depth of about 30 m. School snapper and kahawai are also common catches, along with the odd kingfish.

A little further offshore, in 45 m to 50 m, snapper dominate the catch. Most fishing is by drifting, anchoring and berleying once fish are located.

As well as the reef structures around Whale and Rurima, there are several other reefs within easy striking distance of Whakatane. These produce the usual fish species, with tarakihi the main catch in winter.

Kohi Point is popular with shore fishers but also offers boat fishers good snapper at times, kingfish and kahawai.

To the east, Ohiwa Harbour provides sheltered, tidal water with excellent shellfish resources and good flounder fishing. It can also produce school snapper, kahawai and kingfish for those prepared to fish light tackle in shallow water. Outside the bar there's good fishing on the sand off Ohope Beach, with gamefishing offshore in summer.

Throughout the region, from Tauranga to Opotiki, shore fishing, particularly surfcasting, is hugely popular. The Bay of Plenty is one of New Zealand's premier beach-fishing locations.

A series of wonderful beaches sweeps around the coast as far as Opotiki, before the shore turns rocky. Most beaches produce a variety of good fish throughout the year, with snapper the most sought-after. Popular venues include Matata Beach, the mouths of the Tarawera, Rangitaiki and Whakatane Rivers and dozens of possies in between. Most have road access, though keen beach fishers use four-wheel-drives or all-terrain vehicles to get to the section of beach they want to fish.

The eastern bay's offshore fishing is one of its biggest attractions. The grounds around White Island produce excellent deep-water fishing for hapuku, bass, bluenose and other bottom-dwelling fish, sometimes in as much as

400 m, while White Island's giant kingfish are legendary.

The fishery around White Island and offshore reefs, as well as East Cape and Ranfurly Banks well to the east, support Whakatane's large charter fishing fleet. Careful husbandry and voluntary conservation by most of the skippers and crews has ensured the fishery remains in good shape.

During summer the Bay of Plenty normally experiences New Zealand's best and most consistent yellowfin tuna fishing, though runs in recent years have been poor. Tuna is the main focus for much of the offshore fishing effort during this time, with marlin and sharks also regularly caught. Most charter boats and many private boats overnight at Whale or White islands, or further down the coast, to be close to hot fishing.

Things to do

The combination of ocean, rivers and bush mean that Whakatane is an outdoors-oriented town. There's plenty of good hunting in the ranges and forests, for red and rusa deer and wild pig, with guided hunting available.

River kayaking is popular and guided trips down the Waioeka are suitable for families, or go sea kayaking on Ohiwa Harbour with KG Kayaks. Whale and dolphin watching trips, excursions to Whale Island and boat or helicopter trips to White Island are Whakatane specialties, all available from the charter base down by the wharf. Walking on a live volcano and peering into White Island's crater is an experience not to be missed.

First-class trout fishing can be found throughout the region and there are serious tramping opportunities close by, with numerous DOC huts and other shelters scattered through the bush country behind Opotiki.

Closer to Whakatane, walkers can enjoy rather less-gruelling routes, including the 'Footprints of Toi,' a seven-hour, 14 km walk that takes in Kohi Point, several major pa sites and the Ohope and Mokoroa scenic reserves. It can also be done in smaller sections and is suitable for walkers of all ages and fitness levels.

There are also several walks in and around Whakatane. The Whakatane River Walk takes in all the sights, including the river mouth and Mataatua waka. The Whakatane Heritage Trail follows a series of plaques through the city and includes many historic sights. It takes about two hours.

Art lovers can explore numerous galleries, studios and workshops in the city and beyond; there are also garden tours and museums.

Six golf clubs and a golf range within 40 minutes' drive of the centre of Whakatane offer the golfer plenty of choice and there's mini-golf for the kids.

For the family there are also skate parks, swimming baths — including thermal baths at Awakeri — a cinema, the Amazing Maze, paintball, rifle and claybird shooting, berry farms, wineries and much more. Eating out is easy; Whakatane and the surrounding region are well stocked with restaurants and cafes. On a summer evening the wharf is of particular interest.

Fishers should make a point of visiting the Whakatane Sportfishing Club, on the main wharf right beside the river. This purpose-built facility is a community focal point and its walls display casts of some of the magnificent fish caught in local waters. It also serves wonderful meals at very reasonable prices, which you can wash down with a beer or two from the bar. Visitors are welcome.

For comprehensive information on where to stay, what to do and where to eat, check out www.whakatane.com, or visit the information centre on the corner of Kakahoroa Drive and Quay Street, 07 308 6058.

Accommodation

There's no shortage of good accommodation in Whakatane, which has dozens of motels and hotels, or in Ohope, Opotiki and elsewhere.

Beach house and bach accommodation can be found in Ohope and Ohiwa, backpacker accommodation in Whakatane and a range of lodge, B&B, budget and campground accommodation within half an hour of town. There's also accommodation available in Murupara, Awakeri and on the coast either side of Whakatane. Marae stays are available by arrangement.

Boat ramps

Whakatane boasts two public boat ramps on the Whakatane River. The bar can be treacherous and boaties must check in with the Coastguard on VHF before heading out. Signs beside the ramps indicate whether or not the bar is workable.

Ohiwa and Opotiki each has a public boat ramp. A private ramp at Rangitaiki River Camp is available to the public for a small fee. Small boats can launch from a number of protected boat ramps but many require river bar crossings to access the open sea. None of these should be taken lightly. Ohiwa Harbour, a few kilometres to the east of Whakatane, has good fishing and safe boat launching inside but it too has a tricky bar, which should be attempted only in good conditions. Further around the coast its character changes from sand to rocky bays and shingle beaches and boats can be launched into the open sea from sites usually tucked into the corners of bays or coves.

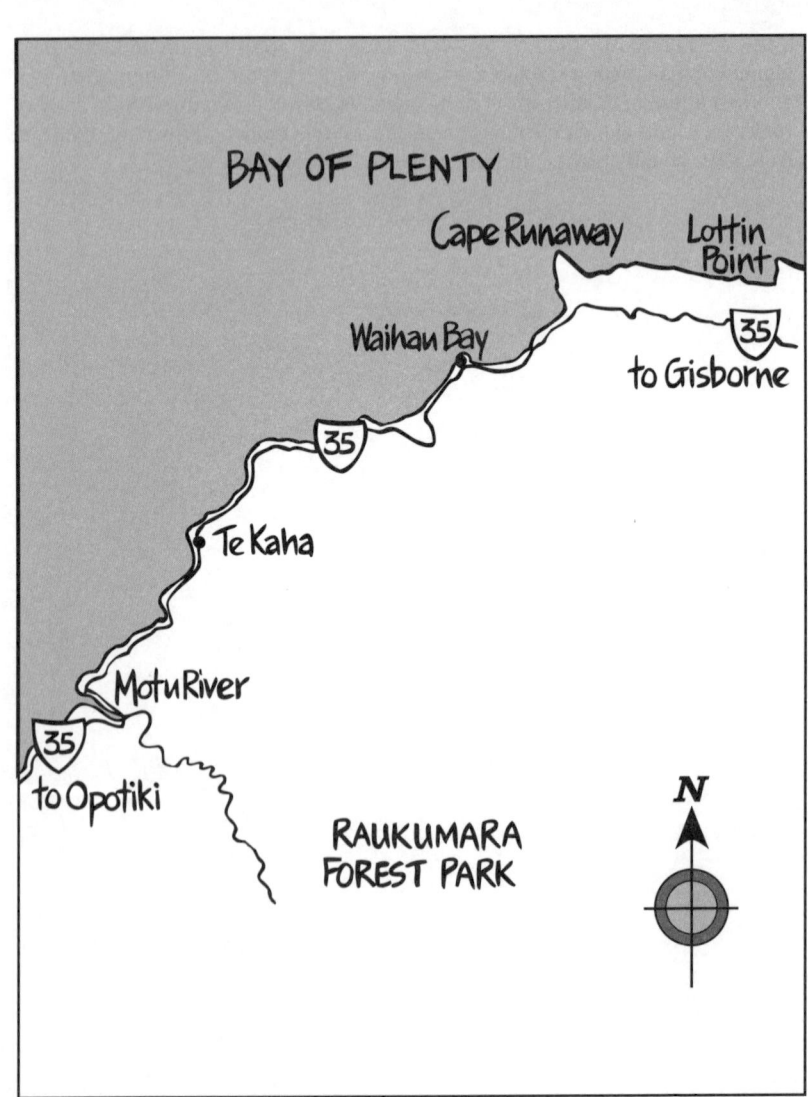

18

Waihau Bay

Waihau Bay is included in this book because I can't think of a fishier place to spend a couple of days. Isolated though it is, the mostly Maori settlement is spectacularly beautiful, dominated by the bulk of Cape Runaway at its northern end with White Island smoking on the horizon. The fishing in the bay and the deep water beyond is wonderful year-round but especially in summer when tuna and marlin come to play.

Fishing and the consumption of seafood is a large part of local culture. Waihau Bay remains relatively undeveloped, though the first of the seemingly inevitable beachside subdivisions is underway and there are plans for apartments on the hill behind the village. I hope development won't spoil the flavour of the place, though I guess that's a forlorn hope.

Waihau is at least three hours' drive on State Highway 35 from Whakatane, passing through Opotiki, Te Kaha and several interesting seaside villages on the way. The road follows the coast, winding around coves and climbing over headlands, every corner bringing fresh coastal views.

The village of Waihau Bay is tucked inside Orete Point at the southwestern end of Whangaparaoa Bay. It consists of a pub and motel/cabins, a general store with fuel, takeaways, a new fishing club and a wharf. A few houses are clustered close to the wharf, with the remainder of the population spread around the bay behind the pohutukawa.

 The fishing

In a word: superb. Waihau Bay is a magnet for small-boat gamefishers during the season and most locals take advantage of the gamefish run to chase tuna and marlin. The Waihau Bay Sportfishing Club has an active membership comprising locals and visitors. The new clubrooms are a credit to the community.

Most years Waihau Bay and the waters around Cape Runaway, Waikawa Point and down to Te Kaha play host to giant blue marlin, along with smaller striped marlin and yellowfin, skipjack and albacore tuna. The big blue marlin are the drawcard for many visiting anglers but yellowfin tuna are the main catch for local and visiting gamefishers, especially early in the season. In some years they come right into the bay and have been caught by anglers fishing the reefs for kingfish.

Skipjack tuna also come in close and are sometimes taken by anglers spinning from the shore. A small boat is all that's required to troll for these exciting speedsters — we once caught dozens of them from my 3.5 m dinghy during an Easter weekend break. The bottom fishing and diving is excellent too. Snapper is the main catch in summer but the area is also famous for its blue moki run in late winter. Good hapuku fishing in winter and spring and excellent fishing for kingfish round out the boat-fishing options.

Shore fishers can target snapper, kingfish, trevally, kahawai and a variety of other species from the rocks and beaches. Kingfish are usually caught by suspending live kahawai under a balloon close to the rocks. The Te Kaha to Lottin Point area, including Waihau Bay, has some superb rock ledges for land-based fishing. Access is generally over privately owned farmland and many of the locals are less happy about granting access than they used to be, however. Permission should be sought before crossing fences to get to the shore.

The river mouths of the region, including the Whangaparaoa, Kereu, Raukokore and particularly the Motu experience good runs of kahawai at times. The Motu was once famous for huge numbers of kahawai, which chase the whitebait run into the river mouth in spring. Commercial netting has greatly reduced these runs in the last 20 years, though there has been something of a resurgence in kahawai numbers over the last few seasons. Kingfish often follow the kahawai, adding a bit of spice to river-mouth angling.

Lottin Point and Cape Runaway offer a wealth of opportunity for land-based fishers. With ledges that drop off into deep water, they have the potential to produce fish of almost any species. If ever a marlin is taken from the shore in New Zealand, it may well come from one of these rocky promontories. Already, keen anglers have spun up small yellowfin tuna from these locations.

 Things to do

If you're not much interested in fishing it's hard to think of many reasons to visit Waihau Bay, though the drive around the coast is worth it for the scenery, and the bay enjoys a relaxed coastal lifestyle in a superb climate. Many visitors taking the Pacific Coast Highway stop in Waihau Bay for the night on their way to Gisborne.

For those keen on trout fishing, there are plenty of rivers nearby, as well as magnificent native bush and farmland for deer and pig hunting, camping, horse trekking and tramping. Jetboating, scenic flights and boat charters are also available. Excellent diving for crayfish, kina — even paua — can be found up and down the coast, from Whanarua Bay right round the cape to Hicks Bay. Oruati Beach has safe swimming and good surf at times. A number of coastal walks — to Cape Runaway or Lottin Point, to name two — will challenge the fittest walkers and there are plenty of tramping tracks into the bush-covered ranges of the East Cape.

The Waihau Bay Lodge is a good place to enjoy a beer and a bistro-style meal and during fishing contests the fishing club puts on a great feed.

Accommodation

One of the best things about staying in Waihau Bay is meeting the locals, who are happy to share their lifestyle. Homestays are recommended for this reason — the food and hospitality are hard to find anywhere else.

For such a small village, Waihau Bay has a surprising number of reasonably priced accommodation options, including B&Bs and the aforementioned lodge. There are self-contained motel-style units available around the bay. The motor camp has tent and caravan sites. The campground opposite the beach is popular in summer so book ahead — roadside camping is no longer allowed. In fact, it's wise to book ahead for any accommodation.

The website www.holidayhouses.co.nz/waihau_bay is a good place to start, or Google Waihau Bay for more options — they're well spread among numerous accommodation websites.

Boat ramps

A three-lane concrete ramp and jetty opposite the lodge is the main boat-launching facility. There's a marked channel out through the rocks opposite the ramp — take care to keep within the markers, especially at low tide. Some locals launch off the beaches and small boats can be launched beside the Whangaparaoa River mouth. The Gisborne/Tatapouri Sports Fishing Club maintains a narrow ramp at Lottin Point, suitable for boats up to 6 m in good conditions.

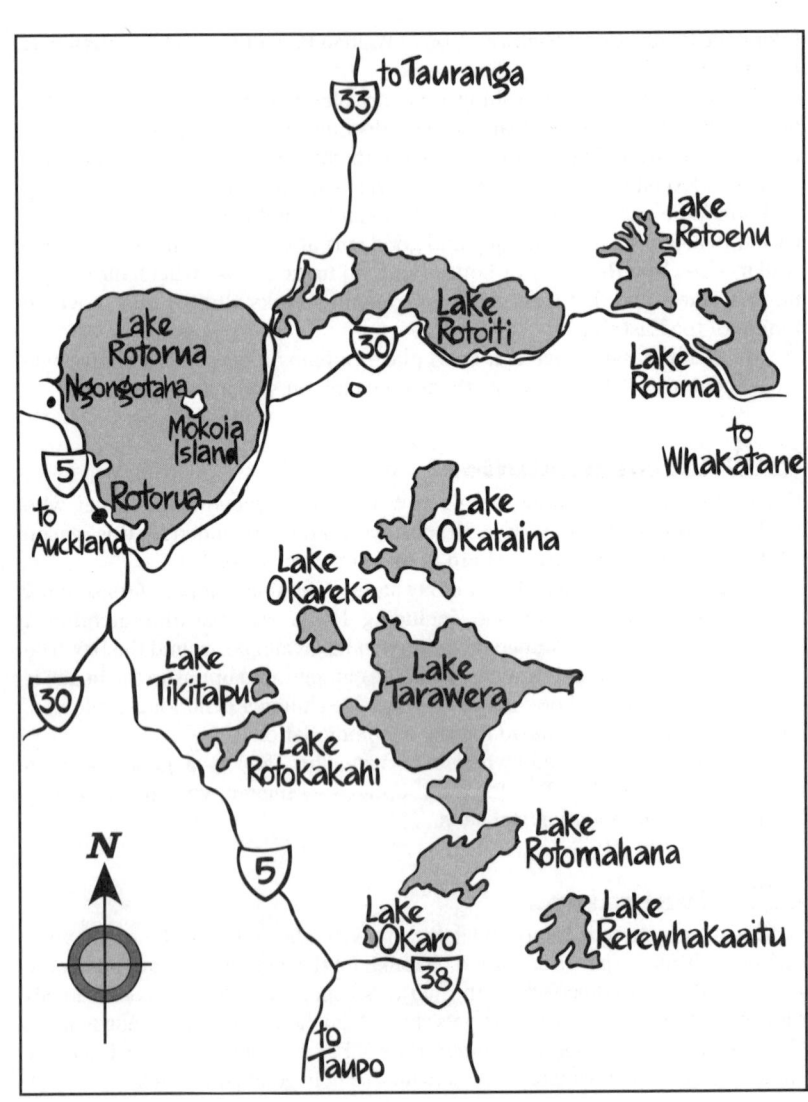

Rotorua

The Rotorua region is such an exciting one for the trout fisher it's really several destinations rolled up into one.

Offering perhaps the largest variety of trout fishing opportunities in New Zealand, the Rotorua region packs them all into an area of manageable size, allowing the weekend angler to sample a variety of waters and fishing styles. That it's also one of New Zealand's most popular tourist destinations is a real bonus.

For the fisher, a huge variety of lakes, rivers and streams are within easy striking distance of a Rotorua base. Of course, many of these places are angling destinations in their own right, many with excellent accommodation options of their own. But an angler based in Rotorua for the weekend can easily drive to most of the region's best fishing inside an hour, returning at the end of the day to all the attractions of a modern city. And for non-fishers, Rotorua has more to offer than perhaps anywhere else in New Zealand.

About five and a half hours' drive from Wellington, two and a half hours from Auckland, one and a half hours from Hamilton and Whakatane, and less than an hour from Tauranga, all on good roads, Rotorua is central and easy to get to.

Rotorua's major lakes

New Zealanders are polarised by the town of Rotorua; they either love it or hate it. One of the few places in New Zealand where tourism is king — Queenstown is another — Rotorua can come across as loud and rather brash, even tacky. For many Kiwis it's too commercial, the coffee's too expensive and there are too many foreigners.

On the other hand it's vibrant, the shops, restaurants and bars are nearly always open and there's a range of accommodation and entertainment that no other New Zealand city of this size can offer. I love it.

The city of Rotorua hugs the shores of the lake of the same name. Famous for its geothermal attractions, Rotorua and the surrounding area has always been a sought-after place to live. The Arawa people settled there early, using the hot springs and geysers for heating, cooking and medicinal purposes. Europeans quickly recognised the area's unique thermal attractions too and a thriving tourist industry was well established by the latter part of the 19th century.

The Rotorua we see today was built as a spa town — somewhere well-heeled Victorians could visit by train to 'take the waters'. The spectacular buildings down by the lakefront remain from Rotorua's days as a sanatorium. Spas operate in Rotorua to this day and its many thermal baths are still valued for their purported medicinal qualities.

Rotorua's fishing begins right in town. Lake Rotorua is a trout factory producing huge numbers of good-sized fish that can be caught using a variety of methods. Additionally, the rivers and streams that enter the lake, many flowing through the city and its suburbs, support trout fisheries of their own, as well as playing host to the annual spawning runs of lake fish. The Ngongotaha River is an excellent year-round fishery.

Around Lake Rotorua, nine major lakes and several smaller ones each offer a different fishing challenge in completely different surroundings. Further afield, a number of other lakes, large and small, as well as superb river and stream fishing opportunities mean an angler need never be bored.

Details of flyfishing-only waters, spinning opportunities, fish sizes, access and hints and tips for the Rotorua fishery are contained in an excellent Fish and Game Lake Rotorua pamphlet, available from Fish and Game Eastern region, see www.fishandgame.org.nz.

 The fishing

Lake Rotorua is the most prolific of all the region's lakes in terms of fish numbers. Popular with boat and shore anglers, it's a seasonal fishery with quite different winter and summer characteristics.

During summer the lake's relatively shallow waters become too warm to be comfortable for trout, forcing the lake's fish to stack up off the various stream and river mouths, which debouch relatively cold water into the lake. These fish provide great angling opportunities for land-based flyfishers who often wade out into the lake near river and stream mouths to target these fish.

Particularly in summer, but also during the rest of the year to a lesser extent, river mouths and the shallow areas close by are the haunt of Rotorua's giant brown trout. While rainbows average 1.5 kg, browns sometimes exceed 5 kg, and 3 kg or 4 kg fish are relatively common.

Browns are eminently catchable but canny enough to fool most anglers. A few big-brown specialists enjoy good success on dark nights with big flies fished slowly on a floating or intermediate line.

Spinfishers can also take advantage of the summer fishing, though most river and stream mouths are restricted to flyfishing. Nevertheless, fish often patrol up and down the shore well beyond the flyfishing-only limit, marked by striped poles.

Boat fishing in summer is more difficult. Unlike other lakes in the region, most of Lake Rotorua isn't deep enough to form a thermocline so the fish can't escape the heat in deeper, cooler water below the temperature break. For this reason, techniques such as downrigging, leadline fishing and jigging, which work well elsewhere, are not applicable to Lake Rotorua.

However, harling is effective early in the morning before the water heats up too much. Harling is shallow trolling, using threadline (spinning) or flyfishing tackle, in a few metres of water along the weed banks and drop-offs. It's particularly effective from a kayak, rowed dinghy or a craft propelled by an electric motor, though outboard-powered craft still enjoy success.

In winter the fishery changes. Adult fish leave the lake to spawn in the tributaries, starting with the browns in autumn, leaving behind smaller, immature fish. Trout are at their best just prior to spawning and can be taken by a variety of methods as they prepare to make their annual migrations upriver to breed.

During autumn and winter trolling comes into its own, using high-density, fast-sinking flylines or a few colours of leadline to get down 5 m or 6 m. Rainbows are the main catch and, since they spawn later than browns, they're available throughout the lake for longer. Limit bags are not uncommon on Lake Rotorua.

As the spawning run gets underway in earnest, boat fishing drops off and flyfishing comes into its own. The spawning run provides excellent river and stream fishing, some of it within the city limits.

The upper reaches of most rivers and streams close on June 30, to protect spawning fish, opening again on October 1 or December 1 — check the regulations carefully because they're complex and specific to each waterway. Lake Rotorua and the lower reaches of all its rivers and streams are open for fishing year-round.

The Ohau Channel, linking Lake Rotorua to Lake Rotoiti, is famous for its run of fish moving from one lake to the other seeking spawning streams. On Lake Rotoiti opening day, October 1, the Ohau Channel is lined with anglers and every year it produces several fish in excess of 6 kg. The fishing remains good for the first few weeks of the season and the channel is worth fishing again towards the end of the season when early spawners begin to move through it at the start of their runs.

Lake Rotoiti is one of the deeper and larger lakes in the region with a reputation for large fish. Lake Rotorua empties into Lake Rotoiti via the Ohau Channel before the conjoined waters make their way to the sea down the Kaituna River.

In recent years Lake Rotoiti has been in the news for the annual appearance of unsightly and sometimes dangerous algal blooms, which mostly affect the Ohau Channel–Okawa Bay end of the lake.

Rotorua's water quality went steadily downhill for more than 100 years until an effort to clean up the lake began in the 1970s. Since then it has improved markedly, though it still suffers from nutrient overload caused by run-off from farming and other human activities. Nutrient-laden water from Rotorua has been entering Rotoiti, which is now suffering the cumulative effects of years of nutrient enrichment. In the short term summer algal blooms are here to stay, though there are plans to reduce the nutrient load so the lake can recover.

While it sounds (and looks) bad, the algal blooms appear to have had little effect on the fishing. Most years blooms are restricted to small parts of the lake, the rest remaining clear.

Lake Rotoiti is primarily a summer fishery for boat anglers. The best boat fishing is usually early in the season, which opens to all methods on October 1, with shallow trolling and harling particularly effective.

As the water warms and the trout retreat to cooler, deeper water, boat fishing becomes more difficult. Harling can still bring success early in the morning but daytime fishing is the preserve of deep trollers, who use lead or wire lines, downriggers or jigs to access fish.

Jig fishing has proven especially effective, as it has in all of the deep lakes in the region. The most popular rig doesn't incorporate a jig at all, or if it does, the jig carries no hook; rather it consists of a sinker tied to the rig's terminal end and up to three droppers on the trace armed with a selection of streamer-type flies. The rig is worked very slowly near the bottom. The best jig fishers target fish they can see on the fishfinder from a drifting or anchored boat, but it's possible to successfully jig without a sounder by drifting through areas of known depth, chosen from a bathymetric chart.

In winter the lake is closed to boat fishing but flyfishers may fish from shore from Ruato Bay to Hinehopu. They catch some spectacular fish — Rotoiti consistently produces the biggest rainbow trout of any of the Rotorua lakes. Pre-spawning fish can be targeted by flyfishers as they congregate near the Ruato stream mouth, the Pipe and a few other locations along this stretch of shoreline. Fishing with luminous flies between dusk and midnight is the most popular method, though some anglers enjoy success early in the morning.

Lakes Tarawera and Okataina share many similarities with Rotoiti — both are deep, filled with large trout and closed to fishing, except for small strips of shoreline, between June 30 and October 1.

Okataina is the smaller of the two, and arguably the most beautiful lake in the region. Surrounded by high, bush-covered hills, it's accessed via a narrow road that branches off State Highway 30 at Ruato Bay and winds down through mature native forest to the lake. Okataina Lodge is the only building on the lakeshore except for a DOC hut in bush at the southern end. The lodge is a great place to stay, with fishing at its doorstep, a cosy lounge, an excellent restaurant and views up the lake to die for.

Flyfishers can fish the beach and jetty at the road end of the lake year-round and many trophy-sized fish have been taken this way. During the open season the Log Pool (actually the mouth of a small stream) is a great fish producer, especially early in the morning.

The lake offers plenty of opportunities for trolling lures and flyfishing from an anchored boat. Deep trolling works best during summer, though there is some scope for harling at Dogger Bank. Jigging also works well in Okataina, often taking larger fish. Though the lake once produced trout of more than 5 kg, the average size is closer to 2.5 kg these days, but there are still enough 3 kg-plus rainbows to keep the fishing interesting.

Tarawera is one of the largest of the Rotorua lakes, second only to Rotorua itself. In character it's much more like Okataina than Rotorua or even Rotoiti though, like Rotoiti, it produces superb fish, sometimes of trophy size.

Tarawera can be fished in almost any wind as the hills surrounding it offer plenty of shelter. Trolling is by far the most popular fishing style on the lake but flyfishers also do well from the shore or from anchored boats. Jigging is a new technique that's paying dividends in summer.

Opening day on Lake Tarawera, October 1, is a tradition that draws many hundreds of anglers each year. The night before there is a 'piping in the haggis' ceremony at Tarawera Landing, usually well attended no matter the weather. After the festivities many attendees stay the night on their boats, moored in the bay or pulled up onto the beach, in preparation for an early start. Accommodation around the lake is scarce around this time.

Lake Tarawera is a short drive from central Rotorua. The road is scenic, skirting Lakes Tikitapu (Blue Lake) and Rotokakahi (Green Lake). Lake Okareka (see page 122) is also accessed from the Tarawera road.

 Things to do

With so much superb fishing on offer day and night, finding time for other activities may prove difficult. However, Rotorua has so much to offer that you won't be short of options. As New Zealand's tourism capital, Rotorua is crammed with entertainment options for the whole family. Outdoor adventure tourism is high on the list, with activities from bungy jumping to whitewater rafting on offer. Gentler pastimes include lazing in thermal spas, walks, lake cruises, sightseeing flights, museum and art gallery visits and shopping.

Rotorua's thermal wonders have long been the basis for its popularity with visitors. Many of the natural thermal attractions can be seen in public spaces in the city and around the lake for free. Care should be exercised to avoid injury — keep to marked paths and stay behind barriers.

Larger areas of thermal activity include Whakarewarewa, with its Maori arts and crafts centre and carving school, which is worth a visit of its own, and Waimangu Valley, to name just two. There is an entry fee for these attractions but the mud pools, boiling water and geysers are worth every cent.

Rotorua also offers some of New Zealand's most professional Maori cultural shows. Staged primarily for overseas visitors, they are well worth seeing. Tamaki Maori Village just out of town is also excellent.

At night Rotorua comes alive with a thriving bar, restaurant and dance scene. Many establishments are open 24 hours on weekends, attracting visitors and locals alike. The city's website, www.rotorua.co.nz, has all the information you could possibly need to ensure an enjoyable stay in Rotovegas.

Accommodation

If more is better, Rotorua is the best. With more beds than any other city in New Zealand except Auckland, one would expect that finding somewhere to stay wouldn't be too great a challenge. However, Rotorua services such a large volume of tourists, most staying just a night or two, that securing a bed is not always easy. It can pay to book ahead — I've been caught out a couple of times and had to settle for cabin or campground accommodation when all the motels in town were full. Rotorua's accommodation options run the full spectrum from luxury hotels and exclusive lakefront lodges to budget backpackers, camping and cabin accommodation. There's something for every taste and most budgets. See www.rotorua.co.nz for listings or try www.tourism.net.nz/region/rotorua.

Boat ramps

The larger lakes are well served with boat ramps, most of which are suitable for trailer boats of all sizes. Lake Rotorua has six public boat ramps and numerous private ramps; Rotoiti has four ramps; Tarawera has five; Okataina has one (narrow and exposed).

20

Minor lakes and surrounds

The larger, better-known lakes carry the region's trout fishing reputation and absorb much of the fishing pressure but there is far more to Rotorua lake fishing than just the 'big four'.

Several quieter lakes offer different angling opportunities within easy reach of the city. Some, such as Rotoma and Rerewhakaaitu, are actually as large as Okataina.

 The fishing

Lake Okareka is a small lake in an attractive setting, a popular dormitory suburb of Rotorua. A relatively shallow lake, it offers good shoreline flyfishing and safe, sheltered boat fishing for rainbows averaging 1.5 kg. The lake is open year-round and has a good boat ramp at Acacia Bay.

Lake Rotoma has clear water and extensive weed beds, though the water level fluctuates naturally depending on inflow and outflow, most of which occurs through fissures in its bed. Trolling and flyfishing can both be rewarding, though long leaders are recommended in the lake's clear water. Tiger trout — brown trout/brook trout (char) hybrids — offer an intriguing alternative to rainbow trout. Rotoma is about 30 minutes' drive from Rotorua on State Highway 30 heading towards Whakatane.

Lake Rotoehu, between Rotoiti and Rotoma, is an interesting, moderate-sized lake that produces smaller fish than the bigger lakes but with higher catch rates. Shallow trolling or harling give the best results.

Lake Tikitapu (Blue Lake) has an all-weather boat ramp on the main beach, meaning excellent boat fishing is accessible. Harling is the most productive method, from rowed or powered craft. Shoreline fishing is good too, and a walking track runs right around the lake. Flyfishing off the beach at the western end can be excellent in heavy rain. Blue Lake also has a few brook trout, an attraction for species hunters.

Lake Rotomahana is less known and less fished than many Rotorua lakes. Access is via Rotoehu Forest from Waimangu Valley Loop Road. A forest permit is required but is worth the effort for the quality of the fishing. Permits are available from Independent Security Consultants, 66 Tarewa Road, Rotorua, 07 347 8880.

Trout here average around 1.3 kg and are susceptible to the same techniques used on the other lakes. Volcanic activity in the lake means fish are full of mercury and should not be consumed in any quantity, however. Catch and release is the safest option.

Lake Rerewhakaaitu lies in the shadow of Mount Tarawera in a landscape still showing the scars of the 1886 eruption that killed many of the local inhabitants. Access is off State Highway 38 with a good boat ramp in Homestead Arm off Brett Road. Rerewhakaaitu can be bleak in winter but the fishing can make up for the cold.

There's excellent boat and shoreline fishing for rainbow trout of around 2 kg. Flyfishers enjoy great fishing year-round in the lake's shallow margins where fish can often be seen feeding on smelt or insects. Harling or shallow trolling over weed beds is the favoured boat-fishing method and some fishers enjoy good success from float tubes or flyfishing from boats.

A number of other minor lakes, rivers and streams are also within striking distance of Rotorua. The small lakes Okaro, Ngahewa and Ngapouri lie on the fringes of the major lakes. They contain good populations of small fish and provide entertaining float-tube fishing. Okaro is also suitable for shoreline and small-boat fishing. They're best early in the season before the water gets too warm.

Lakes Aniwhenua and Matahina are hydro lakes on the Rangitaiki River. The Rangitaiki system is a prolific trout producer and includes excellent rivers and streams, as well as Flaxy Lake and its associated canals.

Lake Matahina is deep and narrow, with few shore-fishing opportunities. It fishes best from a boat. Aniwhenua is the opposite, with shoreline fishing the most popular and effective method.

Famous for trophy rainbows in the mid-1990s, Aniwhenua is now much altered by silting and changes to its underwater flora. The big rainbows are gone and much of the upper lake is now difficult to fish from a boat, but shoreline angling has really come into its own. The lake still holds plenty of trout — good anglers can catch 10 fish or more in a session — but the ratio of browns to rainbows has swung in favour of browns, especially for shore fishers. Cruising fish can be spotted and cast to and some browns are 4 kg-plus.

Aniwhenua fish, along with fish from the Rangitaiki River, enter the Rangitaiki's smaller tributaries to spawn in winter. For a month or two either side of the closed season, streams such as the Horomanga, Waihua and others offer small-stream angling for large fish in stunning surroundings.

The Rangitaiki River is fishable throughout its length but gets the most attention above the town of Murupara. Flyfishers can enjoy superb dry-fly and nymph fishing in the river's upper reaches and its tributaries deep inside Rangitaiki Forest, but they are a fair way from Rotorua and better targeted by anglers staying closer by. A forest permit is required to access the river's upper reaches, the Whaeo Canal and Flaxy Lake.

The latter is an excellent fishery with superb flyfishing for large brown and rainbow trout. Accessed via forest roads from Murupara, it's an ideal spot for a float tube. The adjoining Whaeo Canal has brilliant flyfishing too.

Other fisheries of note include the Whirinaki River, which empties into the Rangitaiki at Murupara. This river has tens of kilometres of fishable water that runs through rough farmland, exotic and native forest. Its upper reaches are accessible only to helicopters or committed trampers. Flyfishing on the Whirinaki is good throughout its length and some stretches are among the most scenic in the North Island.

Accommodation

There's always Rotorua, but the more adventurous can often find vastly more interesting places to stay out of town, many of them close to superb fishing. Given the choice, I always gravitate to these sorts of places, not least because their prices are often much less steep than those in town.

Although it's only 45 minutes from Rotorua, visitors to the Aniwhenua/Rangitaiki fishery often choose to stay nearby. Several well-priced backpacker-style lodges and other lakeside accommodation are available, as well as luxury lodges, a free lakeside camping ground off Black Road and motel accommodation in Murupara. For those wanting to fish the Rangitaiki Forest, camping is available at Te Awa beside the Rangitaiki River.

See www.rotorua.co.nz and www.tourism.net.nz/region/rotorua.

Boat ramps

Rotoehu has two ramps; Rotoma four and Okareka and Tikitapu have one each. Lakes Matahina and Aniwhenua have one each (a second gravel ramp launches into the Rangitaiki River above Aniwhenua, but access to the lake is now difficult due to silting) and Lake Rerewhakaaitu has two.

It's possible to launch small craft into some of the smaller lakes, including Flaxy Lake, though some of these are better left to shore fishers or float tubes. Lake Rotomahana has a jetty but no formed ramp.

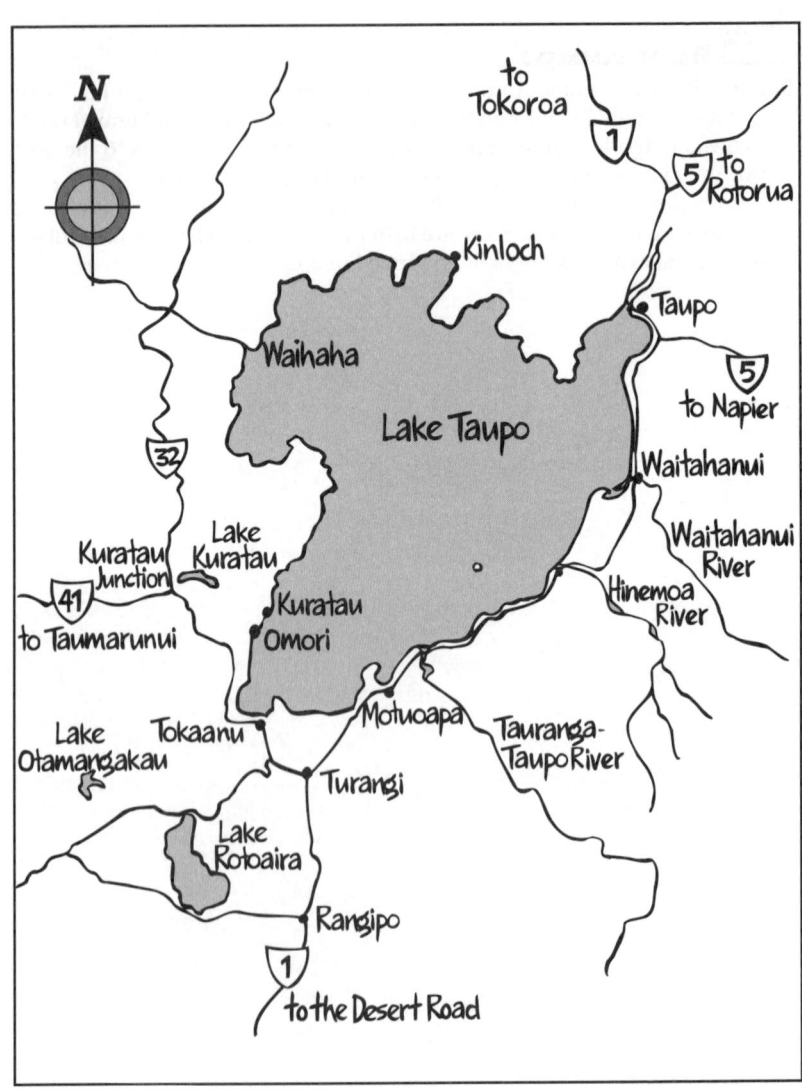

Taupo

Lake Taupo is the largest body of fresh water in New Zealand. Formed inside a caldera after possibly the world's largest and most violent eruption in the last 10,000 years, it is also New Zealand's deepest lake.

Lake Taupo is at the geographic heart of the North Island; Maori consider it the heart of Te Ika a Maui — the great fish of Maui.

For most people travelling north or south through the North Island, Taupo is on the way. State Highway 1, the most direct route between Wellington and Auckland, passes through the town, which has grown from a village on the northern shore of the lake to a thriving service town, resort and tourist attraction in its own right.

Since trout were introduced to the lake in the 1880s, Taupo has been a firm favourite with anglers. The rivers feeding into the lake, particularly the Tongariro at the lake's southern end, are world famous for their winter runs of spawning rainbow trout. River and lake fishing are truly world-class, attracting thousands of overseas anglers every year.

Lake Taupo is a vast body of water and the Taupo district is large too. There's so much fishing available from a base at Taupo, Turangi or elsewhere around the shores of the Great Lake, it seems sensible to break the fishing into sections.

Most of the fishing in the region requires a Taupo District fishing licence, administered by DOC, but you'll need a current Fish and Game licence to fish some of the waters on the fringes of the region. It pays to make sure you're carrying the right licence for the water you're wanting to fish.

Lake Taupo

The vast majority of angling effort in the region is directed towards Lake Taupo. There are numerous other lakes close by, each attracting bands of the faithful, but for most people fishing at Taupo consists of trolling on the big lake.

 The fishing

Boat fishing on the lake accounts for about 90 per cent of the fishing effort in the region. Some of the boat fishing techniques that evolved on Lake Taupo are used elsewhere in New Zealand, though the character of some of the region's other lakes is so different that totally different fishing techniques are needed (more on that subject later).

Traditionally, boat anglers have harled Lake Taupo — trolled a fly on light tackle using sinking flylines — during spring and into summer, fishing the shallows up to 10 m. Taupo trout feed primarily on smelt, a small native fish introduced from Lake Rotorua in the 1920s, so they're particularly susceptible to trolled fish imitations, lures or flies.

Later in the season and through winter deep trolling using lead-cored or wire lines accesses water up to 40 m deep, though harling can be productive year-round, especially in early morning or dusk.

In recent years the use of downriggers has changed the nature of deep trolling. A heavy lead ball is used to take the fly/lure to the desired depth, where it's trolled on a release clip. When a fish bites the clip releases the line and the angler is ready to play the fish to the boat. Downriggers can be used in conjunction with light nylon or superbraid lines and sporting tackle, since the rod doesn't have to resist the drag of the heavy trolling line and lure. Downrigging is popular with the more innovative Taupo anglers and indispensable for the large fleet of charter operators on the lake.

The other new method that's really making waves on Taupo is jigging. Jigging evolved out of a successful sea-fishing method using metal lures or jigs fished vertically in the water column. Today's freshwater jigging, Taupo-style, bears little resemblance to its saltwater progenitor but it's still about vertical fishing.

Rather than using a metal jig at the business end of the tackle, most anglers now use a lead sinker and up to three short traces branching off a backbone. A selection of streamer flies is attached to the branches and a small swivel used to attach the rig to the main line. Lightweight 2–2.5 m graphite rods are used in conjunction with small baitcasting (overhead) reels and fine-diameter superbraid line.

The fishing technique is not difficult — flies are lowered to the required depth from a drifting or anchored boat and worked using gentle lifts and twitches of the rod. Finding fish is the key to success and a good sounder/fishfinder and/or an in-depth understanding of the lake floor's underwater topography are essential. With a bit of practice most jig fishers soon learn the areas to target and a hydrographic chart of Taupo becomes their best friend.

Jigging is most successful during the heat of summer when the fishing is hard using most other methods. When surface water temperatures rise, trout school beneath the thermocline, which may be as deep as 40 m — beyond the reach of other fishing methods. Jig fishers can target these fish and often experience spectacular fishing.

Harling concentrates on areas of shallow water around the lake. The bays on the eastern side of the lake, many close to river mouths, are the most productive areas. Horomatangi Reef, a complex of shallow rocky reefs well out in the lake off White Cliffs, is another popular venue, as are the extensive shallows at Otutere, Motuoapa and Stump Bay.

Deep trolling concentrates on drop-offs where shallow water falls away into the depths of the lake. The edges of the banks mentioned above produce good fishing, as do the fringes of Horomatangi Reef and hundreds of headlands and bays where it's possible to troll along the 30 m contour line.

There is some flyfishing from boats at most of the lake's major river mouths and also where the Tokaanu tailrace enters the lake. Boats generally anchor on the lip where the river empties into the lake or where shallow water drops into deep. Plenty of current is desirable. Fast-sinking lines are used with streamer or smelt flies, glo-bugs or boobies. Flies are cast out into the current, allowed to sink and slowly retrieved. Takes can come at any point in the retrieve, right up to the boat.

Glo-bugs and boobies can be fished static — simply cast out and left —

with good results but fish often get deeply hooked and must be kept.

Boat fishers can come into conflict with shore fishers competing for space at the river mouths. The several mouths of the Tongariro are favoured by boaties because the lips are generally too treacherous to wade, keeping shore anglers away. The Tauranga-Taupo river mouth is another favourite for similar reasons.

Apart from at river mouths, for some reason flyfishing from a boat is seldom practised in Lake Taupo. It's not because it doesn't work — I've had some excellent fishing drifting over near-shore shallows casting to hungry trout chasing smelt. Nearly all the flyfishing effort in Lake Taupo is conducted from shore, primarily at the mouths of numerous rivers and streams entering the lake. Much of the effort is directed at night fishing using large, luminous streamer flies cast and retrieved from shore on dark nights. Stream-mouth fishing is largely an autumn and winter pastime, targeting fish gathering prior to their upriver spawning runs, but good results can be had at any time of year.

In recent years spawning runs have become less concentrated and the peaks are coming later in the season — in September rather than July. There is also a considerable summer run into most rivers so it's worthwhile fishing river and stream mouths any time of the year.

In spring, smelt move inshore to spawn and the trout follow. This is the golden time for shore anglers, who can walk the beaches and bays casting to marauding trout feeding on smelt. This can be done at any time of day and the fishing can be fast and furious, though the fish themselves are often not in the best condition after their recent spawning efforts.

Shore fishers can also target the mouths of smaller streams around the lake, all of which produce good fishing, especially at night. The mouths of the rivers flowing into the western side of Lake Taupo produce legendary fishing at times. A boat is the easiest way to access Waihora or Waihaha.

Shore fishers also do well from many of the lake's rocky headlands and anywhere there's deep water within casting range. There's excellent flyfishing right in town, under the lights of Taupo's many waterfront motels.

Things to do

With all that wonderful fishing I'm not sure how you'd find time for anything else but the truth is most visitors to the region are there to enjoy its many other attractions. As well as being stunningly scenic, Lake Taupo is strategically positioned to take advantage of the region's many outdoor activities. In winter the skifields to the south are a great drawcard and many skiers stay around the lake — some of them combine fishing and skiing.

Other outdoor activities include whitewater rafting, kayaking, tramping, hunting, mountain climbing, gliding, parachuting, four-wheel motorbikes, horse trekking, paintball, sailing and other water sports on the region's lakes and rivers and much more. The volcanic activity around the geothermal power plant at Wairakei is a popular attraction and there are safe walking tracks between mud pools, hot-water springs and multi-coloured fumaroles. Thermal baths can be enjoyed at Taupo, Tokaanu and in Lake Taupo itself.

The region also encompasses Tongariro National Park and magnificent native forests including Pureora and Kaimanawa, home to rare native flora and fauna as well as exotic animals popular with hunters, such as pigs and deer. The Tongariro Crossing is acknowledged as one of the world's great walks. Taupo also offers numerous attractions celebrating its Maori heritage.

Family-oriented activities include boat hire, lake cruises, jetboating on the Waikato, excursions to Huka Falls, scenic tours, parks, gardens and reserves and more. Wairakei is one of New Zealand's premier golf courses.

The township of Taupo has plenty to interest the visitor, including a very lively restaurant, bar and cafe scene that pumps, summer and winter. The town centre has been redeveloped into an attractive, pedestrian-friendly place and there are a few special shops that surprise: the wine shop tucked around the corner behind the carpark opposite the lakefront has some wonderful and otherwise hard-to-find wines. With a go-ahead council, Taupo hosts numerous events, which means there's something of interest happening on most weekends of the year.

Accommodation

Whatever your budget, Taupo can accommodate you, from backpacker hostels to luxury lodges with a variety of international-standard hotels, homestays, motels, farmstays, and B&Bs in between.

There are five holiday parks/campgrounds in Taupo, two in Turangi and one each in Wairakei, Motuoapa, Motutere and Tokaanu, most offering a range of facilities including cabins. Timeshares are a feature of the Taupo area and many people with investments there regularly trade a week or more for accommodation elsewhere.

One style of accommodation Taupo-Turangi does especially well is the fishing lodge. Most accommodation pays at least lip service to fishing, especially in Turangi, but a few lodges are aimed totally at the angler. They provide accommodation, guiding and meals in a setting that's all stuffed trout on the walls, old photos and antique tackle — marvellous! Prices range from reasonable to wow! depending on the services and luxury provided. Some are self-catering.

Boutique and luxury lodges include Huka Lodge, acknowledged as one of the best in the world — BYO helicopter. Huka Lodge is right beside the Waikato River and offers fishing as part of the package.

Probably the most popular type of accommodation is holiday homes and cottages. These are scattered through Taupo, Turangi, Kinloch and the many villages clustered around the lake's eastern shore. Many are available to rent. They're a great way to enjoy a few days at the lake, offering home comforts in often stunning surroundings.

Demand for accommodation is high year-round — in winter skiers and anglers compete for beds, in summer holidaymakers and overseas tourists are the main customers. The Taupo region is better serviced with beds than most areas but it can pay to book ahead. Lake Taupo's excellent website, www.laketauponz.com, lists hundreds of activities and a huge range of accommodation options. Also useful are www.laketaupoaccommodation.com and the Taupo page of www.tourism.net.nz.

 Boat ramps

Lake Taupo is well endowed with good-quality concrete boat ramps, but a ramp permit is required to use them. Permits are available from most service stations around the lake.

There are ramps at Taupo (two), and Two Mile Bay, Three Mile Bay, Mission Bay, Motuopa Bay, Tokaanu, Kuratau, Kinloch and Acacia Bay. Launching is also practised at several other locations across the beach into the lake.

Marinas at Taupo, Motuopa and Kinloch, recently extended and upgraded, cater to permanently berthed boats.

Taupo lakes and rivers

The Taupo region contains many other lakes, though none as imposing or popular as Taupo itself. Hydro and natural lakes to the north and south offer a range of options.

Anglers should take care to note when waters are closed in the Taupo region because the season varies greatly from water to water and even on the same water.

River fishing around Lake Taupo is fly-only, though spinfishing and even baitfishing is allowed below the control gates on the Waikato River north of Taupo. Most river fishing occurs during the winter months when the traditional runs of spawning trout pass through the region's major rivers on their way to the headwaters and tributaries to spawn.

 The fishing — minor lakes

The upper Waikato River hydro lakes to the north of Taupo — Whakamaru, Maraetai, Waipapa and Arapuni — offer good fishing, using fly, spinner or trolled lure. The lakes respond to most methods but fluctuating water levels, high summer water temperatures, a lot of weed and considerable water flow make for challenging and inconsistent fishing. Lake Arapuni is the best of them.

To the south of Taupo, several excellent lake fisheries are within easy reach of anglers based in Turangi or Taupo. Lake Kuratau is a small hydro lake not far from Turangi on the upper Kuratau River. Home to a large population of aggressive rainbows, it can provide superb flyfishing to nymphs or streamers fished among the sunken timber at the top of the lake. There's reasonable shore fishing but results are best from an anchored dinghy or float tube.

Over the hill from Tokaanu, heading in the direction of National Park, is Lake Rotoaira. Also called 'The Maori Lake', this medium-sized body of water has excellent fishing, especially early in the season. A special permit is required, in addition to your Fish and Game licence, to fish Rotoaira. It's not always easy to come by but is normally available from one or other Turangi tackle store or from the camp and boat ramp on State Highway 46. Harling and flyfishing both work well in this shallow lake.

A little further to the west, at the base of Mount Tongariro is Lake Otamangakau. This is a small hydro lake with a reputation for big fish, both rainbows and browns. Many double-figure rainbows have been taken here over the years, though average size fluctuates from season to season. It's flyfishing only with opportunities for boat anglers, shore fishers and float tubers.

The fishing — rivers

Taupo is a large lake that holds millions of fish so the spawning run each year is huge. That's just as well, because Taupo's major rivers host thousands of anglers each year and, while a three-fish bag limit is strictly imposed, anglers still have considerable impact on spawning fish numbers. Nevertheless, according to DOC the fishery is in good health and the quality of fishing remains high.

Taupo river rainbows — actually lake fish visiting the river — average more than 1.5 kg most years and more than 2 kg in exceptional seasons. Bigger fish are common.

Brown trout also run the rivers in good numbers but are less commonly caught. They're often big fish — 5 kg or more is not uncommon — but they remain the preserve of a few knowledgeable anglers who target them, mostly at night. There's a good summer fishery for brown trout in the lower Tongariro. They're hard to catch but respond to well-presented nymphs or dry flies.

Most effort is devoted to the larger rivers, particularly the Tongariro, which has many kilometres of fishable water. The most popular river is the Tongariro, followed by the Tauranga-Taupo, Waitahanui and Hinemaiaia. The smaller rivers are less popular but can fish well to anglers prepared to downscale their gear.

In the Tongariro, upstream nymphing using heavy bombs to get down near the bottom of the river's boisterous flow is the most popular method these days but downstream wetline fishing with sinking lines and streamer flies remains popular and effective.

The same methods work in the smaller rivers, though nymphing dominates and is the only practical method in smaller streams such as the Waiotaka and Waimarino.

Rivers on the western side of the lake flow though private property and access can be difficult, as it can be on the Waitahanui and to a lesser extent the Tauranga-Taupo.

The Tongariro is well served by a network of vehicle and walking tracks, bridges and marked angler-access points. It's a big enough river that you can always find a piece of it to yourself, no matter how crowded the main pools.

Accommodation

See the information on pages 131–132, or websites www.laketauponz.com, www.laketaupoaccommodation.com and the Taupo page of www.tourism.net.nz for a huge range of accommodation options.

Boat ramps

Lake Kuratau has a gravel launching ramp, accessed through a gate over a paddock, Lake Otamangakau has ramps at either end and Lake Rotoaira has ramps at the penstock end of the lake (two) and at the camping ground, which also features a jetty.

Each of the Waikato hydro lakes has public launching facilities. Ramps are generally concrete and some of the lakes, like Karapiro, have several.

Lake Waikaremoana

Lake Waikaremoana isn't a place you pass through on your way to somewhere else. As isolated as it's possible to be in the North Island, it's a destination, not a waypoint.

Lake Waikaremoana is one of my favourites — for its trout fishing and its scenery. Like few other places in New Zealand, Waikaremoana has a presence — a sort of spirituality or spookiness that's hard to deny. On a dark winter's night with the black waters reflecting starlight and the silhouettes of mountains all around, it's easy to understand why Waikaremoana holds a special place in the hearts of the local Tuhoe tribe, known as the children of the mist.

Tuhoe have always invested the steep mountains, deep lakes and dark forests of their Te Urewera home with spirit beings, fairies and other mythical creatures. The possibility of their existence doesn't seem too far-fetched when you're standing in the lake in the dark listening to the noises of the night.

Lake Waikaremoana is in a valley high up in the Huiarau Ranges, deep inside forested Te Urewera National Park. The closest town of any size is Wairoa, itself a long way from any major cities.

I usually travel to Lake Waikaremoana on State Highway 38 through Rotorua, Murupara and up into the ranges via a narrow, winding and only recently sealed road. Most of the route is through deep forest. Te Urewera has some of the best native podocarp forest in the country, much of it never milled, with outstanding wildlife, including kiwi, kokako, kaka, native parakeets and other rare birds.

On the way to the lake you cross some of the best trout streams in the North Island, starting with the Whirinaki River, which empties into the Rangitaiki River at Murupara. The Whirinaki is fishable throughout its length, from the outskirts of Murupara to the willow-lined stretch through Te Whaiti and the river's gorgeous upper reaches above Minginui, where tall native trees stand guard on the banks.

Other notable streams include the headwaters of the Whakatane River, which the road crosses and travels beside for several kilometres, the Waikare River and several rivers draining into Lake Waikaremoana itself.

Small clearings in the bush — the villages of Ngaputahi and Papueru — punctuate the drive before the more substantial settlement of Ruatahuna, once home to Te Kooti and a centre for the Pai Marire cult. Motorists need to look out for horses tethered beside the road or simply wandering free. Children on horseback are a common sight; in the rugged, roadless Urewera hinterland, horses are still the best way to get around.

Te Urewera remained closed to European settlement well into the 20th century and its people played an important role during the wars of the 19th century, standing fast and raiding the coast from their mountain homes. Even today few Pakeha inhabit the region.

The fishing

As well as offering pristine and spectacular surroundings unlike any other fishing venue in New Zealand, Waikaremoana has exceptionally good fishing. Many anglers visit year after year to enjoy its superb shoreline angling, stalking wary brown trout around the lake's margins. Lake Waikaremoana holds both brown and rainbow trout, both growing to respectable sizes. Average fish weigh 2 kg, with larger specimens, especially browns, commonly taken.

A variety of fishing methods are used, including shoreline flyfishing and trolling from boats. Jigging is a new technique that works well in summer.

Another popular pastime is to fish the various stream and river mouths where they empty into the lake. Stream and river-mouth fishing is particularly good in autumn when the fish begin to gather for their spawning runs. The Hopuruahine and Mokau streams are the most popular for stream-mouth angling, which is fly-only.

River and stream fishing is also good, especially as soon as the season opens on November 1 — a month or two later than most other places in the North Island, in deference to Waikaremoana's cool climate and late-spawning fish.

Early season gives stream and river fishers the opportunity to target these late-spawning fish, while lake fishers are assured of plenty of action from spent fish returning to the lake, though they are generally in poor condition.

A boat can be a real bonus on Waikaremoana, even for the flyfisher. It allows you to reach parts of the lake and shoreline not otherwise accessible. Moving from place to place and relocating if the wind changes is also easier by boat.

Walking tracks all but circumnavigate the lake but high bluffs mean much of the shoreline is inaccessible to walking anglers. DOC huts scattered around the lake offer accommodation for the tramping angler, though they become crowded in summer and bookings should be made. Free camping, once a summer tradition among boaties who would clear their own lakeside campgrounds in the location of their choice, is no longer permitted.

Waikaremoana's weather is changeable and can be fickle at any time of year. It's a big lake with plenty of fetch, especially when the wind blows from the west, which it mostly does. High bluffs and a generally mountainous topography contribute to some violent storms, including spectacular summer thunderstorms. Boaties need to take care: small boats can easily be caught out by sudden squalls or unforeseen changes in the weather. It's not a safe place to fish from a dinghy or a float tube.

Luckily, Lake Waikaremoana isn't the only fishing option. As well as the stream and river fishing already mentioned, there's good lake fishing at Lake Waikareiti, a 45-minute walk through bush from the visitors' centre at Aniwaniwa. A much smaller lake than Waikaremoana, it's sheltered and offers good fishing for rainbow trout. Dinghies are available for hire and trolling or flyfishing from small boats is the most popular option. Float tubes or inflatable float boats that can be carried in are also useful.

A little to the south, Lake Whakamarino at Tuai offers a completely different environment. This small hydro lake holds huge trout — fish up to 12.5 kg have earned the lake a reputation for producing trophy trout.

Shoreline fishing and flyfishing from an anchored boat are both popular. Motorised craft are not allowed.

The rivers near State Highway 38 on the way out to Wairoa are also worth fishing. The Waiau River holds good fish and there are other smaller streams worth investigating not far from the road.

Fish and Game's excellent Waikaremoana pamphlet, available free from Fish and Game offices, covers the Waikaremoana fishery in detail. Check out www.fishandgame.org.nz/eastern.

Things to do

One of the things I like about Lake Waikaremoana is there's not too much to distract the fisher. As well as spectacular bush walks and some serious tramping challenges, it's all about the lake and the fish that live in it. The 'Great

Walk' is a 46 km three- to four-day tramping track that follows the lakeshore for most of its length. Magnificent forest scenery and plenty of opportunities for swimming and fishing are features of this world-renowned walking track.

Some visitors come to Lake Waikaremoana to sail and indulge in other water sports — kayaking is a great way to explore the lake, provided you keep a weather eye open — but most lake users spend at least some of their time fishing. Other options include horse trekking and guided eco-tours.

A small marina at Waikaremoana accommodates boats and launches permanently domiciled on the lake but most boats are trailered in either from Hawke's Bay via Wairoa, or via Murupara and the long, winding road through the bush. Take care when towing through the forest. The road can be challenging, especially in bad weather, and it's best to tank up before you leave Murupara or Wairoa. Fuel is available at the lake, but it's not cheap.

Accommodation

Accommodation around the lake is limited to Lake Waikaremoana Motorcamp, with power and tent sites, self-catering chalets, a bunkhouse, a family unit and four- or five-bunk fisher's cabins, along with a store, fuel and boat ramp. The store stocks fishing licences and a selection of flies and tackle. Just a few minutes' walk from the DOC Information Centre at Aniwaniwa, it's the base camp and starting point for most activities on and around the lake, including the Great Walk.

A new camping ground at Big Bush has cabins, tent sites and motel-style accommodation. There are a couple of lodges: the luxury Whakamarino Lodge on Lake Whakamarino to the east of Lake Waikaremoana and the affordable Byre B&B at Tuai, five minutes from Lake Waikaremoana. DOC huts are strategically placed along many of the national park's tracks, including the ones around Lake Waikaremoana. Some have associated campsites. Facilities are limited and may or may not include water, which is generally drawn from streams or the lake. Huts need to be booked in advance and demand is heavy, especially in summer.

Boat ramps

There is an excellent boat ramp at Waikaremoana settlement. Boat launching is also available at the head of Mokau Inlet.

Napier

To be perfectly honest, Napier wouldn't be my first choice as a fishing destination. There's good fishing close by but the main reason it's in this book is that it's one of my favourite places for a weekend getaway. I always manage a bit of fishing while I'm there, either in one of the wonderful rivers nearby or in Hawke Bay itself, but there's so much to do in the city and surrounding region that the family never gets bored.

Napier is best known for its wonderful art deco architecture. The preponderance of 1930s buildings is an accident of fate — the Napier earthquake on 3 February 1931 flattened the old town and killed 258 people.

The earthquake tilted the land under the city, raising the seabed by 2 m and draining Napier's inner harbour. The whole nature of the coast changed; lagoons and coastal swamps drained away and a new harbour had to be built to service Napier's coastal trade. A second, modern harbour able to service ocean-going ships has since been constructed on reclaimed land.

The rebuilt city of Napier sits right beside the sea. Its Marine Parade and promenade are popular with visitors and residents alike.

Hawke's Bay is the driest and one of the sunniest parts of the North Island. The hinterland, made up of broad river valleys and coastal plains backed by steep hill country, is a patchwork of vineyards and orchards, with sheep farming still predominant in the hills. Hawke's Bay is New Zealand's second-largest wine-growing area after Marlborough and the largest red wine producer. If you like wine, a wine trail or two is a must during your stay.

Napier may be the premier city in Hawke's Bay but its sister city of Hastings is just a few kilometres down the road. As the cities have grown they've all but merged geographically, though each maintains a fiercely independent identity. It takes only a few minutes to travel from one city centre to the other.

Getting to Napier/Hastings is straightforward enough. It's a fair hike from Auckland. Most people follow State Highway 1 down-country to Taupo and then take State Highway 5 — the Napier–Taupo Road. Put aside a good six

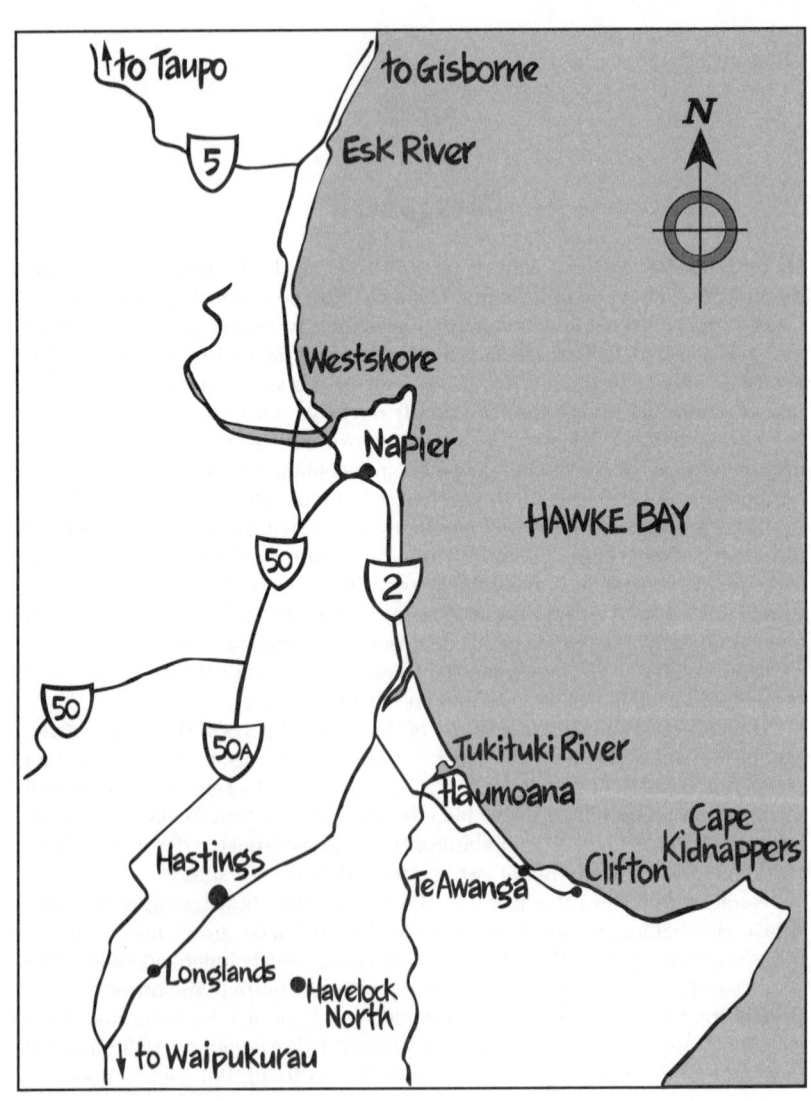

hours for the journey. Wellingtonians have it slightly easier, most choosing State Highway 1 to Levin, State Highway 57 to Woodville then State Highway 2 through Dannevirke, Waipukurau and Hastings. The trip generally takes four and a half hours.

 The fishing

Napier is near the middle of the great sweep of Hawke Bay, a natural rocky bluff forming the basis for its harbour. There's good beach fishing to the north and south, particularly towards Cape Kidnappers. Te Awanga Beach to the south is a firm favourite with local surfcasters and beaches to the north such as North Shore, Tangoio and Whirinaki produce good catches of snapper, gurnard, kahawai and trevally. In spring many popular Hawke Bay fishing beaches experience a run of big snapper, which the local surfcasters have become expert at targeting. Most of the river mouths emptying into the bay produce good kahawai fishing during the whitebait run, with trout also getting in on the act in the rivers' lower reaches.

Close to the city itself, Pandora Bridge across the inner harbour is a good place to target kahawai and barracouta, with parore a common catch for kids using baits of shellfish or dough. Perfume Point, named for the sewer outflow that used to enter the sea here, is a good spot for snapper, kahawai, gurnard, trevally, john dory and large rays. The occasional kingfish is taken, usually on small back-hooked livebaits set for john dory.

A little further round the point to the west, Perfume Point Beach produces a similar range of species, with gurnard predominating. With plenty of car parking nearby, the beach and point are easy to access.

Other shore-fishing spots close to town include Town Reef on the eastern side of the port reclamation. Short casts are all that's required for snapper, kahawai, barracouta and the odd kingfish. Shellfish baits will attract blue moki.

There are a couple of man-made rocky outcrops on the other (western) side of the reclamation. The locals call one 'The Rocks'; the other does not appear to have a name.

The Rocks juts out to sea off Hardinge Road. Fish a floating bait over the foul ground or, better still, fish baits under a float for kahawai and small kingfish in summer. Livebaits are best.

The second outcrop juts into deeper water off the reclamation proper. The same techniques work as for The Rocks, with the addition of blue moki in the evenings, best targeted with shellfish baits. Small boats can also be launched here just beside the rocks.

Boat fishers have the whole bay to choose from, plus inshore spots north and south of Napier. The closest recognised fishing spot to Napier, and one of the few reef areas in the bay, is Pania Reef. This extensive reef complex is an excellent spot, with all sorts of species turning up at times. There's also good crayfish diving.

Bigger craft can head out wide to chase gamefish in summer — tuna and marlin are summer visitors in most years — or bottom-fish Lachlan Banks for hapuku and bass. Charter boats are available.

Bottom fishing in Hawke Bay is often conducted on the drift. There's little in the way of structure to hold fish so boats tend to drift until they get bites, then anchor. A good fishfinder is a real bonus and any structure at all is worth fishing.

There are a few more reefy areas that produce a variety of fish around Cape Kidnappers, a fair run from Napier, though there are boat-launching facilities at Clifton. Most can only be fished in calm conditions.

Trout fishers have plenty of scope in Hawke's Bay. Several famous rivers empty into the bay, including the Ngaruroro, Tukituki and Tutaekuri. The best fishing in the lower reaches is usually in spring, before the rivers get too low and warm. Hawke's Bay's hot, dry summers are a challenge for lowland trout, though most of the region's rivers hold good heads of fish in the upper reaches.

Most Hawke's Bay rivers have shingle beds and are flood-prone, which affects the quality of the fishing from year to year. After a period of stable flows, most can provide good fishing for predominantly rainbow trout averaging 1 kg to 1.5 kg.

The Esk River offers good fishing for brown trout, which are also present in the bay's other rivers to a greater or lesser extent.

Bright silver, hard-fighting, sea-run browns are a feature of the lower reaches of many Hawke's Bay rivers. They are easiest to catch when the whitebait are running.

 Things to do

A lot! Napier is full of interesting sights and things to do. As well as enjoying the exquisitely restored architecture, visitors can dine out at dozens of fine restaurants and cafes, sip a beer on the pavement or in one of the city's many trendy bars, or take a drive or a guided tour to one or more of the region's many wineries. Most offer superb restaurants as well as tastings and sales.

If the whole family is in tow, make sure you check out Marineland. It no longer has its once-famous dolphins but there are plenty of other marine creatures to see.

In a similar vein, Napier's National Aquarium is a must-see, with hundreds of New Zealand fish on display in the modern oceanarium. Divers feed the fish at set times daily.

Children will also enjoy the Napier Aquatic Centre, the seaside mini-golf course on Marine Parade and of course the beaches.

In keeping with the art deco theme, Napier is home to more antique shops than anywhere else in New Zealand. It's an especially good place to find 1920s and 1930s jewellery — ask my wife!

There are a number of guided tours, bay cruises, walks and other activities starting right in town — Napier is compact enough that you can park the car and walk almost anywhere.

A trip by tractor to the gannet colony at Cape Kidnappers and a drive and walk to the top of Te Mata peak overlooking Hastings are Hawke's Bay signature activities.

Accommodation

Probably the most fun place to stay is one of Napier's wonderful art deco hotels — you'll be surprised at how little this costs. Other options include the usual range of self-catering motels, cottages, hotels, campgrounds, B&Bs and homestays. Luxury lodges are a popular option and certainly a great way to treat yourself and your partner.

Book well ahead if you're planning to stay over a long weekend or at peak times, including Art Deco Weekend (the third weekend in February) and during Harvest Hawke's Bay (the first weekend in February).

Many wineries have accommodation and can provide the perfect setting for a romantic stay. Wine and romance — two good reasons to choose Hawke's Bay for a getaway weekend!

Campgrounds are plentiful, with many taking advantage of the coastline.

For information and accommodation options, see www.napier.govt.nz and www.hawkesbaynz.com.

 **Boat ramps**

Napier city has three public boat ramps and there is one each at Clifton Beach and Waimarama Beach, south of Cape Kidnappers.

The town ramps can accommodate the biggest trailer boats but the smaller ramps down the coast are better suited to boats under 6 m. Using a tractor or four-wheel-drive is advisable.

Castle Point

Castle Point has always been a popular holiday and weekend destination for Wellingtonians. Its sweeping sandy beach and dramatic Castle Rock headland, lighthouse, reef, caves, lagoon and steep sand dunes also draw visitors from much further afield. The beach is among the best on the Wairarapa coast, with generally safe swimming.

Castle Point held a great fascination for me as a boy. My parents took me there on several occasions at a time when my interest in fishing was just beginning to blossom. My father was never very keen on fishing but he was happy to walk with my younger sisters and me along the reef on calm days so I could quiz fishers lined up along the reef.

In time I scrounged a length of 30-pound nylon — which I wrapped around an old plastic Vim bottle — a few nondescript hooks of various sizes and several lumps of polystyrene. I would pack the lot into an old sports bag and carry it onto the reef to try my luck for kahawai.

Often it was too rough to fish the lower parts of the reef so I was forced to trek further up Castle Rock's ramparts to cast my hand line. My mother, though always more sympathetic to my piscatorial urges than my father, would watch worriedly, occasionally even gripping my legs as I lay flat on the edge of the cliff, my line dangling into the water many metres below.

Regularly my lump of polystyrene would race across the sea before diving below the surface as a big Wairarapa kahawai took the bait. Once I briefly hooked a huge green-backed, yellow-tailed kingfish, a fish so monumental and powerful that it shaped my whole fishing future.

Like the kingfish, most of the kahawai I managed to fool into eating my bait found their freedom. Even when they stayed attached to my line, an interminable hand-over-hand haul up the sheer side of the cliff usually resulted in the fish falling off the hook, sometimes within centimetres of the top. I learned a bit about the euphoria of fishing success at Castle Point, but a lot more about its bitter disappointments.

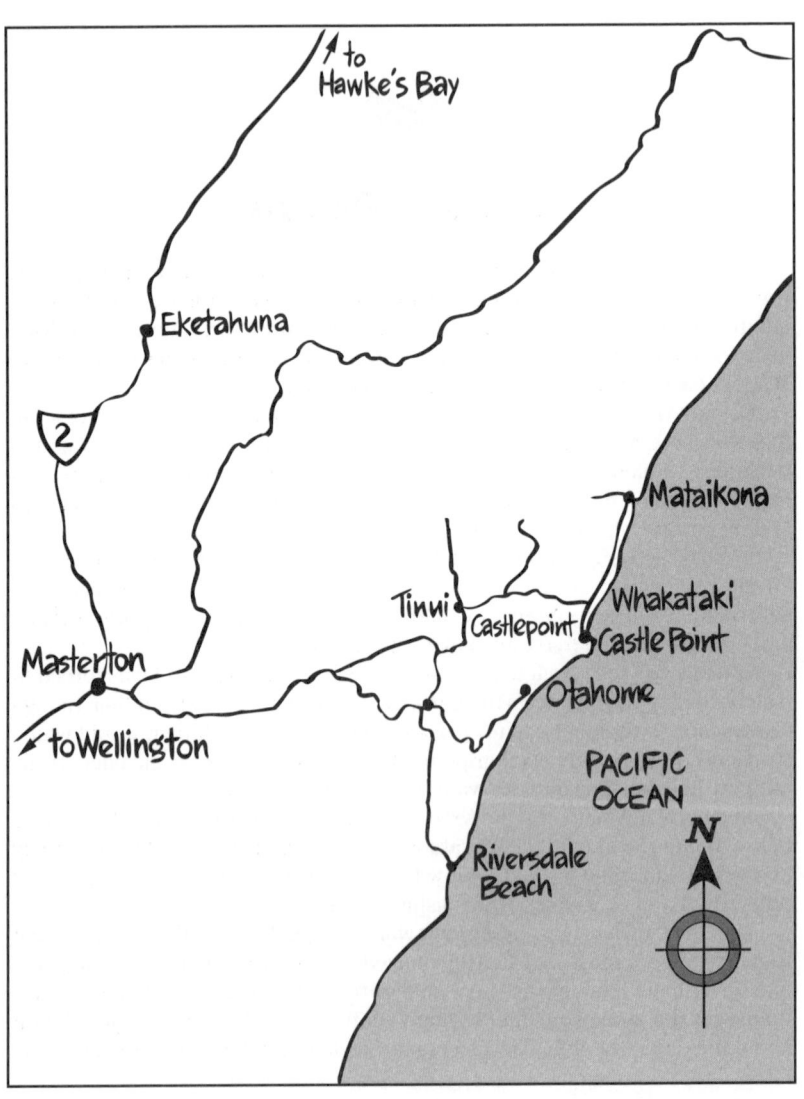

When I grew older I continued to travel over the hill from Wellington to the coast at Castle Point. Sometimes my friends and I would drive there to fish overnight during fishing club contests, returning to Wellington on Sunday morning to weigh our bounty. Often the catch wasn't too exciting — a few gurnard, the odd kahawai and, in winter, red cod or skate — but the fishing was generally better than we could expect from the shore in Wellington Harbour and there was always the chance of snapper, kingfish and other 'glamour' species to keep us coming back. Much later I took advantage of several opportunities to boat-fish out of Castle Point, launching into the lagoon and braving the narrow gap through the reef to access the open sea.

The fishing

It's fair to say that the fishing at Castle Point isn't what it was, especially for land-based fishers restricted to casting from the reef or the main beach. In the past they landed snapper, kingfish and even the occasional hapuku off the rocks. These days such catches are rare, though kingfish can still be targeted by patient fishers prepared to fish live kahawai under balloons on suitably heavy tackle. Anglers using conventional rigs and baits can also catch snapper.

More common catches these days include gurnard and red cod (especially in winter), kahawai, the occasional blue cod close to the rocks (though they're seldom of legal size), jack mackerel, barracouta and conger eels. The best fishing is probably in spring and early summer.

Some large skates are taken in winter, along with assorted dogfish, and the occasional summer school shark will give the average surfcasting outfit a thorough working-over. Large bronze whaler sharks are also occasionally hooked off the reef in warmer months. They invariably find their freedom after a short struggle.

At high tide, yellow-eyed mullet and sometimes kahawai can be caught from the wooden 'bridge' across the lagoon. The same species can also be caught in the lagoon itself, along with flounder and sometimes rays.

Fishing off the reef is weather- and sea-dependent. If there is any sort of swell running, the lower portions of Castle Point Reef can be extremely dangerous. A plaque set into the reef commemorates the many fishers who have lost their lives here, and signs on the beach and the reef itself warn visitors of the dangers.

I once attempted crossing the lowest portion of the reef to reach friends who had crossed earlier in the tide. A wave caught me, washing me into the lagoon. I was able to scramble back onto the reef before the backwash could suck me over the rocks and into the open sea or out through the narrow gap at the lagoon's southern end. The dunking gave me quite a fright and dampened the enthusiasm of my mates, with whom I spent the next six or seven hours, soaking wet and shivering, waiting for the tide to turn and drop sufficiently for us to make our way back to safety.

In general, the fishing off the reef is better at night. I've enjoyed some good sessions but anglers need to take even greater care, as it's all but impossible to see the swells. Fishing from the beach can be OK at times; the most common catch is kahawai.

Boat fishing used to be the exclusive preserve of commercial fishers, except for a few dinghies launched into the surf during holidays. A reasonable-size fleet of crayfish and longline boats still fishes out of Castle Point, launching into the lagoon off special trailers drawn behind modified tractors or bulldozers.

These days recreational boats often join them, especially on weekends. Many of these are also launched using tractors, and trailers with extendable drawbars have been copied from the commercial boys.

The fishing offshore can be good. Boats generally need to travel a fair way up or down the coast to find large blue cod, and hapuku are some way out to sea on deeper pins and drop-offs, though the Wairarapa coast experiences a run of school hapuku every spring that come into water as shallow as 20 m to 30 m.

Other popular species for recreational anglers include kahawai and trumpeter, barracouta, conger eels and the occasional summer kingfish. Snapper are rarely caught but they're usually large, and john dory are an unusual but sought-after catch.

Charter trips are also available.

 ## Things to do

The village of Castlepoint is a collection of beachside houses, many of them baches or holiday homes, a motor camp and motel, a general store/cafe/bar and a pub down the road at Whakataki. Most of its activities revolve around the beach and its rock pools and caves, Castle Rock and the lagoon. The swimming is good in summer if there's not too much surf and there's reasonable scuba diving to the south.

A scramble around the rocks at low tide will reveal the opening to a good-sized cave. Climb inside and it opens up into a magical grotto. The floor is strewn with large boulders covered with silcrete. Stalactites hang from the high ceiling and stalagmites stand proudly upright on the cave floor beyond the reach of visitors. The cave is not without its dangers. When seas are high, water comes right through the cave.

There's a chance to spot seals, dolphins or little blue penguins from the reef or Castle Rock, as well as numerous seabirds whose number and species changes with the seasons. Watching the fishing boats navigate the tricky 'gap' into the calm waters of the lagoon to unload their catch on the wharf is always popular with visitors; or you can charter your own fishing trip. You can also enjoy fresh fish on the local pub menu.

A wind-in-your-hair walk to Castle Rock, through the pines of Castlepoint Scenic Reserve or over the dunes, provides stunning coastal views. In winter Castle Point can be a wild place but I've always enjoyed trips at this time of the year, when wind and waves are king.

The beaches of Otahome, Mataikona and Riversdale are not far away; Riversdale is a popular holiday destination in its own right. The Castlepoint Races, held on the beach every year since 1872, usually in March, are a huge drawcard and a fun day for the family. Betting is by equalisator — a sweepstake style, making it perfect for a casual flutter.

Accommodation

Apart from private beach houses and baches, some of which are available for hire, accommodation is limited to the Castlepoint Holiday Park, which offers a diverse range of accommodation, including caravan and tent sites, cabins, motels, cottages, houses, flats and a lodge. It's right on the beach and is a great place to stay summer or winter, though bookings are advised in summer, 06 372 6705, email holiday@castlepoint.co.nz.

For information and accommodation in Wairarapa and Castlepoint, try www.wairarapanz.com.

Boat ramps

There's beach launching into the lagoon or into the surf off the main beach. Tractors and trailers with long drawbars are recommended, as the beach has very little fall.

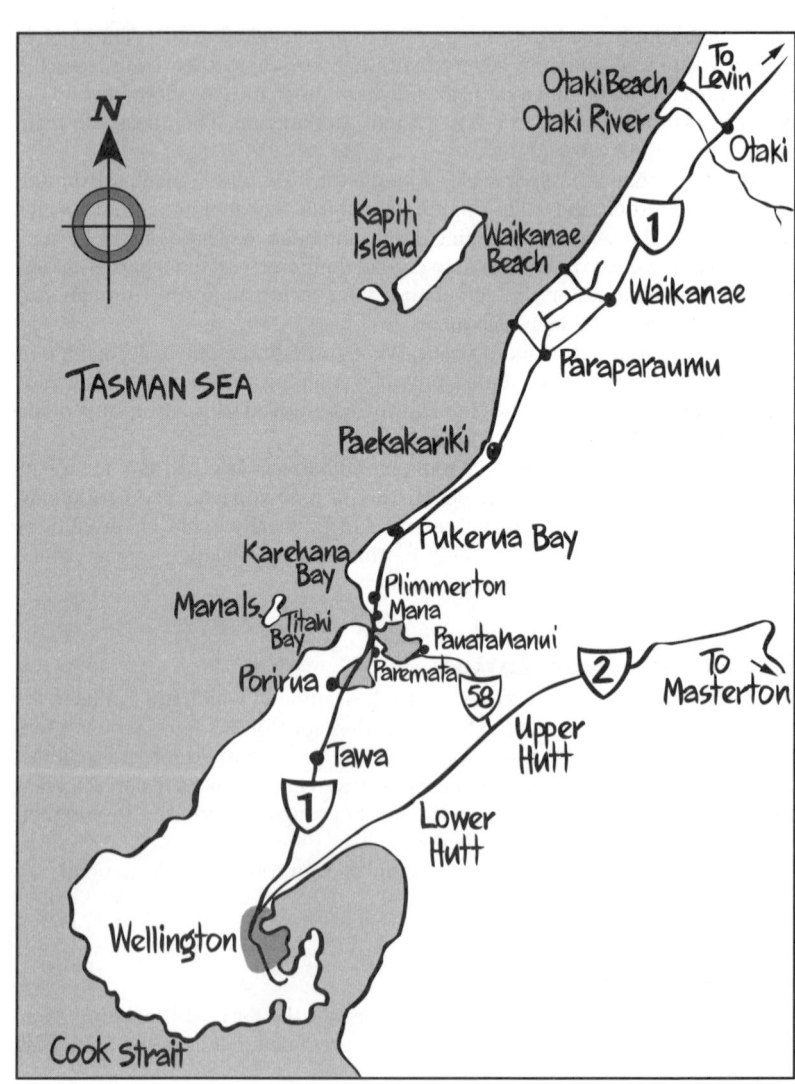

Kapiti Coast

When I was a boy growing up in the Hutt Valley there was no such place as the 'Kapiti Coast'. We used to go to 'Pram' (Paraparaumu), Plimmerton, Paremata or Waikanae.

Nowadays this popular coastal region goes by the name 'Kapiti Coast'. I've never been too sure of its geographical limits but always assumed it included the stretch of coast opposite Kapiti Island, a few kilometres offshore, and the coast to the south — an area often called Mana. Mana's distinguishing features are Mana Island just offshore and two safe harbours sharing an entrance at Plimmerton. So perhaps this entry should be called 'Kapiti-Mana'.

Whatever it's called, the region has expanded hugely in recent years as Wellingtonians retire to the coast. Improved road and rail links mean many residents happily commute to Wellington city or the Hutt Valley, and the growth and gradual gentrification of Porirua, Tawa and Titahi Bay has removed some of the stigma once attached to the area.

Although only 50 km or so from central Wellington, the Kapiti Coast has a much better climate. It's both warmer and drier than the Harbour City and has less wind — both of which attract Wellingtonians.

The area was important to early Maori, who valued its climate and fertile soils. Ngati Toa chief Te Rauparaha descended from Kawhia to conquer the local tribes in the 1830s, setting up his headquarters on Kapiti Island. From there his followers raided and settled the area around Wellington and the South Island. The Kapiti Coast and the coastal plain just to the north were once full of Maori gardens. Later they became market gardens, with a large Chinese community settling around Otaki, growing vegetables for the Wellington market.

Although a lot of visitors pass through on their way north or south or come just for the day, the Kapiti Coast is a popular weekend getaway. It offers a complete break from the city but is close enough to be convenient — if you leave Wellington after work on a Friday you can be enjoying a glass of wine watching the sun set behind Kapiti Island less than an hour later.

The fishing

One of the biggest attractions of the Kapiti Coast for me is the exceptional boat fishing around Kapiti and Mana islands. They're far enough offshore to discourage small craft — though Kapiti-Mana has better weather than Wellington, Cook Strait is just around the corner so conditions can change extremely quickly.

The fish caught are an interesting mix of southern and northern species: blue cod, wrasse, Maori chiefs and warehou are common, but so are snapper, trevally and kingfish. There's good fishing for tarakihi, hapuku and kingfish as well, with barracouta, red cod and dogfish common in winter. Add conger eels, gurnard, kahawai and rays to the mix and its clear there's a diverse and interesting fishery awaiting the keen angler.

A clearly marked marine reserve protects nearly half of Kapiti Island's coast. Fortunately, the remainder offers good fishing — in shallow water for snapper and blue cod, kahawai and reef species, with the deeper water offering up tarakihi and kingfish. Warehou are common in winter.

I have had the privilege of working on Kapiti Island. It's an important wildlife reserve and visitors require a permit to land. Thus the island's rocky shore hasn't been denuded of life like so much of the rest of New Zealand's coast. I didn't fish from the island while there — it didn't seem right — but we regularly gathered the largest paua I've ever seen to supplement our rather bland diet. Gathering them barely involved getting our feet wet — large paua clung to the rocks all the way up to the low-tide mark.

Paua can still be found on the mainland coast and at Mana Island but not in the numbers or size we found at Kapiti. Poachers have taken their toll, but also relentless pressure over generations has ensured that stocks are a shadow of their former abundance. Nevertheless, it's still possible to gather a feed using snorkel gear in many places along the rocky stretch of coast between Karehana and Pukerua bays.

Some of the best snapper fishing in the Wellington region can be found inside Mana Island. In summer good runs of snapper turn up on this coast. They respond to deep berleying and ledger or weighted strayline rigs. The entrances to Porirua and Pauatahanui harbours can turn up some good snapper fishing at times, with smaller fish caught inside, and red cod during winter. Hunter Bank between Mana and Kapiti islands is also good fishing.

Shore fishers can cash in on the snapper too. The best fishing is from the rocky shoreline between Pukerua Bay and Paekakariki. The rocks and beach below the Fisherman's Table Restaurant is a popular spot that in summer yields spotty sharks, tope, gurnard and rays, along with snapper and kahawai. On calm nights, fishing for flounder with a spear and a light can be good, as is drag-netting during the day.

Further north, rock gives way to sand. Surfcasters do catch fish from the beaches at Paraparaumu and Waikanae but it can be a long time between drinks. The water is shallow for a long way out and paddle crabs are a nuisance. Kahawai are the most common catch.

Well offshore, boat anglers can target hapuku and bass in deep water. Favourite locations include Fisherman's Rock, several miles west of Mana Island, and many rises or ridges a similar distance from shore to the north and south.

Much closer in, hapuku can be taken from holes and banks a couple of miles behind Mana and wide of Kapiti Island. This is easier fishing, though less consistent. When the 'puka are there, though, they can be present in good numbers.

Rounding out the coast's fishing options, there's interesting, though challenging, trout fishing in the Waikanae River. Good-looking pools greet the angler from the main road bridge, drawing him or her upriver into a scenic river valley. There are good trout living in the pools and runs, though the numbers are not high so there can be a fair bit of walking involved. It's sometimes possible to spot fish but prospecting the better-looking water with a lightly weighted nymph is the best way to go.

There are fish in the Otaki River too but they're even harder to find and catch. For both streams, the best fishing is during the annual whitebait run when trout gather in the sections below the road bridge, close to the sea. Swinging a smelt fly through the pools near the river mouth at dusk in October or November can bring the best results of the year.

Things to do

With Wellington providing a captive clientele so close by, the Kapiti Coast has been quick to develop the sorts of attractions that will hold visitors in the area.

It offers a host of activities ranging from exhilarating outdoor adventures, eco-tours and marine activities to excellent and varied shopping. There's one of New Zealand's top golf courses, a fascinating rail museum, including magnificently restored trams, easily accessible nature reserves and arts and crafts that match the best in the country, to list just a few.

Kapiti Island tours are recommended, leaving from the beach at Paraparaumu. A visitor's permit is part of the deal and the adventure involves boarding the boat through the surf and landing at Kapiti, where you can experience a guided tour, superb coastal forest and fascinating native bird life.

Adventurous attractions include River Rock Outdoor Escapes and Kapiti 4x4 Adventure. You can also go gliding, parachuting or learn to fly at Kapiti Aero Club.

More sedate activities include visits to numerous art and crafts studios, the Lindale Centre, a tourist complex with a farm theme, and Nyco Chocolates for the kids or those of you with a sweet tooth. There's also a good museum in Waikanae.

Eating out is easy enough. Many of the better motels have their own dining rooms but there are plenty of options in Paraparaumu, Waikanae or even Levin, a few kilometres further up State Highway 1.

And if none of these entertainment options appeal, Wellington City is less than an hour away by train — it's more than feasible to head to town for a relaxed day's shopping from a base on the Kapiti Coast.

Accommodation

The Kapiti Coast has plenty to offer, with a preponderance of charming B&Bs particularly popular with Wellington folk seeking an overnight getaway.

Other options include homestays and plenty of motels. The Sand Castle Motel, perched right on the edge of the ocean on Waikanae Beach, boasts unique architecture, direct beach access and sea views from most units. There are also numerous holiday homes for rent.

The Kapiti Coast page of www.tourism.net.nz has plenty of accommodation listings and www.kapiti.org.nz has accommodation options, activities, places to eat and much more.

Boat ramps

Boat ramps at Plimmerton (two), Paremata Bridge (beach), and Porirua Harbour (Mana Marina) take care of most of the boat launching for the region. Several smaller ramps or beach-launching venues are also used but most are wind- and/or tide-dependent.

Boats are also launched off Paraparaumu and Waikanae beaches in good conditions. A tractor is required. Mana Marina has berths and swing moorings for bigger craft. The marina boat ramp is the best in the district.

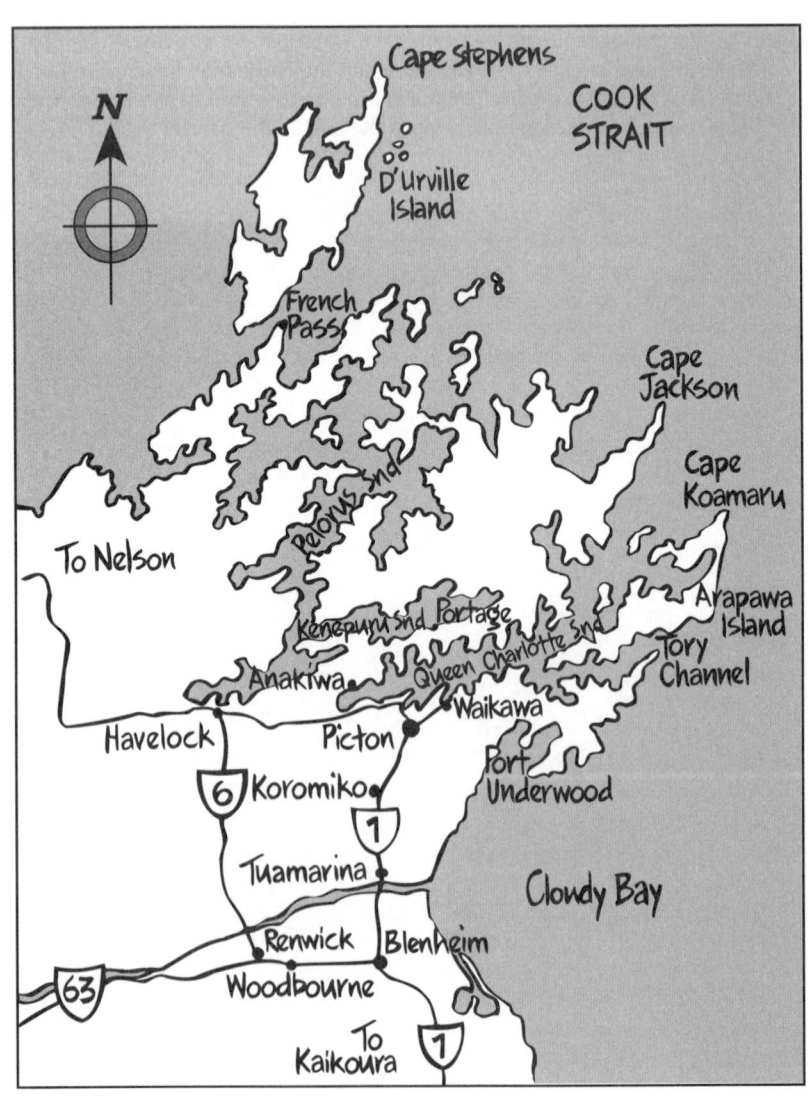

Marlborough Sounds

**Captain Cook was quick to recognise the value of the Marlborough Sounds'
many deeply indented sea-arms. Sheltered and deep, they offered him and
his crew a safe haven where they could recuperate and repair ships after
their world-spanning journeys.**

The same qualities that attracted Cook draw a huge number of visiting and
resident boaties today: miles of deep, sheltered water, thousands of bays and
coves, bush-covered slopes, beaches, islands, reefs and superb natural
anchorages. The fishing's not bad either.

Visitors coming from the North Island have an advantage when approaching
the Marlborough Sounds by sea, as most do. The ferry ride from Wellington to
Picton takes passengers through spectacular maritime scenery. On a good day
the Cook Strait crossing is a doddle and you might be left wondering what the
fuss is all about; on a bad day you'll quickly understand why the strait deserves
its ugly reputation. The crossing takes about three hours in good weather —
more when it's rough — and travellers with vehicles need to check in at least an
hour before departure for loading.

Visitors can fly in, too, from Christchurch, Wellington or Auckland. There's
a busy provincial airport at Blenheim, just a few kilometres by road from
Picton at the head of Queen Charlotte Sound. Once again North Island visitors
get the better deal when it comes to sightseeing; the route often flies directly
over the sounds, allowing a wonderful bird's-eye view of its cruising grounds
before the plane lands among the vineyards that surround Blenheim.

27

Queen Charlotte Sound

Queen Charlotte is the longest and most populated of the Marlborough Sounds. With Picton at its head, it's the entrepôt for Cook Strait ferries and the railhead for the South Island. A bustling port, Picton/Waikawa is also a thriving tourist and holiday destination.

New housing developments are proceeding apace, many aimed at the holiday home market. Marinas at Picton and Waikawa Bay cater to a growing fleet of large pleasure boats that call the sounds home and there are excellent launching facilities for trailer boats. Picton offers a full range of boat-building, chandlery and marine service facilities and is one of New Zealand's most boat-friendly towns — you can drive your boat right into town, tie up and go shopping.

Boats play a huge part in the life of the sounds. Most of the holiday properties are accessible only by boat, so boats of all shapes and sizes are ubiquitous. Bach owners with properties close to Picton may own just a small runabout but many have much larger craft, especially if they travel further down the sound or into Tory Channel. Most properties have their own jetties and many have boathouses where small craft can be stored.

Tradesmen use boats to service hundreds of baches in the sounds. Water taxis and regular tours and passenger boats leave from Picton and Waikawa. In summer the sound buzzes day and night with boat traffic, and during holiday weekends it can seem as if the whole of Christchurch is resident in Queen Charlotte.

Fortunately there is a lot of water and an uncountable number of bays, arms, islands and beaches, so there's always somewhere to yourself, but the fishing is certainly more challenging when boat traffic is at its most dense.

The fishing

The fishing inside Queen Charlotte Sound isn't nearly as good as it once was and is probably the least rewarding of all the sounds. Its popularity with visitors and holidaymakers and its relative accessibility have brought a fair amount of fishing pressure over the years from both commercial and recreational fishers.

Blue cod, the predominant and most sought-after catch, have particularly suffered. Legal-sized fish — 33 cm and over — are rare in the inner sound and the recreational bag limit has been reduced to three. Further down the sound things improve and legal fish are easy enough to come by, but anglers generally need to travel to the waters at the mouth of Queen Charlotte and beyond to find the 50 cm-plus cod once caught close to Picton.

The cod fishing has actually improved over the last few years as the bag and size limits, and the exclusion of commercial cod fishers, have started to make a difference. However, a visit to the small marine reserve at Double Cove shows what's been lost — big blue cod cruise up off the bottom to devour offerings of bread or fish. Fish of this size are no longer caught in the inner sounds. Nevertheless, persistence will usually produce a feed of cod these days; when they're biting, catching three fish doesn't take long.

Further out it's more like the old days. A trip to Cape Jackson or around Cape Koamaru to the Brothers Islands can provide full-on fishing for big cod, some well over 50 cm and 3 kg.

Cod fishing doesn't require much finesse and they will bite on almost any sort of bait. Flasher rigs are a popular option, usually sweetened with fish or squid bait. Many people use heavy tackle for cod, though it's not needed to subdue the fish — they're not the greatest fighters in the ocean. Much of the fishing takes place on the drift in areas of high current so gear needs to be fairly robust. Plenty of lead is the norm.

In more sheltered water, lighter gear works better and, in my opinion, catches a better class of fish. I've also had great success using soft plastics, either fishing the wash close to the rocks or in deeper water using dropshot rigs. The size of the cod taken on artificials (metal jigs also work well) has been a pleasant surprise, and was a revelation to the locals I fished with.

But Queen Charlotte, and the sounds in general, are not just about blue cod. There's good fishing for a variety of species in the sheltered waters of the sound and Tory Channel. Tarakihi and gurnard are common, kahawai can be taken most of the year and hapuku are available in the deeper water at the mouth of Queen Charlotte and out in Cook Strait beyond.

In summer snapper are fairly common, though not often fished for, and trevally, john dory, kingfish and other northern species make an appearance.

Less desirable species are also common: dogfish, school sharks, barracouta and red cod, along with various wrasses, scarpies (banded perch) and other bottom dwellers.

The beauty of fishing the sounds is that you can find a variety of great table fish in mostly sheltered waters, often just a few metres from shore. In addition, scallops and mussels are abundant, cockles can be found in most sandy bays and crayfish are taken inside the sounds by those in the know. The entrance to Tory Channel is a good spot at slack tide.

Inside Queen Charlotte Sound, fishing the edges of the channels can be productive. Small baits take tarakihi and gurnard, with blue cod over the rubble just before the drop-off. Tarakihi are also present close to the islands and reefs of Queen Charlotte. They favour the edges of the reef over sand. Use light tackle, small hooks and cut fish baits.

Hapuku are the target of fishers dropping large baits in the deeper holes of the outer sound. They can sometimes be taken closer in, especially from June to September, but most of the fishing takes place well out in Cook Strait.

Shore fishing in Queen Charlotte is limited and for the most part requires a boat to get from place to place. There is reasonable beach fishing in many of the bays for the usual sounds species of cod, gurnard and tarakihi. Kahawai can be taken off the breakwater at Waikawa Bay and Grove Arm produces snapper and kahawai from shore. Bach owners often have success from their own jetties, taking snapper on summer nights in sandier bays and a variety of fish in rockier bays. Many of the points fish well for blue cod, kahawai, the odd snapper and even kingfish. Endeavour Inlet has reasonable scope for the shore fisher.

Things to do

Most of the activities in the Marlborough Sounds revolve around the water. Picton has an excellent tourist infrastructure offering all manner of sightseeing tours, boat trips, excursions, yacht and launch charters, water taxis, dive trips, dolphin and seal watching, sea-kayaking and much more.

The town is well serviced by restaurants, bars and cafes, though they tend to be a bit pricey (also true of the accommodation).

Boaties can visit the many resorts scattered around Queen Charlotte Sound, stopping in for a drink, lunch or dinner — or a night or two. A visit to the eco-resort in the Bay of Many Coves is recommended. It blends beautifully with the hillside and its food and wine are first class.

The 71 km Queen Charlotte Track is one of New Zealand's great walks. From Picton it winds around the head of Queen Charlotte Sound and along its eastern side to Ship Cove, taking in dozens of bays, headlands, coves and beaches over four or five days. Accommodation ranges from campsites and backpacker lodges to luxury lodges and hotels.

One of the advantages of this trek is that you can catch a water taxi if you want a break from walking. The taxis can also carry your gear. The track is also popular with mountain bikers and certain sections can be biked year-round.

The bustling provincial city of Blenheim, capital of the Marlborough province, is a short drive from Picton. Furnished with a busy airport, it's the entry point for many visitors to the sounds.

Marlborough is famous for its vineyards and Blenheim is the gateway to the region's world-renowned wineries — wine tourism, including cellar visits and guided wine trails are a Marlborough speciality.

The city is also endowed with a good range of dining and accommodation options, excellent shopping and a full range of services.

Accommodation

In my opinion the very best Marlborough Sounds experience involves staying in a beachside bach accessible only by water. Getting to and from your accommodation is half the fun and, once there, whipping into town is usually not an option. It's enforced relaxation but, with water lapping at your doorstep, that's no hardship for a fisher.

Many of the sounds' baches are palatial these days and increasingly occupied year-round. But there are still plenty of modest examples, most of which have been in the same families for generations. Some have electricity, particularly those in bays close to Picton, but many rely on diesel generators, and some of the more remote use other sources for lighting and cooking. Water is often piped from streams in the hills.

As is the case with holiday houses everywhere, you often need to know someone to rent such places but there are agencies that specialise in renting baches in the sounds. Start your search with websites such as www.holidayhouses.co.nz/marlborough_sounds.asp.

The second-best option is a sounds holiday by boat. A few days cruising and fishing the Marlborough Sounds is about as relaxing a holiday as I could imagine. There are plenty of charter operations available, self-drive or skippered, you may bring your own boat or you may be lucky enough to be the guest of someone with a suitable craft. Picton and Waikawa marinas are packed with wonderful sounds cruisers, among the brasher, more modern craft. A cruise on one of the old girls is recommended.

Another option for the visitor with his or her own boat is to stay at one of the many resorts or lodges scattered around Queen Charlotte Sound, mooring your boat each evening and retiring to the comfort of the lodge. Endeavour Inlet boasts Punga Cove Resort, Endeavour Resort and Furneaux Lodge.

Picton and Marlborough offer a range of long- and short-term accommodation, including timeshare and apartments for rent, some waterside. Demand for accommodation is particularly heavy in summer when tourist numbers peak. I have been caught out before, unable to find a motel bed in either town. On that occasion I finally found accommodation at the Grovetown Country Hotel between Picton and Blenheim, enjoying a wonderful evening's entertainment, a good meal and a clean, reasonably priced room. Country hotels are often overlooked but they can offer outstanding value and a better-than-average chance of enjoying a slice of local colour.

Boat ramps

The excellent public boat-launching facilities at Picton and Waikawa Bay require a permit or the payment of a day charge. Security is reasonably good, so leaving vehicles and trailers overnight or longer is not normally a problem.

Pelorus and Kenepuru sounds

In many ways I prefer Pelorus Sound to Queen Charlotte — there are fewer visitors and far fewer baches, resorts and other tourist infrastructure. I prefer the fishing, too. The summer run of snapper, some very large, appeals to my North Island sensibilities and there are plenty of opportunities for the shore-based angler.

Kenepuru extends off Pelorus Sound with no opening to the sea at its northeastern end. This nearly landlocked body of water provides some excellent snapper fishing at times.

In most respects, Pelorus is similar to the other sounds: a boat is required to really explore it and the best fishing tends to be out towards Cook Strait. Outer Pelorus is less heavily fished than outer Queen Charlotte Sound so the fish are bigger and more plentiful.

At the head of Pelorus Sound — actually the head of Mahau Sound, but they are all interconnected — is the town of Havelock. Founded during the Wakamarina gold rush years of the 1860s, the town boomed before dwindling into relative obscurity as the gold was exhausted. Havelock is the birthplace of Sir Ernest Rutherford, the famous physicist who first split the atom.

Havelock has accommodation, fuel, boat-launching and shops. Picton is only 30 minutes away by road and Blenheim is only marginally further on State Highway 6. Havelock is en route to Nelson and you need to pass through it to explore Croisilles Harbour from Okiwi Bay. A boat ramp there allows access to French Pass and d'Urville Island, saving a long run by sea from Havelock.

Kenepuru Sound can be reached by road from Linkwater, between Picton and Havelock, but most visitors come by sea.

The fishing

The head of Mahau Sound at Havelock has large areas of shallows, as do the upper reaches of Kenepuru Sound. These shelly, sandy areas attract good numbers of snapper in summer and fishing here is quite unlike fishing in Queen Charlotte.

Kingfish are also relatively common, along with kahawai and john dory. Mussel farms throughout the area provide good fishing and most of the points are a go for kingfish.

The many points of Kenepuru Sound are popular with land-based fishers, who cast into the channel or close to reefs running off the points for big snapper. A boat is needed to access most locations but shore fishers often catch more and bigger fish than boat fishers in the same area. The tidal flats of Kenepuru Head can provide excellent beach fishing at night over a high tide.

Further out in Pelorus Sound proper, the fishing becomes more like that of Queen Charlotte and the other deep-water sounds but snapper and kingfish are much more abundant. Port Ligar is a good spot for kingfish, as is Danger Point, which can be fished from shore.

As you head further out, blue cod begin to dominate, along with tarakihi. Gurnard and dogfish patrol the channel edges and there is a good possibility of hapuku on the pins and holes in the outer sound and around the Chetwode Islands. There's good crayfish diving too, though strong currents demand respect.

As with Queen Charlotte Sound, good scallop beds can be found in many of the bays — Ketu Bay was particularly good last time I visited.

 Things to do

Pelorus Sound has many of the same attractions as Queen Charlotte, only they're rather less commercialised. If you have your own boat, or access to someone else's, you've got it made. (There's fuel in Havelock, at Portage and also at Wilson Bay.)

Havelock is the green-lipped mussel capital of New Zealand — the sheltered waters of the inner sounds are ideal for farming mussels and much of the town's infrastructure is geared to supplying the mussel industry. Havelock has a busy port with plenty of marine services available to visiting boaties. Havelock Marina is home to many commercial and recreational boats.

Popular Havelock-based tours include a trip on the mail boat (an excellent way to see Pelorus Sound), mussel farm cruises (which include tastings of the local produce), an eight-hour nature cruise to French Pass and more.

Bare-boat and skippered charters are available from Havelock, as are half- and full-day fishing charters. Diving trips go to the outer sounds and the wreck of the *Mikhail Lermontov*, and helicopters fly hunters and fishers to remote spots.

Active recreation includes a number of walks, mountain biking and sea-kayaking, while visitors looking for more sedate activities can take in the town's museum with its interesting record of Havelock's gold-rush boom years, or one of the many award-winning gardens in the region. For more ideas, see www.havelock.co.nz.

Accommodation

Kenepuru and Pelorus Sounds offer the usual range of motels, backpackers, B&Bs, an upmarket hotel, a scattering of basic DOC campgrounds and more than their fair share of motor camps.

Bach rentals are also available, some of them — as in Queen Charlotte — accessible only by boat. Farmstays are another option.

Numerous lodges scattered around Pelorus and Kenepuru sounds range from self-catering to fully serviced luxury accommodation. They are usually beside the water and are often nestled in superb native bush. They include Pelorus Lodge, St Omer House, Raetihi Lodge, Okiwi Bay Lodge and Te Rawa Resort.

For details, see www.destinationmarlborough.com.

Boat ramps

There are concrete boat ramps at Havelock, Portage and several in Tennyson Inlet, at Duncan Bay, Penzance, Elaine Bay and Cissy Bay. Beach launching is also possible here and there.

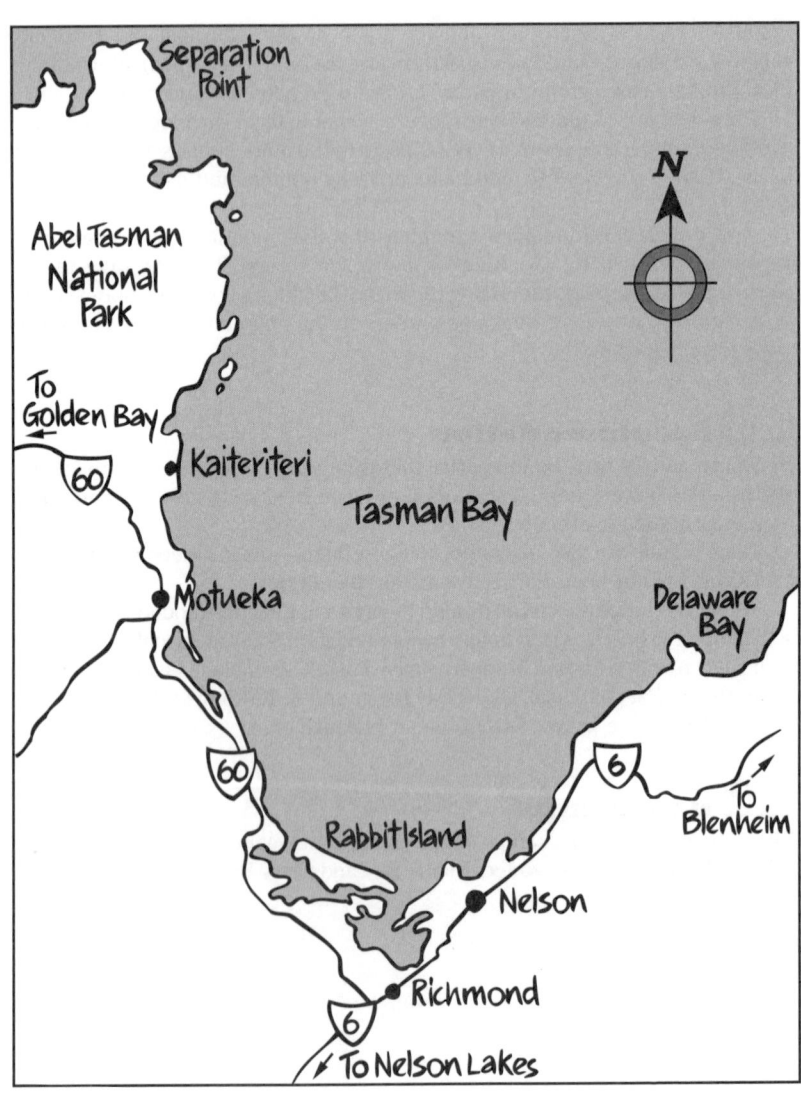

Tasman Bay

Tasman Bay was named after the Dutch explorer Abel Janszoon Tasman, who in 1642 led the first European expedition to reach New Zealand. It is quite a contrast to the island-strewn Marlborough Sounds on its eastern boundary.

From a base in Nelson, there's plenty to explore in Tasman Bay and the region's rivers, streams and the Nelson Lakes offer excellent trout fishing. What's more, laid-back Nelson, with its vineyards, galleries and good weather is regularly rated as one of the top spots to visit in New Zealand.

The city of Nelson is set between the Maitai Valley and Tahunanui Beach. Mount Richmond Forest Park is on its doorstep and Rabbit Island Beach is just a short drive away.

Blessed with fertile soils and a benign climate, Tasman Bay and Golden Bay (over the Takaka Hill) have always been attractive places to live. Early Maori settlers had to fight to hold the area from other Maori desirous of its resources, including argillite and greenstone. A succession of iwi lived in the area, each in turn pushed south or absorbed by subsequent settlers.

Ngati Tumatakokiri took to their waka and attacked Abel Tasman in Golden Bay, killing four of his men, but these fierce warriors had themselves been displaced by the time Cook visited the area in 1770.

Pakeha settlement began in earnest in 1842 with the first two shiploads of settlers arriving to take up land surveyed by the New Zealand Company. The discovery of gold at Aorere (Collingwood) and later in the back country towards Murchison, as well as copper and chromite closer to Nelson, saw the port develop quickly, shipping minerals out and miners in. Nelson grew steadily and today it's a bustling port and a lively provincial city.

The fishing

Nelson is blessed with top-quality fishing right on its doorstep. An hour to the east are the Marlborough Sounds, while an hour's drive inland takes the angler to the world-renowned wilderness of northwest Nelson, its rivers and streams full of trout.

Boat fishers and shore anglers both enjoy good fishing for a range of species, including snapper, kingfish, kahawai and trevally, as well as blue cod, tarakihi, gurnard, warehou, sharks and rays. Summer fishing is generally better and more consistent, particularly for the glamour species like snapper, but blue cod are available year-round over rocky inshore reefs. Red cod are winter visitors, preferring shallow sand/mud bottoms. They're commonly taken by beach fishers inside Nelson Harbour and near the mouths of major rivers.

Croisilles Harbour, the last outpost of the Marlborough Sounds, is less than an hour from Nelson by road. There's a boat ramp at Okiwi Bay and good shore fishing here and there. The harbour is sheltered from southwesterly winds and its rocks, reefs and shallow sandy bays offer a variety of fishing. Mussel farms dot the more sheltered bays, attracting fish of many species. There are good blue cod on most of the reefs, while snapper patrol headlands, islands, reefs and the sandy areas in between. Kingfish and kahawai are also common.

Tarakihi can be targeted off most of the points, especially around Cape Soucis — use small baits and 1/0 hooks. Croisilles Harbour is known for its good-sized snapper, especially in spring and autumn.

The coast between Croisilles and Nelson is mostly rocky, punctuated by a series of points that provide good fishing. Many of the points are associated with extensive areas of shallow reefs, offering boat fishing for cod, snapper, trevally, tarakihi, kingfish and kahawai. There's also some shore fishing at Hori Bay.

Closer to Nelson, Delaware Bay turns up large early-season snapper in close, as well as gurnard, kahawai and flounder, while Pepin Island is an obvious drawcard. Shore anglers and boat fishers enjoy good fishing for a variety of species here, including blue moki.

In and around the port of Nelson, anglers can sample excellent snapper fishing along Nelson's famous Boulder Bank and in the deeper channels of the harbour entrance. The Boulder Bank is accessible to shore anglers but more commonly fished from boats in 5 m to 10 m of water. Shore anglers can also choose between a couple of accessible downtown spots, including one — The

Fishing Platform — constructed especially for their use. They can also fish into Blind Channel, which runs into the Waimea estuary to the west of town. Blind Channel is also a good spot to fish from a boat.

Small snapper, the odd kingfish, small trevally and kahawai, frequent the inner harbour, which offers safe fishing from small boats. Several sheltered spots around Rabbit Island also produce surprisingly good fishing in shallow water. Rabbit Island is especially popular with surfcasters. Kina Beach on the eastern side of the Moutere Inlet is another worthwhile and very scenic surfcasting spot.

Much of the boat fishing around Nelson is in shallow water but a run of 5 km to 10 km out to sea from Moutere Bluffs finds deeper water and some excellent snapper fishing in summer.

The coast between Anawera and Separation points is a succession of rocky bays and coves, interspersed with sandy inlets, islands, caves and rock stacks. Largely included in the Abel Tasman National Park, it's uncommonly beautiful.

The fishing is good for most species and there is a marine reserve at Tonga Island that has good diving.

Trout fishers based in Nelson have an abundance of good waters to sample. They range from easily accessible rivers such as the Motueka and Wairau to more remote waters, including the upper Pelorus and the Buller.

Rising in steep, bush-covered mountains, the Pelorus traverses gentle farmland before emptying into the sea at Havelock. It's primarily a rainbow trout fishery, though there are sea-run browns in its estuary and trophy browns in the headwaters.

All of the major rivers have numerous feeder streams, most producing good fishing at times. The Nelson Lakes are also popular with boat fishers and there are numerous other lakes, reservoirs and mountain tarns to sample.

Things to do

A compact yet scenically diverse area, the Tasman Bay region includes the national parks of Abel Tasman, Kahurangi and Nelson Lakes. Just over the Takaka Hill you will find the famed coastline of Golden Bay and the charming towns of Takaka and Collingwood. Nature lovers can enjoy Abel Tasman National Park, New Zealand's best-known and arguably most spectacular coastal park, and wonderful tramping, fishing and hunting in Kahurangi

National Park, with Nelson Lakes offering boating and skiing in season.

Nelson city provides a varied shopping experience, with the Saturday outdoor market a fun and atmospheric stop for food, jewellery and crafts.

Like so many New Zealand cities, Nelson offers a host of outdoor activities: swimming, cycling, sea-kayaking, rock climbing, whitewater rafting, mountain biking, sailing, golf, horse trekking, four-wheel biking, multi-day hikes and skydiving, to name a few. There are more than 22 walks around the city and outlying area.

Among the many walks, the Heaphy Track, starting in Kahurangi National Park, is world-famous. The Tasman Coastal Track in Abel Tasman National Park takes three to five days and the spectacular beaches and dramatic coastal scenery make it a favourite with sea kayakers.

Nelson city, Richmond, Motueka and Takaka in Golden Bay are the main shopping areas of the region. They offer a full range of services, including banking.

Accommodation

Nelson's accommodation options range from backpackers to luxury lodges, with everything in between: international-standard hotels with Nelson's hallmark of relaxed personal service, seafront motels, historic B&Bs, rambling rural holiday parks, restored cottages and homestays on picturesque farms and orchards. The city and surrounds are especially well endowed with self-contained and serviced accommodation, including some very upmarket options, wonderful beachfront properties and more than a few eco-themed cottages.

Some of the most spectacular accommodation is up towards Abel Tasman National Park. Much of it is beachfront or nearly so, mostly nestled into the hills and bush.

For more details, see www.nelson.co.nz, www.harlequin.co.nz/nelson and www.nelsoncitycouncil.co.nz.

Boat ramps

Boaties have plenty of launching options in Tasman Bay. Nelson's main boat ramp is on Akersten Street at the northern end of Port Nelson. There's another ramp near the southern end of the airport in the suburb of Monaco, giving access to the Waimea Estuary and the open sea beyond. The town of Mapua has good launching facilities close to scallop beds, while small-boat launching is possible in Ruby Bay and Kina Point to access Rabbit Island.

In the other direction, there's limited beach launching in Cable Bay, close to Pepin Island, and excellent facilities at Okiwi Bay, an hour from Nelson, in Croisilles Harbour.

Many people launch from suitable beaches up and down the coast, but local knowledge and the permission of property owners is needed. Some coastal campgrounds have basic launching facilities.

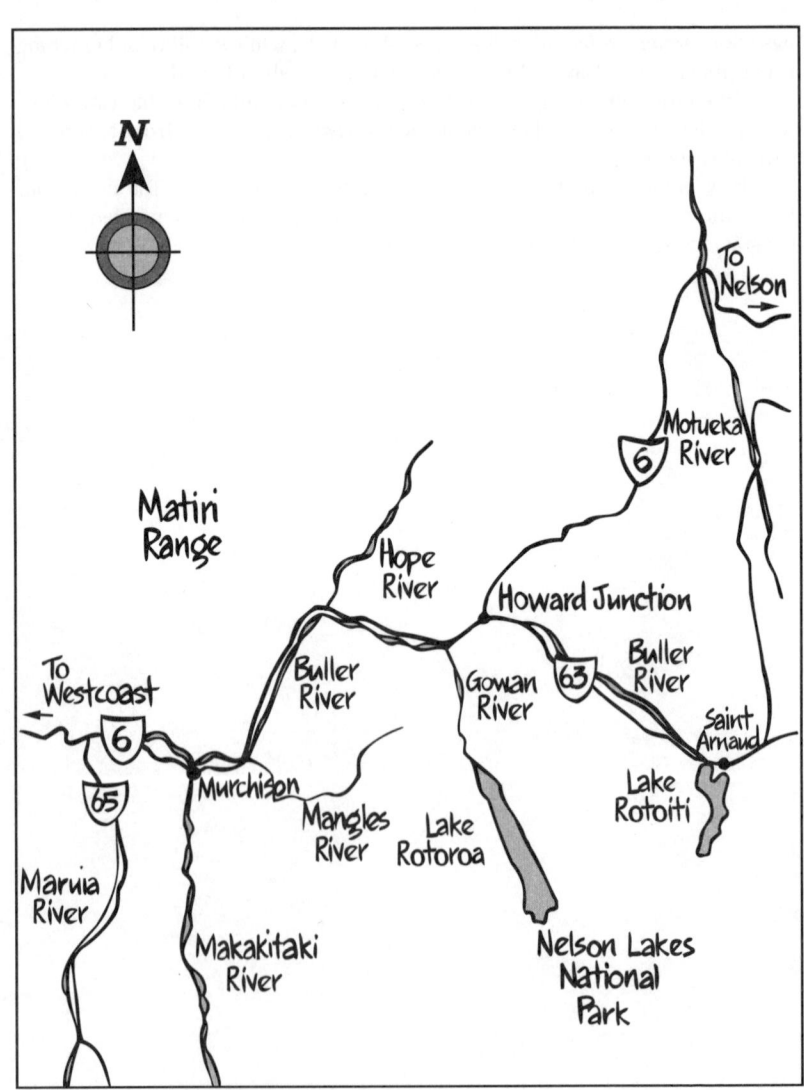

Murchison

Here and there in this book I've included a stopover that is a lot more about fishing than it is about other attractions. Murchison is one of these. It's got plenty more going for it, but the trout fishing in and around the town is so good that everything else pales into insignificance, at least in my mind.

Two or three days in Murchison hardly does it justice but my wife will usually grant me that much without protest, finding enough alternative activities to keep her interested if she elects not to join me chasing trout.

The town of Murchison is on one of New Zealand's more spectacular routes, linking Blenheim and Nelson with the West Coast. This spectacular drive follows the course of the Buller River to the sea at Westport. On its way the mighty Buller bisects the Paparoa and Brunner ranges and it is surrounded by mountains along its length. Many of the slopes are covered in pristine native forest, a mixture of beech on the higher slopes and less fertile land and mixed podocarp in the valleys. The stunning scenery attracts many movie and documentary crews.

The best land is farmed but the high altitude makes it a hard life, so much of the countryside is still wild. It's a marvellous place. Murchison is an outdoors centre, extremely popular with kayakers, whitewater rafters, hunters, trampers and climbers, as well as anglers. Some of New Zealand's best trout fishing guides are based in Murchison, while the skifields of St Arnaud and lakes Rotoiti and Rotoroa are not far away. The residents of the former frontier goldmining town have developed a certain measure of self-reliance, due to their geographical isolation. Their can-do attitude is reflected in the way the town has embraced the adventure tourism industry.

The fishing

Where to start? The Nelson region, which includes Murchison and its immediate surroundings, has on average the largest brown trout in New Zealand. There are waters in the region to reward and challenge anglers of any skill level, from raw beginners to master flyfishers.

Several major river systems are accessible from Murchison, though most anglers concentrate on the Buller and its tributaries. The Motueka and Buller have good runs of sea trout, though anglers based in Murchison mostly fish the middle and upper reaches for resident fish.

In the Motueka system, popular feeder waterways include the Wangapeka, which holds big trout, the Pearse, Tadmor, Baton and Dove rivers. Larger fish are generally found above the Wangapeka confluence.

The Wairau is fishable for 140 km of its length, encompassing runs and pools in its upper reaches and a braided bed lower down. It discolours regularly but still holds a good head of resident fish.

Sea-run browns are common below Tuamarina and small numbers of salmon also run the river. Trout average 1.5 kg, with larger specimens in the middle and upper reaches. From Murchison the upper reaches of the Wairau are less than an hour away.

The Buller is remote and beautiful. New Zealand's fifth-largest river, its special value has been recognised by a water conservation order, making it illegal to extract water, dam the river and otherwise interfere with it.

Trout range from 1 kg to 3 kg throughout the Buller system, with sea-runners common lower down. Major tributaries such as the Maruia, Matakitaki and Mangles rivers are spectacular fisheries in their own right, and most of the minor tributaries also provide good fishing, many in a wilderness setting. Rainbow trout are present in the Maruia above the Maruia Falls.

The Gowan and the upper Buller above the Howard confluence are almost always clear; other rivers and the rest of the Buller can discolour after heavy rainfall.

Boat fishers can enjoy excellent harling and deep trolling in Lake Rotoiti, with the shoreline angling also good. Lake Rotoroa has similar angling opportunities, plus the attraction of the Gowan River that feeds it from the north and the Sabine that drains it in the south. Other rivers of note include the Owen and Matiri.

The invasive exotic algae didymo is present in several rivers in the region, including the Gowan, Matiri and Owen. It's also present in the Buller itself, though so far the infestation appears to be light.

Dealing with didymo

Didymo is the single biggest threat facing New Zealand's lakes, rivers and streams. It has the potential to destroy the country's reputation as a world-class trout-fishing destination.

First detected in Southland in 2004, didymo, or **Didymosphenia geminata**, is a freshwater algae that can smother a riverbed with an unsightly mass of grey, harming stream life and making the river impossible to fish. Didymo has been confused with New Zealand native algae, but the main difference between didymo and native species is the way it feels. Native algae feels slimy and will break apart in your fingers, whereas didymo is strong and feels like wet cotton wool. Also known as 'rock snot', it's easily spread between water bodies by anglers.

At the time of writing, didymo had been detected in 42 rivers and streams and five lakes, all in the South Island. To prevent it spreading further, fishers and other water users need to take precautions.

Whenever possible you should restrict equipment, boats, clothing and other items to exclusive use in one waterway. Take extreme care if moving gear between rivers, streams and lakes, since individual algal cells are invisible to the eye. All fishing gear, waders, clothing and other equipment must be thoroughly washed and anglers should treat every waterway they visit as if it were infected, taking suitable precautions.

Most affected waters have signposts listing the precautions users must take to prevent the spread of didymo, and there are didymo cleaning stations at strategic points throughout the South Island, including at Picton. Specific cleaning methods have been developed for some freshwater activities. Anglers crossing to the North Island on the Interislander ferry have no excuse not to clean their gear — the cleaning service is free.

The mantra for avoiding the spread of didymo is: **Check, Clean, Dry.**

Check

Before leaving a waterway, check items for clumps of algae. Leave any debris found at the waterway.

Clean

Clean all items for at least one minute with one of the following:
- Hot (60 °C) water
- 2 per cent solution of bleach
- 5 per cent solution of salt
- 5 per cent solution of dishwashing liquid
- 5 per cent solution of antiseptic hand-cleaner
- 5 per cent solution of nappy cleaner

(A 5 per cent solution is 500 ml of product, with water added to make 10 litres. A 2 per cent solution is 200 ml of product, with water added to make 10 litres.)

All these items can be found at your local supermarket. It is recommended that you use biodegradable products.

Dry

If cleaning is not practical, wipe the item until it is dry to the touch and then leave drying for an additional 48 hours.

(Information courtesy of Biosecurity NZ. For more information and advice on dealing with didymo, see: www.biosecurity.govt.nz/didymo, www.fishandgame.org.nz, and www. rivers.org.nz/article/didymo).

 Things to do

Murchison is an outdoor adventure kind of town. Most of the activities focus on the rivers, mountains and bush.

Aside from fishing, visitors can hunt for red deer and chamois on the tops and remote valleys, and wild pigs and possums lower down. Guided hunting trips can be arranged.

Rafting, including guided trips, is popular with tourists; superb stretches of river offer grade two to grade five runs through magnificent scenery.

Kayakers can find stretches suitable for family fun, or challenging water for the skilled canoeists on the Buller River and its tributaries.

Jetboating is also popular.

Trampers can take advantage of good high-country and valley tracks. Of particular interest are those in the Nelson Lakes region, the Matakitaki Valley and the Matiri range.

For the less committed walker, an interesting variety of bush walks start within a short distance of the township. These range in length between 20 minutes and two hours, taking in some of the history, flora and fauna of the region.

Mountain bikers have a variety of trails to choose from and bikes are available for hire.

Exceptional bluffs and dramatic landscapes add to the pleasures of mountaineering in the region. Climbs are graded for the novice through to the experienced climber. The area also offers some of the finest caving in New Zealand, especially in the Mount Owen region, which has the largest underground cave network in the Southern Hemisphere.

On a slightly less active note, gold panning, an activity as old as the township itself, is a relaxing way to spend a few hours, or you can take in the nine-hole golf course just north of the township beside the Buller River.

You might try a bit of tennis at the public courts or play some bowls. There's also boating available at Lake Rotoroa, including a water taxi service. The website www.murchison.co.nz has plenty of useful information on things to do in the region.

Murchison's central location in the top of the South Island means there are many day trips within an hour and a half's drive: the Abel Tasman, Nelson Lakes and Kahurangi national parks; waterfalls, walks and hot springs at Maruia Springs; Nelson's artistic and viticultural attractions; New Zealand's longest swing-bridge; earthquake history and a seal colony on the coast at Cape Foulwind.

Accommodation

For a town of just 750 inhabitants, Murchison has plenty of accommodation options. Many of them fall into the lodge category, most with an outdoors or sports theme, and some are geared exclusively to anglers.

There are also luxury lodges (Lake Rotoroa Lodge is one of New Zealand's finest), self-contained accommodation, B&Bs, homestays and holiday homes.

See the Murchison pages at www.tourism.net.nz/region/nelson.

 **Boat ramps**

Jetboats launch into the Buller and other rivers in the region from unformed ramps/chutes.

There's a boat ramp at St Arnaud on Lake Rotoiti and boats can also be launched over the beach at Rotoroa beside the lake of the same name. Kayaks and canoes can be launched directly into most of the rivers and lakes.

31

the West Coast

The South Island's west coast stretches from Farewell Spit in the north to Jackson Bay in the south. It's so large that it can't really be considered a distinctive region and there is considerable variation in topography.

However, a few things are constant: it rains a lot, the scenery is superb, the sandflies are voracious, its few residents are incredibly friendly, and the beer is good and plentiful.

Rainfall on the coast is some of the highest in New Zealand, especially in the south. The mountains of the South Island's alpine interior block the prevailing westerlies, forcing moist air to rise. The clouds dump their moisture on Westland's narrow coastal strip and the western side of the foothills and mountains, ensuring lush forests and green grass year-round.

Despite its reputation for precipitation, my most recent visits to the coast have been during extended periods of fine weather. On the last occasion the weather was stunning — fine and warm with little or no wind. The West Coast certainly had its best face on and when it's in that kind of mood it's a simply gorgeous place to visit.

Even when it's raining — and rain is a reality if you spend more than a day or two on the coast — it's a magically beautiful place, empty and remote and dominated by mountains, forest and sea.

There are four roads through the mountains to the West Coast: Haast Pass, Arthur's Pass, Lewis Pass and the Buller Gorge road.

The southernmost, the Haast Pass, is popular with tourists but otherwise little travelled. State Highway 6 winds through magnificent country, passing lakes Wanaka and Hawea then climbing high into the Southern Alps before descending the Haast River valley to the coast at Haast.

South Westland is an amazingly wild and unspoiled part of the country. Sparsely populated, it's a must-see for anyone interested in New Zealand's natural history.

The coast's three main towns — Westport, Greymouth and Hokitika — are

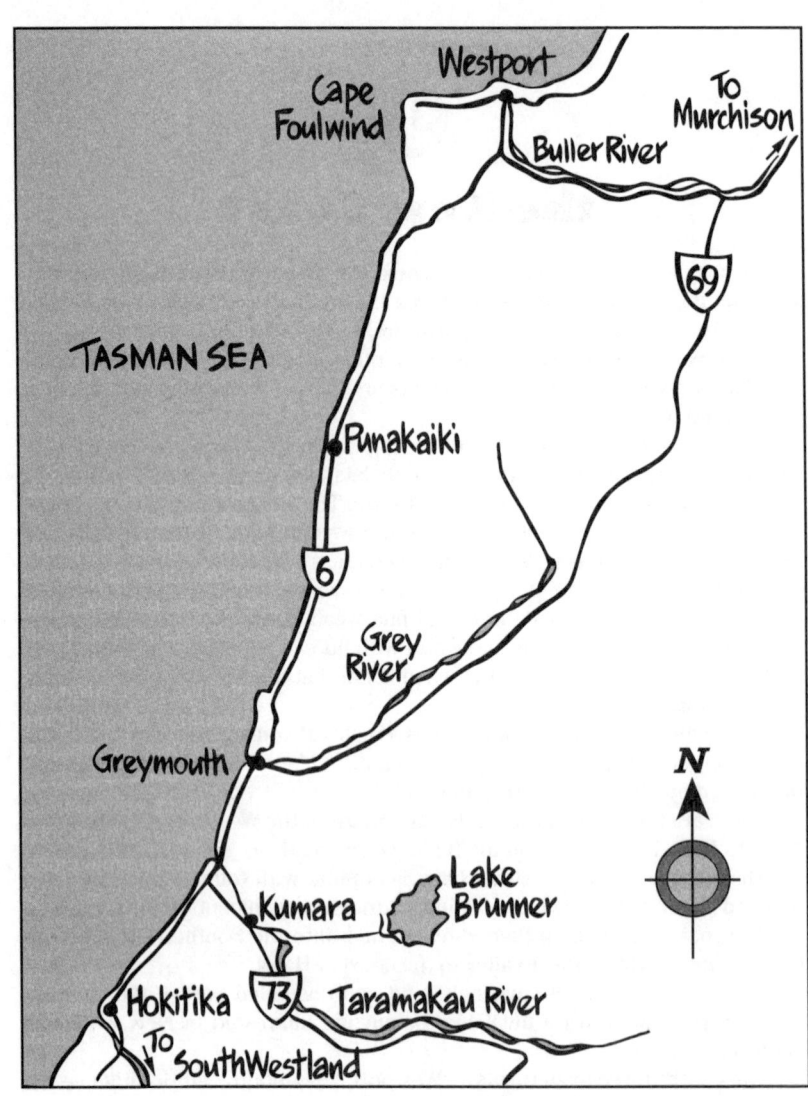

close to the major mountain passes at the mouths of some of the coast's larger rivers, the Buller, Grey and Hokitika respectively. Residents make their livings from fishing, farming, forestry, mining and associated services, with tourism increasingly important.

Westport and Greymouth are homes to considerable commercial fishing fleets that regularly work the treacherous river bars on their way out to sea. Despite the size of the craft and the experience of the crews, numerous lives have been lost. The Grey River bar is particularly nasty, and a bronze memorial at the breakwater's southern tip is mute testament to the many fishers who have lost their lives crossing it.

With so much territory to explore, it's hard to do the West Coast justice. On my most recent trip I concentrated on the area in and around Greymouth, the coast's largest town and commercial centre. There's plenty of accommodation and one needn't travel far from town to find good fishing. If the weather's good and the bar's behaving, you can find excellent sea fishing just off the bar, and a newly discovered winter sportfishery for giant bluefin tuna has really put Westport and Greymouth on the map with anglers.

From Greymouth, Hokitika is just 30 minutes down the road, Lake Brunner is less than an hour away and Westport is a pleasant hour's drive along the coast to the north.

 ## The fishing

I was pleasantly surprised by the quality and variety of fishing available close to Greymouth. When the whitebait are running, every river, stream and lagoon, including those right in town, is targeted, not just by keen local whitebaiters but by schools of large, hungry, sea-run brown trout.

Fishing for sea-run trout is possible year-round but the best results are usually when the whitebait are running. However, with so much natural food for them to hunt, it can be frustrating trying to get trout to bite your artificial. Whitebaiters regularly catch big trout in their nets.

Whitebaiting is almost a religion on the coast, attracting enthusiasts from all over the South Island and further away. Many stay beside the rivers for weeks, even months. Whitebait stands — bankside positions from which to set your nets — are passed down through generations. Many baiters brave the open sea at the river mouths, wading into the surf with scoop nets.

Whitebaiting is more important in South Westland, where catches are larger and many of the stands are amazingly elaborate, but even around the main towns such as Greymouth, whitebait runs can be spectacular in good years.

The coast to the north of Greymouth is beautiful, with bays and beaches, headlands and small estuaries. A northerly drift often means discoloured water since the Grey and many other rivers usually carry a lot of sediment, which is then stirred up by rough seas and strong currents. Diving is difficult. But in settled conditions such as those we experienced on my last trip, the sea is blue, the sand is golden and at times I wondered if I was in fact in Northland.

Beach fishing is possible along the coast and quite worthwhile, by all accounts. Surfcasters catch kahawai, gurnard, rig and school shark, as well as elephant fish and a few good-sized snapper. Small boats can be launched into sheltered estuaries near Punakaiki and Te Miko, or over some of the beaches in Paparoa National Park. Many locals have baches beside these estuaries where they keep their boats.

In recent winters Westport has played host to visiting big-game fishers, with boats also leaving from Greymouth. They come to catch the giant bluefin tuna. Tuna arrive on the coast in June and July when hoki gather at the edge of the continental shelf to spawn. Vast aggregations of spawning hoki attract factory trawlers from all over the world, as well as hungry tuna, who have learned to follow the trawlers, raiding the nets as they're raised and gorging on discarded and lost fish, fish scraps and processing waste. Recreational anglers also follow the trawlers, hoping to catch the tuna, which often reach hundreds of kilos in weight.

It's a specialised fishery, highly weather-dependent but with great potential. The tuna are the largest in the southern hemisphere and they're easy to catch — provided anglers can get out to the fishing grounds. Local boats are available for charter and many sportfishing charter boats from other parts of the country relocate to Westport for the tuna run. Private boats travel to the fishing grounds from as far away as Kaipara and Auckland. One year an 8 m trailer boat made the journey from Kaipara Harbour to Westport by sea!

The Taramakau River is a large and attractive river. There's good fishing for trout in the lagoon at times and for salmon, which run the river during summer. Surfcasters also catch kahawai from the beach beside the mouth and it's possible to catch sea-run trout and kahawai in consecutive casts. Flyfishers fishing the lagoon on a rising tide can be surprised by big sea-going kahawai — I was!

Upriver there's good fishing, with a nymph or wet fly, for resident brown trout. Locals also target salmon in the deep pools with heavy lures and spinning gear. Some of the river's tributaries offer interesting small-stream fishing, though on my last visit near-drought conditions and low water levels meant the fish had all dropped back into the main river.

The Grey River also offers good fishing — superb, in fact — especially in its upper reaches. The middle reaches can be accessed from State Highway 7 or from smaller roads either side of the bridge just before Ikamatua. Most of the tributary streams also have good fishing. The river's upper reaches are also accessible from State Highway 7, with the best fishing requiring plenty of walking.

Lake fishers have plenty of choice within easy reach of Greymouth. Just out of Kumara, a few kilometres from Greymouth, the Kapitea and Kumara reservoirs, also called Dillmanstown Dam, provide good shoreline fishing and easy casting. If the water level is high enough, it's easy to spot and cast to good-sized fish cruising over the weed beds. In summer damsel nymphs work extremely well, though the waters are also open to spinning.

Lake Brunner is magnificent, set in mature beech and mixed podocarp forest, much of it coming right down to the shoreline. Nonetheless, there are plenty of places for shoreline fishing, or you can fish the lake from a boat with a fly or harling. Many guides work the lake and a famous lodge nestles beside it, along with baches and holiday houses. A boat is an advantage since there's no road access to most of the shoreline. There is road access to the northern end and the principal settlement of Moana, and a couple of the route options pass by Lake Poerua, another excellent trout fishery.

Lake Brunner is a brown trout-only fishery. They're wary fish but reward the skilful angler. The slightly tannin-stained waters of the lake lend the trout a wonderful, deep golden-yellow colour with bright red spots. They're among the most colourful trout in New Zealand.

South of Hokitika, Lake Mahinapua on the coast has good fishing for brown trout, while inland Lake Kaniere has trout and perch. The perch can be a nuisance, since they're mostly small, but there are also big predatory trout in the lake. Kaniere is scenic and best fished from a boat. The Kaniere River at the head of the lake also holds trout.

Further south still, but still within an hour or two of Greymouth, Lake Ianthe has good shoreline fishing. State Highway 6 skirts the lake on its eastern margin.

There's good fishing in the Wanganui and Poerua rivers, as well as the

Waitaha, but as usual it's better above the braided coastal section.

The region around Harihari has superb spring creek fishing for large trout in clear water. It gets plenty of attention from fishing guides and their clients but it's usually possible to find water to oneself, especially if you keep away from the better-known streams and creeks.

John Kent's excellent *South Island Trout Fishing Guide* is invaluable for anyone exploring the South Island's incredible trout fishing. The sections dealing with the West Coast are particularly detailed and spot-on. The book is a constant companion whenever I'm travelling in the region.

Things to do

Greymouth is the largest town on the coast, with nearly 14,000 inhabitants. Consequently, it offers most of the conveniences and entertainments one would expect.

Not surprisingly, many of the activities on offer are related to the outdoors — hiking, guided walks and tours, scenic flights, helicopter flights and glacier landings, canoeing, river and cave rafting, four-wheel-driving, mountain biking, dolphin and seal watching tours, caving, surfing and gold panning.

The Point Elizabeth Walkway is a superb coastal track with great views and stunning native forest, and a drive north to the famous Pancake Rocks at Punakaiki is well worthwhile.

One of Greymouth's best-known attractions is Shantytown, a replica of a gold-town from the late 1800s. There is also the Monteith's Brewery tour and there are several galleries and museums. You will find fine jade carving and a variety of dining and accommodation options. The TranzAlpine Express train trip also terminates in Greymouth.

A short drive inland from Greymouth brings you to Blackball, nestled into the eastern side of the Paparoa Ranges. From here a variety of rainforest and heritage walks are accessible. Blackball is a small former mining village with a general store, a hotel/backpackers (with a great public bar) and a salami company that sells its wares throughout New Zealand. Blackball is famous for its rustic charm and militant union past.

For more information on things to do in and around Greymouth, see www.west-coast.co.nz and www.destination.co.nz.

Accommodation

In theory there's plenty of accommodation, but I have twice been caught out for somewhere to stay, such is the volume of tourist traffic during the peak summer season. It is sensible to book ahead.

Greymouth has dozens of motels, a few large hotels, numerous backpacker lodges, a couple of motor camps and more. The motor camps offer cabins at reasonable rates but some of the tariffs in the other establishments are obviously taking advantage of high demand. It's possibly different during the off-season.

There's a hotel and motels at Moana beside Lake Brunner, as well as holiday houses to rent, and a luxury lodge at the other end of the lake. You can also book a seven-berth luxury houseboat and spend a few days exploring the lake from the water.

The last time we were unable to find anywhere to stay in either Hokitika or Greymouth, we backtracked to Kumara. One of the village's two hotels offers accommodation. It's basic but cheap and an evening in the public bar is well worth the hangover. I can recommend the hotel's whitebait fritters — they're huge and oh so tasty. Eat them between two pieces of white bread for a lunch to die for.

Try www.holidayguide.co.nz or www.west-coast.co.nz for accommodation information.

Boat ramps

Boats can be launched into the Grey River at a couple of locations. Boats are also launched at Hokitika and to the north of Greymouth from beaches and river mouths.

Westport has a couple of good concrete ramps. Boats can be launched into Lake Brunner at Mitchells or from Moana. Small craft can be launched at several points around the lake.

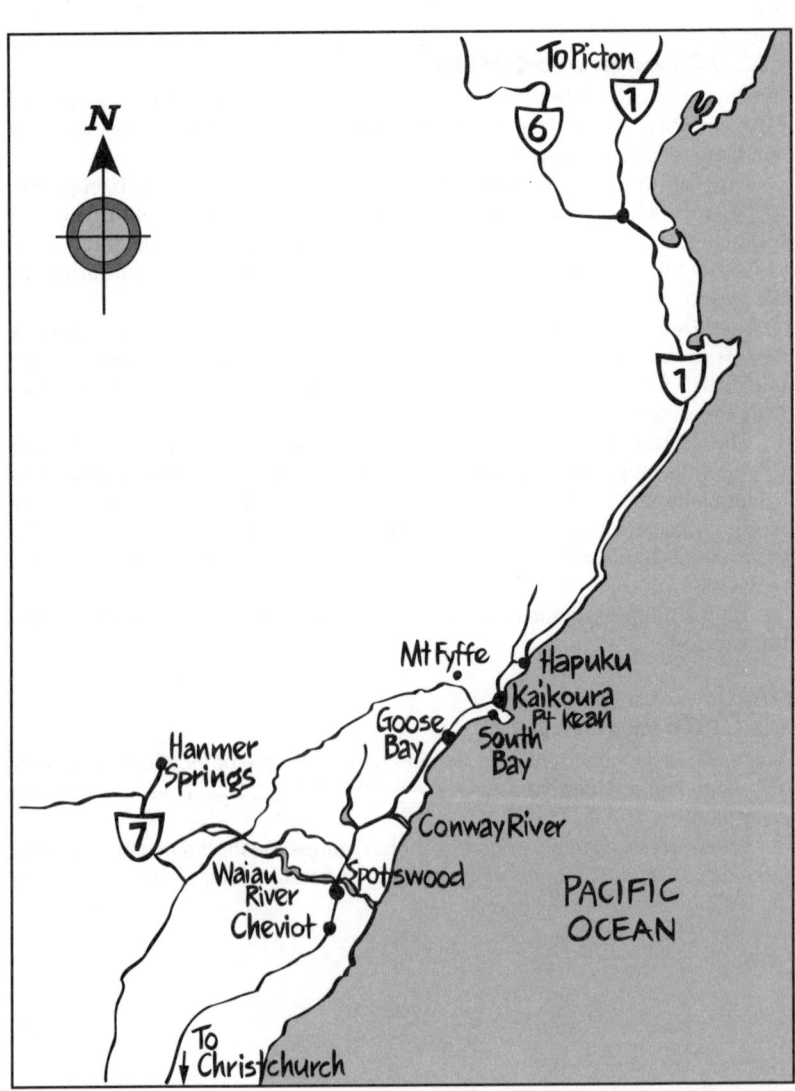

Kaikoura

Nestled between the mountains and the sea, Kaikoura is both wild and beautiful. Today an eco-tourism centre, Kaikoura has always been an important fishing destination, strategically positioned halfway between Picton and Christchurch, close to deep water at the edge of the continental shelf.

Just offshore, cold currents mix with warm water sweeping down from the north. Part of the deep-sea conveyor belt that draws nutrient-rich water from the cold depths near Antarctica, the Kaikoura Current wells up as it strikes the east coast of New Zealand at Kaikoura, mixing with warmer surface waters and dishing up its goodies.

This convergence zone is the richest marine environment in New Zealand, supporting plankton, fish, marine mammals and birds in abundance. The success of Kaikoura's whale-watching industry is thanks to the phenomenal richness of its cold offshore waters, which retain sea mammals year-round.

The area's abundant food resources attracted Maori settlement from early times — there is evidence of 900-year-old moa-hunting Maori settlements at Kaikoura — and the remains of several pa sites can be seen on the peninsula. Kaikoura translates as 'meal of crayfish', a delicacy for which the area is famous.

The riches of the sea attracted Europeans, too. The first shore whaling station was established in 1843. Whale numbers steadily declined after 1850, leading whalers to turn to alternative means of existence, such as farming. Fortunately, the peninsula's lush hinterland supports dairy and beef farming, both important to the local economy.

Today's emphasis has shifted from catching whales to watching them. In 1978, the Marine Mammals Protection Act was passed, providing total protection to New Zealand's whales, dolphins and seals. Kaikoura lies within the Southern Hemisphere Whale Sanctuary.

Several species of whale can be seen off Kaikoura, including huge sperm whales. Other species commonly encountered include orca, pilot whales, southern right whales, humpback whales, dusky and bottlenose dolphins, Hector's dolphins and more.

New Zealand fur seals have also returned in numbers and are a common sight at sea. Colonies breed on the coast close to town.

Attendant on all this abundant sea life are huge flocks of sea birds, including ocean wanderers such as albatross, mollymawk and giant petrel.

Kaikoura is a shining example of a sustainable tourist industry, which allows visitors from all over the world to appreciate life in the ocean.

The town is wrapped around Ingles Bay on the northern side of Kaikoura Peninsula, with the main boat-launching facility on the opposite shore at South Bay. The main road, State Highway 1, bypasses the town's centre, but a sprawl of restaurants, motels, shops and service stations stretches along the main road to the north of the town.

For the recreational angler, Kaikoura is a great place to spend a few days. The burgeoning eco-tourism industry has led to an explosion in the town's service infrastructure so finding somewhere to stay is usually not a problem and there are plenty of cafes and bars.

 The fishing

Kaikoura offers good shore and boat fishing close to the peninsula, on the beaches north and south and over the reefs and drop-offs out to sea.

For the boat fisher, blue cod is the predominant catch. Reasonable blue cod are available to small-boat fishers close to shore among the rocks and reefs scattered all around the peninsula. These areas also hold moki for those anglers with the skills to catch them — shellfish baits are a must — and there are patches of sand offering good tarakihi at times.

Spearfishing and diving for crayfish are also popular — expect greenbone (butterfish) and moki, as well as a few paua. The best paua diving (and shore fishing) is further north, along the relatively lightly fished coast between the Hapuku River mouth and Cape Campbell, though the water is often discoloured.

Goose Bay to the south of Kaikoura has excellent diving off the beach for crayfish, paua, cod and moki. Beach fishing is also good, especially after dark, when big moki are taken. Divers can see seals at Point Kean on the end of the peninsula but care should be exercised, especially when the seals have pups.

They can be quite aggressive, buzzing divers. I'm told the water has a distinctly fishy taste when seals are close by.

The best blue cod are found in deeper water on the edge of Kaikoura Trench and other places well offshore. These areas also produce excellent hapuku, bass and trumpeter. Some of the largest trumpeter in New Zealand come from the Kaikoura region. Bushett Shoals off Goose Bay is famous for XOS trumpeter, hapuku and cod. Charter and private boats from Kaikoura and Goose Bay regularly fish the shoals, the trench and other deep-water marks.

As well as bottom fishing, anglers can enjoy some excellent fishing for pelagic sharks and tuna, mostly albacore, which are summer visitors. Albacore shoals usually turn up mid- to late summer and can be targeted by trolling small lures along the edges of current lines and drop-offs. Sometimes tuna move right in close; at other times they stay well offshore. In winter, surface schools of jack mackerel are common.

Large sharks shadow Kaikoura's whales, seals and abundant fish life. Makos and blues are summer visitors, with white sharks and porbeagles present all year. Big sharks are challenging angling targets and the only big game available to local anglers, though responsible fishers now practise catch and release. White sharks are protected.

Beach anglers can catch kahawai and moki straight off Kaikoura Beach, with the odd salmon taken opposite the railway station. The Kahutara River mouth has good kahawai fishing at times and there is good beach fishing in Goose Bay. Cod can be taken off the shore up and down the coast — target outcrops of reef and rock and cast baits as close to them as you dare. Moki are also present in good numbers, rewarding skilled anglers prepared to fish for them at night. Blue moki are large fish that fight hard and are good eating.

Trout fishers need to travel a bit to find quality fishing as the rivers closest to Kaikoura have beds too unstable to hold many trout. The best fishing is in the Waiau system, which also has a decent run of salmon most years. Access to the river mouth is over private land or by jetboat from Spotswood.

The Conway River also has good fishing, accessible to fit anglers prepared to do plenty of walking.

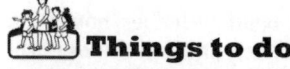 **Things to do**

Any visit to Kaikoura would be incomplete without joining a tour operator for a chance to watch whales, dolphins, seabirds and many other species of marine life. Tours are available by boat, plane, helicopter and on land. Boat trips depart daily, weather permitting. With wetsuits provided, visitors can swim with dolphins and seals in their ocean environment.

There is also excellent snorkelling and scuba diving. When the water's clear, Kaikoura boasts some of the best reef diving in the country, though the water is cold!

Sea-kayaking around the ruggedly beautiful peninsula is popular and kayaks are available for hire, as are mountain bikes.

Scenic flights take in the Kaikoura Mountains and fly over the rocky peninsula and township. In winter it's possible to land atop snow-capped Mt Fyffe and look down to the coast 1500 m below.

Other activities include four-wheel biking, horse trekking, hunting, wine-tasting and marae visits. Visitors can tour local scenic and historical sites, including the stunning Maori Leap Cave, and the Kaikoura area offers walks for all levels of fitness, ranging from 30-minute strolls to half- and full-day walks and more energetic tramps and climbs.

With such a well-developed tourist infrastructure, there are plenty of places to eat in town, some of them excellent, though expect to pay tourist prices. There are also lively bars and nightspots.

Kaikoura's official tourism website, www.kaikoura.co.nz, has all the information a visitor could possibly want, or visit the i-site in the town centre. Most activities and tours can also be booked here, though many operators also have headquarters in town where tour groups assemble and gear up before being bussed to boats at South Bay.

Accommodation

There's plenty of choice in and around Kaikoura, with the backpacker end of the market particularly well served. Much of Kaikoura's tourists are from overseas and many establishments cater almost exclusively to them. It can be a slightly disorientating experience to spend a night or two in a lodge or campground and hardly speak to another Kiwi.

As well as backpacker lodges, there are B&Bs, boutique lodges, hotels and apartments, self-contained units, holiday houses, motels and motor inns (25 of them!), homestays and five campgrounds, some catering specifically to motor homes/camper vans; www.kaikoura.co.nz lists plenty of options.

 **Boat ramps**

Public boat ramps are available either side of Kaikoura Peninsula. South Bay has a breakwater and jetty complex used by commercial operators to manage their passengers. It offers some shelter to private boats too. This is a very exposed coast and the weather changes quickly so launching and retrieving can be challenging. Locals use large four-wheel-drive tractors to launch and retrieve their boats.

There are also small boat ramps up and down the rocky coast, some no more than chutes between the rocks. Some are run by local boat clubs but available for public use with a donation. Most are only suitable for small boats in good conditions.

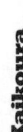

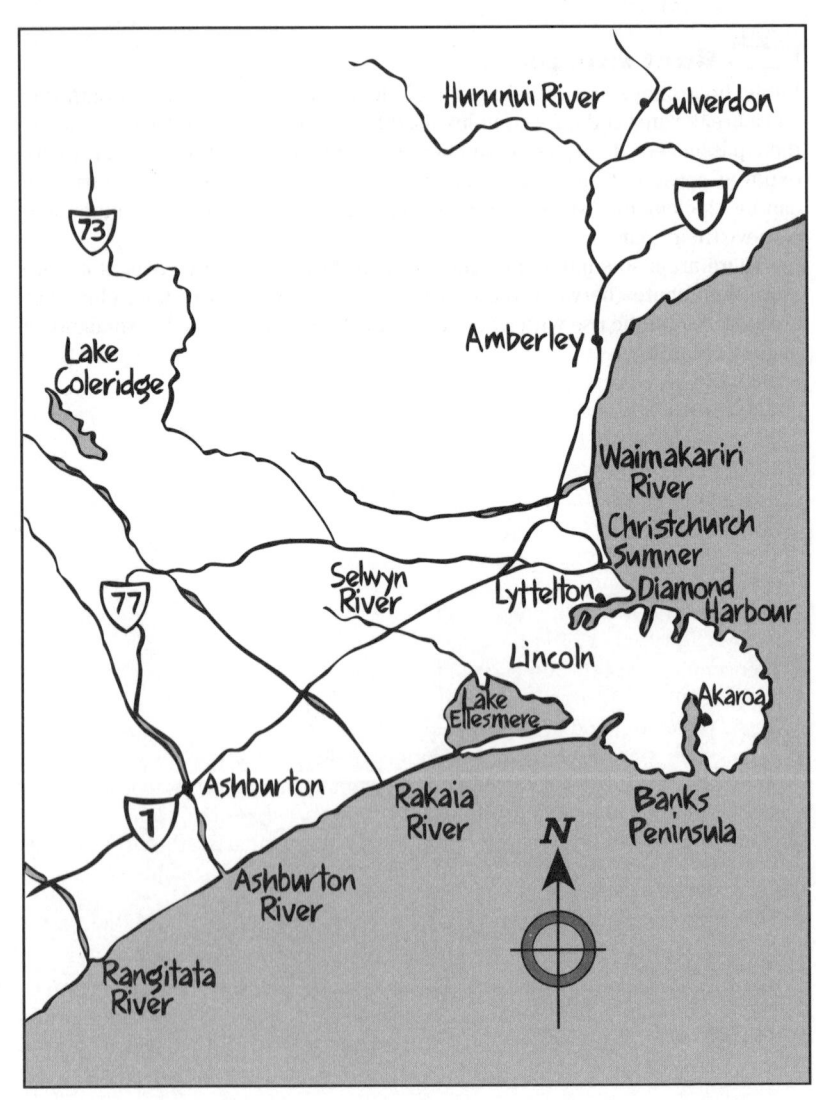

Christchurch

Christchurch is the South Island's largest city. At first it might seem an unlikely venue for a fishing getaway but the city is within striking distance of a surprising variety of fishing opportunities. There's excellent trout fishing close by, New Zealand's best salmon fishing between December and April and some reasonable sea fishing and diving.

Lyttelton Harbour, just over the hill from the city, provides sheltered boating and some fishing, and the bays and headlands of Banks Peninsula are accessible to boaties and shore anglers.

The mouths of Canterbury's great braided rivers are the focus for much of the region's summer fishing, producing salmon, kahawai and sea-run brown trout, while the lakes, rivers and mountains of the high country are seldom more than two hours' scenic drive away.

Christchurch is an interesting city. Reasonably compact, it has an appealing city centre with its cathedral, a superb park — Hagley Park — and the Avon River running right through town. It's a favourite with my family. There's great shopping, plenty of non-fishing activities and all the amenities of a big city. There's plenty of good-quality accommodation too.

In winter Christchurch can be bitterly cold and snow is not uncommon, sometimes covering the sand at Sumner Beach. In summer the city can swelter, especially when the hot, dry nor'wester blows across the plains from the mountains. Temperatures regularly climb into the 30s, making the city's beaches a popular escape. Most of the year humidity is low and sunshine hours are high.

The tidal estuary of the Heathcote and Avon rivers was once an important food source for Maori, who first settled here more than 1000 years ago. Successive migrations took place as North Island tribes pushed southwards.

European settlement began in 1840 and whalers operated out of Lyttelton by 1850. The first organised groups of English settlers arrived in 1850–51, on the 'first four ships' into Lyttelton Harbour. The ability to trace one's ancestry to one of these four ships remains an important distinction for many Canterbury people.

Although relatively cosmopolitan these days, Christchurch retains a certain old-world charm that most visitors remark upon. A rather conservative city, it's very different from the brashness of Auckland or the self-absorbed busyness of Wellington. There's no denying it's a pleasant place to live — 350,000 New Zealanders call it home — and a great place to visit.

The fishing

Reasonable sea fishing is available close to Christchurch. Land-based fishers target kahawai and kingfish in summer from the many headlands of Banks Peninsula — Te Oka and Magnet Bay on the southern side of the peninsula are good — and from Taylors Mistake closer to the city. Kingfish patrol the edge of the kelp and can also be targeted by boat fishers casting jigs and poppers at floating rafts of kelp, which can be found offshore in summer.

Well offshore, fishers can target blue cod — there are a few to be caught around Banks Peninsula as well — hapuku and gemfish. Kingfish are also taken in deep water on live bait. A couple of charter boats work out of Lyttelton.

Lyttelton Harbour turns up a few kahawai and red cod in winter. Flounder and yellow-eyed mullet are also available, as they are in the Heathcote-Avon estuary, though it's Lake Ellesmere south of the city that's the flatfish star. Ellesmere (Waihora) is a huge, shallow body of water that once supported a superb trout fishery, as well as eels and flounder. The sandspit opens to the sea periodically and marine fish enter the lake's brackish waters, where many live out the remainder of their lives.

Irrigation has strangled the lowland rivers that feed the lake, particularly the Selwyn, and nutrient run-off, exotic weeds and an explosion in black swan numbers have combined to degrade the water quality to such an extent that the trout fishery has all but disappeared. A few large sea-run trout are still taken at the mouths of the Selwyn, Halswell and L1 rivers but the runs are a shadow of their former glory.

Ellesmere still supports a commercial eel fishery but even this appears to be in trouble. Steps are being taken to clean up the lake but it's a long-term proposition not helped by ever-increasing demands on scarce water resources throughout the Canterbury region.

There's some beach fishing north and south of the city — Birdlings Flat on

Kaitorete Spit separating Lake Ellesmere from the sea is a prime location — but much of the fishing effort is concentrated on the river mouths.

Several large rivers are within striking distance of Christchurch. The region's major rivers are braided, with dozens of interconnecting channels making their way to sea over broad shingle beds. Rising in the high mountains of the Southern Alps, they carry cold, snow-fed water that deposits its load of silt and gravel in the riverbed on the way to the sea.

These rivers are most famous for the run of chinook salmon that enters them in summer, travelling upstream to the headwaters to spawn and die. Native to North America, the South Island's Pacific salmon population is the only successful introduction of a sea-run population in the world.

Most of Canterbury's major rivers experience a salmon run, along with a few rivers in Otago, Southland, the West Coast and Marlborough, but the bulk of New Zealand's chinooks return to half a dozen Canterbury Rivers. Of these, four are within striking distance of Christchurch: the Waimakariri, Rakaia, Hurunui and Rangitata. The Waiau is a little further north, the northernmost of the region's salmon rivers.

Salmon are generally targeted as they enter the rivers from the sea or at some point during their upriver migration. River-mouth anglers mostly use specialised long-casting tackle that allows them to cast heavy metal lures — called ticers — long distances into the surf of the river mouths where salmon wait just behind the breakers for the right conditions to enter the river.

Upriver, anglers use shorter rods, lighter tackle and smaller lures to fish for salmon already in the river. Upriver gear is used from just inside the mouth all the way up to the river's headwaters. Fresh, shiny river-mouth salmon are always in the best condition — the fish stop feeding when they enter the river and become progressively darker and thinner. By the time they begin spawning they are hardly worth eating.

Salmon fishing has fallen on hard times in recent years, with fish numbers way down. The last few seasons have been the worst on record, though 2006–2007 saw a slight improvement in salmon numbers. The reasons for the decline are unclear, though most fisheries scientists believe unsuitable conditions at sea are to blame. Salmon live in the sea for three to five years feeding on just a couple of food types: krill and small pilchard-like baitfish. These forage species are reliant on plankton, which varies in abundance and distribution from year to year. Many scientists fear that global warming is having an effect on ocean conditions, which is adversely affecting salmon at sea.

Other factors include reduced river flows as the result of water abstraction for irrigation, generally lower rainfall and interference with and dewatering of salmon spawning streams. Stock walking over stream-bed gravel disturb and crush salmon (and trout) eggs, erode river banks and pollute the water by defecating and urinating in it, none of which is good for fish. If didymo finds its way into these precious salmon spawning streams, it may be curtains for the fishery (see pages 177–178 for more on didymo).

Canterbury (and Otago) fisheries face some tough challenges. Water abstraction is a huge issue. Intensive dairy farming is fast taking over from traditional dry-land sheep farming and cropping. Irrigation is the key to high yields and farmers are making huge demands on the regions' water resources. Many of the smaller lowland rivers have been sucked dry as irrigation bores tap into the underground aquifer, lowering the water table. Canterbury's major rivers already carry a huge water-abstraction burden and farmers want still more. The effect on the fisheries the rivers contain is disastrous.

Nevertheless, Canterbury's major rivers still support excellent trout fisheries. The mouths of most rivers, large and small, offer brilliant sea-run trout fishing, especially when 'silveries' (small smelt-like native fish) are running. Silveries are sometimes present in such numbers that ocean waves deposit them in great writhing heaps on the shore.

Silveries run up Canterbury's major rivers to spawn, feeding hungry trout along the way. Kahawai gorge on them at the river mouth and seabirds take advantage of the easy meal. A full-on feeding frenzy in which kahawai, sea-run trout, terns and gulls smash schools of these small silver fish at river mouths is something to experience. Needless to say, the fishing is pretty hot when it's all on.

In general, trout fishing in Canterbury's braided rivers can be challenging. The riverbeds are unstable and ever-changing, so trout move around a lot. The best fishing is in the pools and runs of the main braids, which tend to be more stable, or upstream above the gorges where the rivers narrow.

The Rakaia, Hurunui, Rangitata and Waimakariri rivers are excellent trout fisheries in their upper reaches with both brown and rainbow trout available. The Hurunui is especially scenic, though it's a fair drive from the city.

Of the smaller lowland rivers, the Ashburton and Selwyn can both offer good fishing but water abstraction reduces flows to such an extent in summer that trout suffer from heat stress and even stranding.

Away from the plains the situation improves. Many of the major river tributaries have good fishing and there are dozens of lakes offering excellent flyfishing and spinning opportunities. Knowledgeable anglers find trophy fish in high-country streams but there's often plenty of walking between bites.

Lake Coleridge, near the headwaters of the Rakaia, is the largest of the Canterbury lakes. A couple of hours from Christchurch in the mountains between the Torlesse and Mt Hutt ranges, it contains large rainbow and brown trout, as well as landlocked chinook salmon. It's popular with shore-based flyfishers, spin anglers and boat fishers. The mouths of the Harper and Ryton rivers are the focus of shore-based anglers, many of whom brave the cold and snow of winter to night-fish Coleridge.

Like most South Island waters, it's imperative to check the fishing regulations for season details; they vary greatly from water to water and may change from year to year.

Close to Coleridge a cluster of small lakes — Georgina, Evelyn, Henrietta, Selfe and Catherine — have good fishing while other popular lakes in the region include Pearson, Grasmere and Sarah. Pearson contains mackinaw (North American lake trout, a type of char), as well as brown and rainbow trout.

Another group of lakes, the Ashburton Lakes, includes the Maori Lakes, the Spider Lakes and lakes Heron, Emily, Denny, Emma, Roundabout, Donne, Camp and Clearwater. Lake Emily contains brook trout (fontinalis), a type of char. Many of these lakes are suitable for float tubing and most can be successfully sight-fished from shore. Boats are not allowed on many of the smaller lakes — check the regulations carefully.

For fishing regulations, licences, access and fishing methods, check Fish and Game's excellent website, www.fishandgame.org.nz, or drop into one of Christchurch's tackle stores. Malcolm Bell and the crew at the Complete Angler, on the corner of Barbadoes and Cashel streets, have always been a huge help to me. They're happy to give you the right advice and point you towards the best fishing on the day.

Things to do

Christchurch has all the attractions of a big city including, my wife assures me, excellent shopping.

Christchurch and Canterbury are famous for their natural beauty and offer the visitor a wealth of things to do. There's a lively entertainment scene and plenty of excellent restaurants, pubs, bars, nightclubs and more.

Christchurch

The city's strong cultural heritage is reflected in its architecture, museums and art galleries. Its gorgeous parks and gardens justify Christchurch's 'Garden City' tag and its botanic gardens hold the largest collection of exotic and indigenous plants in New Zealand.

If outdoor activities and sports are your thing, Christchurch has first-class sports facilities, excellent walks, runs and cycling paths, with more demanding routes through the Port Hills, and more.

Canterbury's high country isn't too far away, with snow sports a huge attraction in winter, and harbour and marine eco-tours leaving from Lyttelton. Visitors will see dolphins, including New Zealand's smallest, the rare Hector's dolphin that lives along the Canterbury coast. Dolphin-swimming tours leave from the historic village of Akaroa on the southern side of Banks Peninsula.

There's jetboating on the Rakaia and Waimakariri rivers or punting on the Avon. Catch a rugby game at Jade Stadium, visit the theatre or go to the beach at Sumner or New Brighton — there are activities for every taste.

Among the city's must-sees are the weekend Arts Centre market, Christchurch Cathedral and the International Antarctic Centre. Ferrymead Heritage Park is another favourite with my family, while the ice-skating rink at the Alpine Sport Centre on Moorhouse Avenue is a great place to let off some steam.

Banks Peninsula has many attractions of its own, including an interesting indented coastline. The two largest of its many fiord-like inlets are Lyttelton and Akaroa harbours, at opposite corners of the peninsula. Lyttelton is Christchurch's port, with much of the character of a port town. The harbour is where the bulk of Christchurch's boating is done and there is an active yacht club, rowing club and others. Most of the harbour's bays are overlooked by holiday homes and many have private jetties.

Akaroa Harbour is well worth a visit, though it's a fair drive from Christchurch. On a good day it can be fun to take a boat from Lyttelton and motor right around Banks Peninsula and into Akaroa Harbour for lunch.

Akaroa was originally a French settlement, and it retains links with its French past. It is a popular weekend getaway for Christchurch people, and there are plenty of places to stay, good restaurants, quaint colonial architecture, harbour cruises, interesting wildlife and an excellent museum.

See www.christchurch.org.nz or www.christchurchnz.net.

⌂ **Accommodation**

There's something for every taste and budget in Christchurch. Hotels, motels, luxury lodges, B&Bs, holiday parks, campgrounds, backpackers — whatever suits.

Christchurch gets plenty of visitors right through the year so there's no shortage of beds, though prime central-city accommodation can become scarce on weekends when there are a lot of events on in town. Usually, though, it's possible to find clean motel accommodation a little further out. Christchurch is a compact city with good transport and roads so it's no big deal staying on the outskirts of town.

Often even the big hotels in the city offer good-value deals and it can be fun to treat yourself and your family to a night or three in a luxury hotel, often paying no more than you would for a motel. Find out what's available at www.needitnow.com or www.wotif.com.

For general information and accommodation listings visit www.christchurchnz.net, www.christchurch.org.nz, www.whatsonchristchurch.co.nz or the Christchurch pages of www.fourcorners.co.nz.

⛵ **Boat ramps**

There are public boat ramps at Sumner, Lyttelton and Akaroa. The recently upgraded ramp at Lyttelton is the largest and most popular.

Most of the region's lakes have boat-launching facilities, though some smaller lakes don't allow boating. Jetboats are launched into most of Canterbury's larger rivers and used by anglers to access sections of the rivers difficult to reach by other means. Upriver, salmon anglers rely on jetboats to access the best upstream fishing water and also use them to travel to the river mouths.

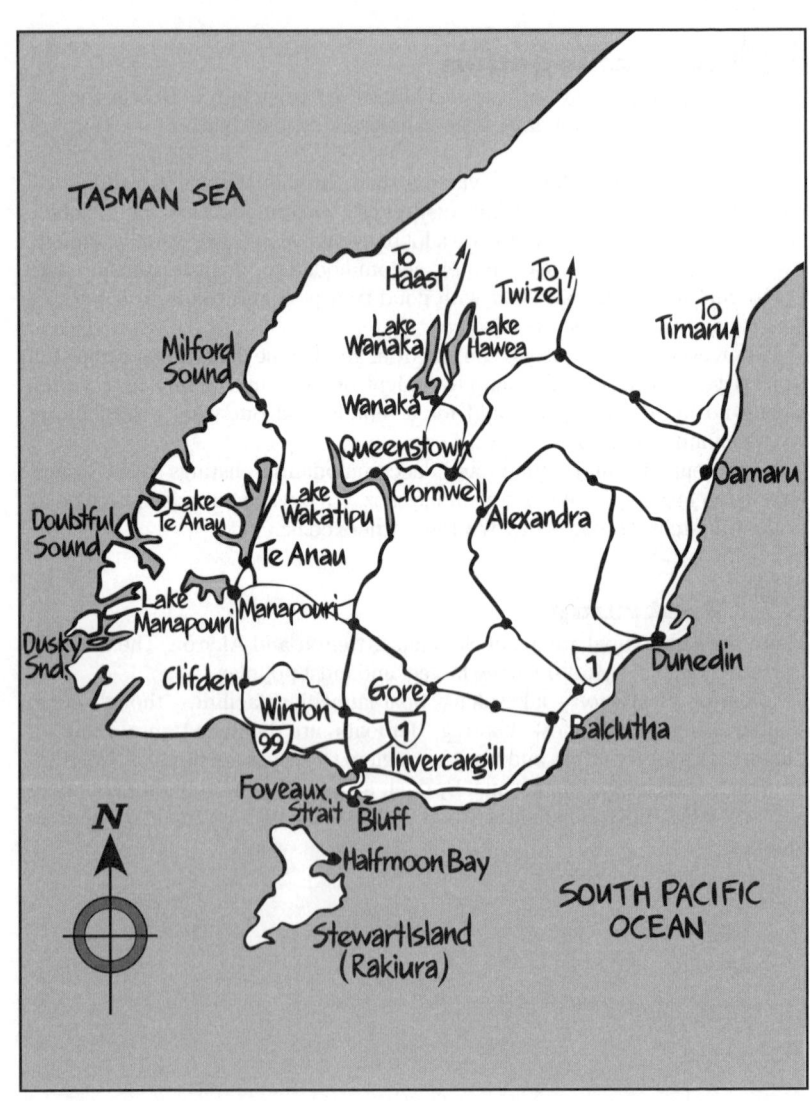

the Deep South

Sparsely populated, the Deep South receives the full force of the 'roaring forties' whistling across the Southern Ocean. It is the first landmass north of Antarctica, so sub-freezing temperatures are possible at any time of year. The mixing of cold sub-Antarctic water with the warm current sweeping down the west coast off Fiordland ensures wild and highly unpredictable weather. Fiordland has the highest rainfall in New Zealand. But for all this, Southland's maritime coastal climate avoids the worst extremes; snow seldom lies on the ground at sea level for more than a day or two, temperatures range from an average high of 18.6 °C in January to 9.5 °C in July, and Invercargill enjoys 1600 hours of sunshine annually (about the same as Dunedin). In midsummer, daylight lasts from 5.00am until 10.00pm, making the grass grow and allowing people to enjoy a wide range of outdoor activities.

To the north lies the alpine wonderland of the Southern Lakes region, in the shadow of the Southern Alps. It enjoys a much drier climate with cold winters and hot summers. Strictly speaking in Central Otago, not Southland, the more northerly of the southern lakes, Wakatipu, Wanaka and Hawea, have become immensely popular with travellers from all over the world. They're all-seasons destinations, with alpine sports in winter and a huge variety of other activities in summer. Queenstown, on the shores of Lake Wakatipu, is one of New Zealand's most popular places to holiday, and Wanaka, beside a lake of the same name, is not far behind.

These days, Southland is going through a transformation. Sheep farming is in decline (sadly, in my opinion). The lowland sheep farms, which were such a feature of the province, are being converted to high-yield intensive dairy farms with many of the evils that entails: pollution, high fertiliser use, soil erosion and an inevitable degradation of water quality in streams and rivers.

However, dairying has returned a measure of prosperity to the province and renewed confidence to its people. Invercargill is beginning to grow again after decades of decline and a progressive city council led by the irrepressible Tim Shadbolt is working hard to make the city an attractive place to do business.

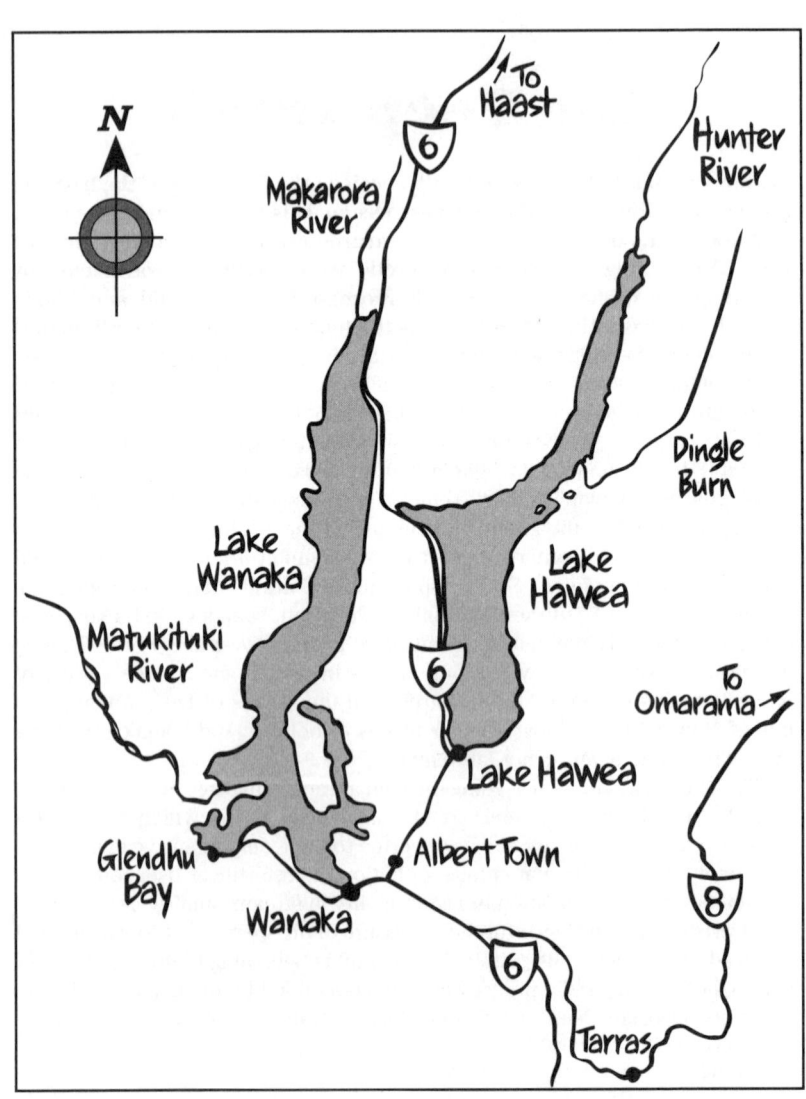

Wanaka and Hawea

Wanaka has grown out of all proportion in recent years, rivalling nearby Queenstown with some of its huge, flash houses overlooking the lake. Property prices have soared and the population continues to grow at well above the national average rate.

The smart money is investing in the next lake up the road, Hawea. Only 20 minutes from Wanaka, it's being tipped as the next Central Otago boomtown. Certainly the property developers are already in there, boots and all.

Wanaka's attractions are self-evident: the setting is gorgeous, the town is nestled beside the lake facing north, with the rugged mountains of Mt Aspiring National Park filling the sky to the west.

There is a growing wine industry centred on Wanaka. Vineyards have charming names such as Mt Difficulty and are producing excellent cold-climate reds and whites. The ski industry provides considerable employment in winter, drawing ski enthusiasts from all over the world and giving the town a cosmopolitan feel.

Wanaka is a town for all seasons. In winter it's an alpine village; in summer it bakes in the dry heat of Central Otago but the cool lakes and high mountains mean it's never oppressive. There's fishing year-round, good places to eat and drink and plenty of activities. It's a place my whole family loves.

 The fishing

Wanaka and its environs offer great trout fishing. Set in truly magnificent scenery, the area boasts three major lakes, a host of small still waters and numerous quality streams and rivers, from small, intimate snow-fed streams to the mighty Clutha River — New Zealand's largest by volume.

Brown and rainbow trout are abundant, as well as feisty landlocked salmon, which can be found in lakes Wanaka and Hawea. The lakes are open to fishing year-round; the rivers and streams have closed seasons. Check the regulations on your fishing licence for details.

The flyfisher can enjoy excellent sight fishing for large, cruising brown trout from the beach right in front of the town. I have a good friend resident in Wanaka who regularly fishes the lake. I once called him on his cell phone while he was fishing before work and he talked me through the stalking, casting and catching of a 2 kg brown trout — I was fishing vicariously.

The best shore-based fishing is in the shallower areas of the lake's margins. The town beach can be good but a short drive around the lake past Glendhu will take you to Paddock Bay, which offers hectares of clear, shallow water. It can be a superb place to cast to cruising browns over the weed beds. Spinning also works well.

Dublin Bay, in the other direction through Albertown, has similar fishing, though it sometimes gets a hammering since it's close to a popular motor camp. A bit further around on the same road you reach Matukituki Station, part of which you need to pass through to reach the mouth of the Matukituki River. The farm road to the river mouth passes through several gates and over cattle stops. I have only been with a local who has a standing invitation to fish there, but by all accounts permission is easily given if sought. Matukituki Station is in the phone book.

Park beside the narrow suspension bridge, cross over on foot and walk the last few hundred metres to the river mouth. You can wade out to fish over the deep drop-off where the river enters the lake, but take care, as the current is swift and the drop-off steep.

Large rainbows can often be seen smashing smelt along the seam where river and lake waters mix. A fast-sinking line and a smelt fly is the way to go, producing rainbows and salmon, which also patrol the river mouth. Boat fishers do well trolling along the drop-off just wide of the river mouth, also taking salmon and trout.

As well as river-mouth fishing, I've enjoyed productive sight fishing on the small beach to the north of the river. Trout cruise right in close and rainbows often crash bait on the surface in deeper water just within range of a long cast. Green or brown Woolly Buggers or smelt flies have worked for me.

The Matukituki River itself has good fishing, especially at the beginning and end of the spawning run, early and late in the season. Resident trout, brown and rainbow, provide entertaining fishing, rising freely to dry flies at times. The bottom section of the river is braided and the fishing variable, becoming more reliable further up. Even so, like most braided rivers, the larger braids and more stable pools often provide good fishing, especially if there hasn't been recent flooding.

At the other end of Wanaka the Makarora River delta is an obvious target for anglers. It's quite a long drive via Lake Hawea on State Highway 6 but is worth it for the excellent salmon and trout fishing at the mouth. Techniques and flies are similar to the Matukituki mouth. Many shore anglers access the Makarora and other stream mouths and known shore-fishing hotspots by boat since road access is either nonexistent or private.

All of the lake's stream mouths are worth fishing, usually with a sinking line and a lure, or with spinning tackle. Better known locations include Boundary Creek and Wharf Stream on the way to Makarora. Boats can be launched over the beach at both these locations.

The Wilkin River enters the Makarora River a couple of kilometres from the mouth. The Makarora has great wilderness river fishing all the way to its headwaters near Mt Brewster, while the Wilkin is one of the South Island's benchmark rivers. It's beautiful with excellent, though challenging, flyfishing to large, sighted fish in clear water. It also has a run of spawning salmon, which adds another dimension to the fishing. Access is by foot only.

For a totally different river-fishing experience, the Clutha River in and around Albertown has superb fishing for brown and rainbow trout. The river here is wide and deep but there's good bank access and easy fishing from Deans Bank right in Albertown village. Fish can often be spotted, rising fish can be targeted with dry flies, or anglers can fish the deep runs and glides with heavily weighted nymphs, Tongariro style. This section of river is open all year with some of the best fishing in winter, when trout spawn in the margins of the main river. I've enjoyed excellent fishing for running and spawning rainbows in July. There's plenty of river to fish within easy striking distance of Wanaka, so there's no need to feel crowded.

Sadly, the Clutha is badly infected with didymo. It's not always apparent and a fresh seems to flush the worst of it downstream for a time, returning the river to its former glory. However, when it's in bloom, so my Wanaka friend tells me, the river is no longer worth fishing, the algae quickly fouling flies, tippets and fly line. The algae is also present in the lake near the Clutha River inlet but it doesn't appear to form the mats it does in rivers and streams.

Anyone fishing in the Wanaka–Hawea region — or anywhere else in the South Island for that matter — needs to ensure they follow the strict gear cleaning and drying regime recommended by Fish and Game to prevent the further spread of this disastrous organism (see pages 177–178).

Lake Hawea has similar fishing to Wanaka. Salmon and trout can be taken spinning or flyfishing from the beach opposite the motor camp in Hawea village or at Johns Creek in Gladstone in the shadow of lakeside cottages and homes.

All the creek mouths are worth fishing. Better-known ones include Timaru Creek and Dingle Burn on the eastern side of the lake and Dinner Creek and Big Hopwood Burn on the western side.

Further down the Clutha River is an excellent fishery with a totally different character. Lake Dunstan is a long, narrow hydro lake built up behind the Clyde Dam. It has some of the best and most consistent fishing in the region, producing brown and rainbow trout to large sizes.

Visiting anglers should check fishing regulations with Fish and Game New Zealand, Otago Region, 03 477 9076, www.fishandgame.org.nz. Cliff Halford is the local Fish and Game officer, based in Wanaka. His contact number is 03 445 4418. There's also an excellent sports shop in Wanaka where you can tap into local knowledge.

Things to do

In winter the big attraction is the skiing. Wanaka is close to a number of world-class ski fields with terrain and levels of difficulty to suit all skiers and boarders. In summer the ski areas are transformed into mountain bike trails and hiking heaven.

Local walks vary in length and difficulty, from 15 minutes to several hours. The three-hour hike to Diamond Lake is well worth the trouble, and serious trampers can choose any number of tramps of one to four days or longer, all set among New Zealand's most spectacular mountain scenery.

With such an outdoors focus, it's not surprising that Wanaka offers a dazzling range of adventure activities. Some really are restricted to the physically fit but people of all ages can enjoy most activities, including jetboat rides, water sports, kayaking, guided fishing, hunting, horse trekking, motorcycle and ATV riding, heli-skiing, four-wheel-drive tours, mountaineering, mountain biking, tramping, skiing, scenic flights, rafting, rock climbing, hang gliding — if it's done in the outdoors, you can do it in Wanaka.

For a taste of what's available, www.lakewanaka.co.nz is a good place to start looking. If you're after something more sedate, there's plenty on offer: wine and brewery tours, garden and farm tours, museums, cinemas, golf and family fun activities, including interactive museum displays and theme parks. And of course Queenstown is just an hour and a bit down the road . . .

Accommodation

Although Wanaka has gone relentlessly upmarket in recent years, there are still a few reasonably priced places to stay. In general, prices are slightly cheaper than in Queenstown. Wanaka has the usual range of backpackers, camping and budget accommodation, including an excellent campground at Albertown right on the lake beside the Clutha River. It's hard to go past if you're a fisher. The campground is also popular with the campervan set but it's such a big place you can usually find a tree to yourself.

There are three more campgrounds in Wanaka itself (Lakeview, Aspiring and Pleasant Lodge), another at Glendhu and a large campground beside Lake Hawea, set in 5 hectares of grounds. Thirty minutes out of Wanaka on the road to Haast Pass and the West Coast, Makarora Wilderness Resort also has camping facilities. Most of the campgrounds offer cabins or tourist flats and Wanaka also has a number of budget lodges.

If it's a bit more pampering you're after or you're visiting during winter, there are hundreds of apartments, holiday home rentals, homestays, farmstays and B&Bs as well as luxury lodges, hotels, motels and resorts. See www.lakewanaka.co.nz or www.wanaka.com for tourist and accommodation information.

Boat ramps

Good boat ramps service Lake Wanaka at Wanaka township, Glendhu Bay, Camp Waterfall and Wharf Stream, though this last is steep and sometimes covered in loose gravel. Boats can be launched over the beach in other locations but beware of loose gravel and soft sand.

Lake Hawea has boat launching in Hawea (concrete ramp) and at The Neck (beach launching over sand). The lake's water level goes up and down with power generation demands. Water travels from the lake down the Hawea River, which also suffers from fluctuating flows, into the Clutha. Anglers on the Hawea River should take care because river levels can rise quickly. Boat launching is generally easier when the lake level is high.

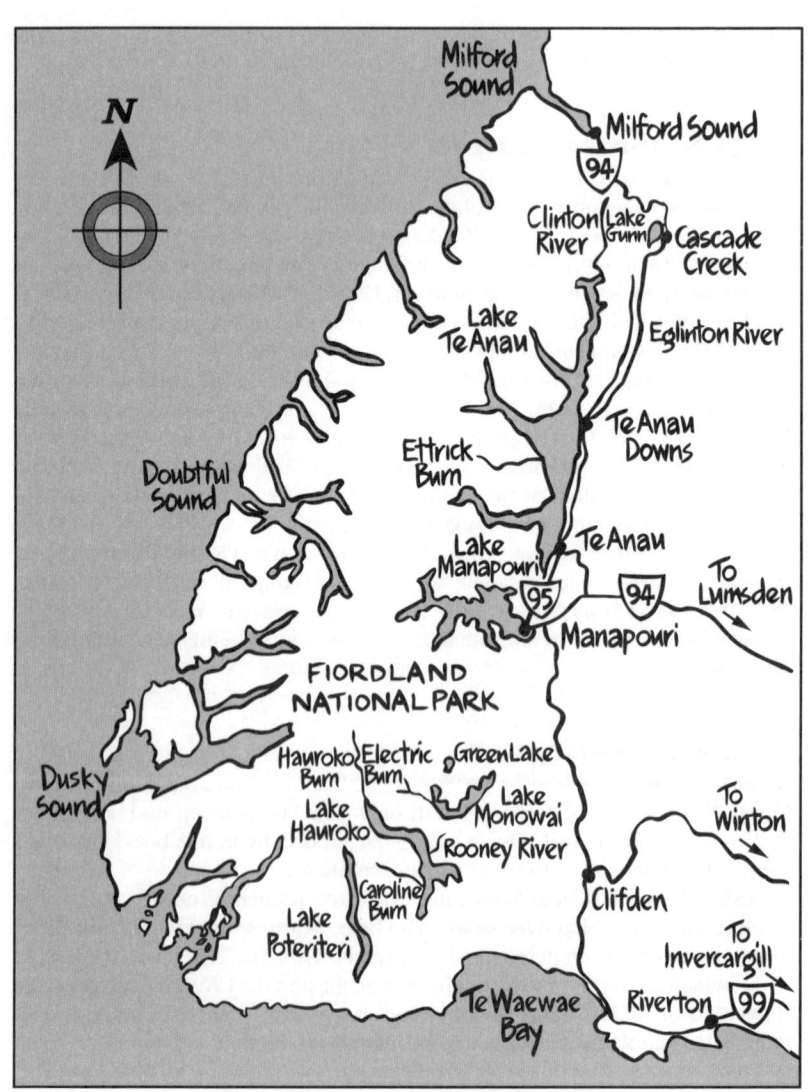

Southern lakes and Fiordland

In such a vast and mostly remote region, it should be no surprise that the fishing opportunities are mind-boggling. There's a lifetime's worth of exploring and fishing in Fiordland alone.

The lakes within Fiordland National Park — Hauroko, Monowai, Manapouri and Te Anau — are all worth fishing, not least for their wilderness qualities.

 The fishing

A boat is needed to access the best fishing, especially on larger lakes such as Te Anau. Lake Poteriteri also has good fishing but access is only by helicopter or foot, or by jetboat from the sea. Lake Hauroko can also be accessed from the sea by jetboat up the Wairaurahiri River — a spectacular trip, not least for the bar crossing at the river mouth.

Lake Te Anau offers salmon as well as brown and rainbow trout. The Eglinton River delta is a great place to target all three species, from the shore by wading or harling from a boat. There is road access from Te Anau Downs but a boat makes things much easier.

A boat is necessary to fish the delta at Ettrick Burn on the western side of Te Anau. Trolling and harling are very productive — lures containing yellow and black colours are especially good.

Rivers running into the lake (and any of the other lakes mentioned here) all offer superb fishing in clear water. The Clinton River at the head of Te Anau's Worsley Arm is a brilliant fishery, passed by thousands of tourists every year walking the Milford Track, which begins here. Few ever stop to fish the river though it has a good head of brown and rainbow trout.

Lake Gunn, on the way to Milford Sound, contains New Zealand's only population of Atlantic salmon. Its outlet at Cascade Creek has some of the highest fish counts per kilometre of any New Zealand river.

Lake Monowai, a contender for the most beautiful lake in New Zealand, contains brown and rainbow trout but no salmon. It is 22 km long, with the best water accessed by boat. The mouth of the Electric River is well worth fishing, from the shore or from a boat, but every stream entering the lake holds fish or attracts fish cruising just offshore.

Lake Hauroko has road access and good fishing in a wilderness setting. It's a big lake with large, hard-fighting brown and rainbow trout. The outlet at the southern end offers good river fishing while the mouths of the Hauroko Burn, Caroline Burn and Rooney River all have good delta fishing. Beware the sandflies!

In addition to the major lakes, virtually every river, stream, tarn and pond has good fishing. Access is generally difficult, meaning most fisheries see little pressure. For the fit and motivated trout angler, Fiordland is a paradise, though the weather is unreliable at best. Bushcraft and well-honed survival instincts are prerequisites to seriously fish the lesser-known waters of the region.

Fiordland's famous fiords or sounds are glacier-cut valleys open to the sea. Further inland these valleys have become lakes, including Te Anau, Wakatipu and Wanaka.

Like these lakes, the fiords offer spectacular fishing in water that is usually sheltered — an important consideration on such a wild coast. Isolation is a feature of the whole of Fiordland; only Milford Sound has road access (via the Homer Tunnel) so boats exploring the fiords usually launch here. Many adventurous Southlanders trail their boats to Milford and then hop from sound to sound down the coast.

But such adventures are not to be undertaken lightly. Great care needs to be exercised when leaving the protection of the fiords — huge seas are often encountered and boats are far from help should anything go wrong. It is also possible to access the fiords from the south coast but it's a long way to travel in a small boat.

Many fishers visit Doubtful Sound, flying in by helicopter to the floating hostelry moored at its head or landing on the deck of one of the sound's resident charter boats. Charter launches offer wonderful diving, fishing and hunting adventures, often exploring well beyond Milford and Dusky sounds.

Each sound is so vast there is usually plenty of good fishing and diving without the need to venture outside. Common catches include XOS blue cod, trumpeter and hapuku, often from very shallow water, thanks to a layer of coloured freshwater lying atop denser saltwater, blocking sunlight and fooling deep-water fish into living in the shallows. It's quite a buzz to hook good-sized hapuku from 25 or 30 m of water, though to be fair such fishing has become rare in the more visited areas. Large parts of the fiords are now gazetted as marine parks. Local operators are well aware of the boundaries but independent visitors need to familiarise themselves with them before fishing.

Outside the sounds, excellent deep-water fishing is possible right in the mouth of most of the sounds. Up and down the coast, the summer to autumn run of southern bluefin and albacore tuna also attracts recreational and commercial fishers. At times large tuna come right into the sounds, and anglers can also catch unusual species such as butterfly tuna, seldom caught anywhere else in New Zealand.

 Things to do

Fiordland is the country's largest national park, which has World Heritage status. Bird watching in the park is especially good, with a wide range of rare bird species around.

Diving in Fiordland is world-class. In the fiords the adventurous diver can see deep-water fish such as hapuku in shallow water under a layer of tannin-stained freshwater that blocks off much of the sunlight. Also present are stands of Fiordland's famous black coral, also in shallow water.

There are now several marine reserves and voluntary protection areas within the fiords. Divers intending to forage should ensure they know which areas are out of bounds. Check out www.fish.govt.nz, and click on 'recreational' for the southern region for information on regulations and reserves.

Lake Te Anau has spectacular mountain and bush scenery. Its northern end is the stepping-off point for the Milford Track, one of the world's great walks.

See www.venturesouthland.co.nz, www.tourism.net.nz/region/southland and www.visit.southlandnz.com.

🛋 Accommodation

Fiordland is one of New Zealand's most popular tourist destinations, so there are plenty of places to stay. Most, however, are concentrated in Milford or Te Anau; and other lakes such as Hauroko. Manapouri and Monowai offer more limited options. Lakes Te Anau and Milford are well served with backpackers, lodges, some to motel standard. Lake Manapouri also has at least three. There are motels available in Milford, Te Anau, Te Anau Downs and Manapouri, along with luxury hotels (in Te Anau and Milford), assorted lodges and self-contained accommodation. Milford Lodge, at the head of Milford Sound beside the Cleddau River, is accessible only by boat from Milford. It offers a variety of accommodation options and activities.

Holiday houses to rent are available in Manapouri, Te Anau, Te Anau Downs and Milford. There are several motor camps in the region: Te Anau has five and Manapouri three, plus there are a couple of more basic 'wilderness' camp sites — Gunn's Lodge in the Hollyford Valley and Knobs Flat on the Milford–Te Anau highway.

In addition, Fiordland has a network of walking tracks with DOC huts placed strategically along the routes. In some locations, camping is allowed beside the huts, though fuel must be carried and open fires are banned. It can pay to book hut space well ahead, particularly in the peak walking season, and you'll need permits to enter the forest parks. The Department of Conservation website, www.doc.govt.nz, has all the information you'll need to plan accommodation and activities within Fiordland National Park. If you're visiting Te Anau, call into DOC Fiordland National Park Visitor Centre, Lakefront Drive, Te Anau, phone: 03 249 7924 for up-to-date information on walking tracks, hut passes and permits, and current weather forecasts.

🚤 Boat ramps

There are ramps at Lakes Hauroko, Manapouri, Gunn and Te Anau (two), and at Milford Sound. Jetboats can be launched into most of the region's larger rivers.

36

Southland and Stewart Island

My first impression of Southland was one of cold, bleak emptiness. I had flown into Invercargill on business and landed in a chill southerly with persistent rain. The temperature struggled to reach double figures, even though it was March.

Fortunately, such a negative first impression didn't stop me going back. I've now seen Southland in all its glory, in summer and winter, travelled to the lakes and fiords of the northwest and enjoyed superb brown trout fishing in the Mataura River.

The town of Gore straddles the Mataura and proclaims itself the brown trout capital of the world — it has a giant statue of a trout to prove it. Fishing in the Mataura and its tributaries is superb and easily accessible, so it's not an idle boast. Fishers visit the river from all over the world.

Even the city of Invercargill has grown on me, not least because of the incredible hospitality of its residents.

 ## The fishing — Southland

Most of the recreational sea fishing in this area is undertaken from Bluff, where there are good launching facilities, or Riverton, which has a sheltered harbour. There's good fishing up and down the coast, though the best fishing is usually some distance from town. Blue cod are the main catch, along with trumpeter. There's good diving for paua (using snorkel gear only) and crayfish close by, as well as scallops and oysters.

Out in Foveaux Strait the many islands, including Ruapuke, offer both shelter and good fishing. In deeper water, large blue cod, tarakihi, big trumpeter and blue moki are taken; school and porbeagle sharks are common, with mako sharks summer visitors.

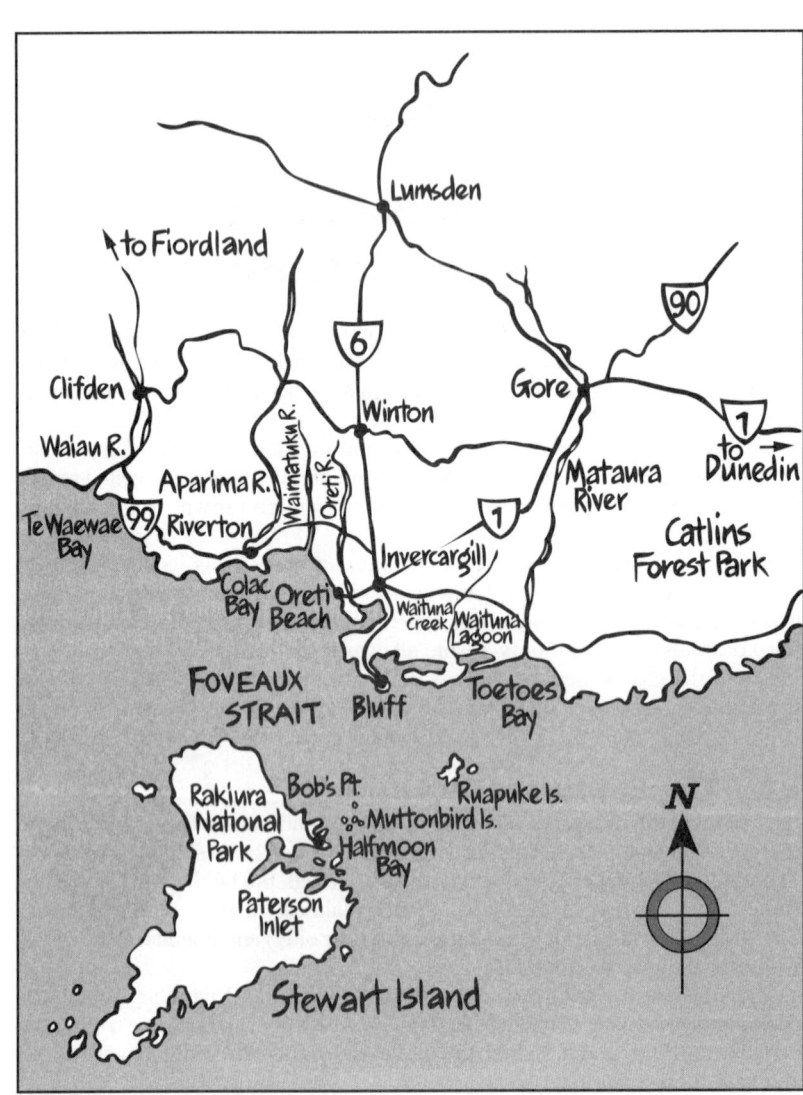

Most fishing is done from drifting boats — shallow water, big swells and sudden rogue waves make anchoring dangerous in all but the calmest of conditions. Locals know the conditions and they almost never anchor in the strait.

For shore-based anglers, there's surfcasting off Oreti and Waituna beaches and at Monkey Island west of Riverton. Beach launching is also possible here in calm conditions.

Beach fishers catch gurnard and rig, with blue cod featuring if there are rocks nearby. Kahawai can be taken in summer and salmon are a regular catch. Other species include school sharks, rays, elephant fish and blue moki, as well as sea-run trout.

All of Southland's many river mouths produce excellent fishing for kahawai and sea-run brown trout. Salmon are also caught. Anglers fish from the beach or, more usually, in the lower reaches of the bigger rivers.

Trout fishers have plenty of flowing water to choose from. The Mataura is the most popular trout stream in the district with arguably the best brown trout fishing in the world. Its mayfly hatches are famous and fishing the evening rise on the Mataura is something every Kiwi trout fisher should try — so many fish but oh so hard to fool!

Most fishers targeting the Mataura use Gore as a base. Some of the best fishing in the river's middle reaches is within easy reach of the town. Further up towards the southern lakes, the Mataura becomes faster and narrower and a little more challenging to fish. In its lower reaches, trout numbers remain high but the river becomes visually less appealing and more difficult to fish as its volume increases. The mouth and tidal reaches have excellent sea-run brown trout fishing. Salmon are always a possibility.

Other lowland rivers of note include the Oreti — close to Invercargill but well endowed with trout and salmon — and the Waituna, which has a lagoon full of fish, including flounder. Very large sea-run trout are caught in the lagoon and the tidal reaches of the lower river, using whole smelt as bait. Saltwater extends 20 km inland on the high tide.

The Oreti is a brown-trout-only river, with clear water and an excellent evening rise. Dry-fly fishing is effective and popular. The upper reaches hold bigger fish but the middle reaches near Winton and Lumsden hold large numbers of smaller trout for entertaining angling.

The little Waimatuku River, not far from Riverton, offers small-stream sight fishing in a lowland setting. The best fishing is in spring.

A bit further west, the Aparima River enters the sea at Riverton, where there's good fishing in the estuary. Upstream, angler access to the river's middle reaches is well marked by signposts.

The lower Waiau River has a good run of salmon and sea trout into its lagoon, with excellent river fishing for 1–2 kg browns and rainbows for 30 km downstream of the Mararoa Weir. Below the confluence with the Monowai River the Waiau becomes too large to easily wade and boat fishing is allowed for the lower 30 km.

The upper Waiau is a much bigger river, draining Lake Te Anau into Manapouri, where most of its flow is diverted for hydroelectric power generation into Deep Cove in Milford Sound. The lower river is a remnant flow, though impressive enough in its lower reaches.

Southland Fish and Game produces a series of excellent pamphlets detailing the fishing, regulations and fishing access in Southland, 03 215 9117 www.fishandgame.org.nz.

 ## The fishing — Stewart Island

Stewart Island is one of New Zealand's last frontiers. The fishing is legendary, even from the town wharf in Oban. Blue cod can be taken off the rocks. Trampers and hunters often carry a handline on the island's many wonderful coastal and bush tracks, stopping off to catch big cod from the rocks where tracks meet the shore.

Boat fishing is exceptional. Many recreational boats make the 22 km crossing from Bluff to cruise Stewart Island, diving and fishing as they go if weather permits. Most of the attention is concentrated on the northern part of the island around Paterson Inlet (parts of which are being targeted for a proposed marine reserve) and the Muttonbird Islands out in the strait. The rest of the island's extensive shoreline sees little recreational fishing pressure. Charters are available from Bluff or with Stewart Island commercial fishers from Oban.

Oyster diving is popular. The area around Bob's Point is part of a commercial exclusion zone and is consequently particularly productive.

 ## Things to do

With so much good fishing, finding time for other activities is difficult. But there are plenty of options in the deep south, beginning in the city of Invercargill.

From shopping to lively cafes, restaurants and bars, Invercargill has all the benefits of city life with few of the drawbacks. Invercargill boasts museums, art galleries and parks, and a short trip takes you to one of the many bush reserves, beaches or gardens on the city's outskirts.

Bluff is close by and well worth the short drive. Try blue cod and chips from the restaurant overlooking the busy port. It's one of the best tastes in the world, especially with a stiff southerly blowing in across Foveaux Strait.

No visit to Bluff is complete without sampling the oysters. In fact you're unlikely to escape this part of the world without eating your fair share, especially during the harvest season, March 1 to August 31. Keen oyster lovers can visit a processing plant to see the little critters being shucked and taste them straight out of the shell. The Bluff Oyster Festival takes place each April, offering an array of Southland seafood, fine wines and entertainment. See www.bluff.co.nz.

Southland offers the usual range of outdoor and adventure activities. The province is also home to New Zealand's newest national park, Rakiura, covering most of Stewart Island.

From Bluff visitors can go whale and seal watching, or diving for the pot in the cold, clear waters of Foveaux Strait in the company of seals — crayfish and paua are abundant.

Only an hour's ferry ride across Foveaux Strait from Bluff lies Stewart Island, one of New Zealand's premier eco-tourism destinations. The island's solitude, stunning scenery, diverse wildlife and the small community of Oban attract travellers from around the world. The island is also offers excellent walks and tramps and whitetail deer hunting. The strait crossing is weather dependent however — Foveaux Strait has some of the roughest water on the New Zealand coast.

Another popular area for eco-tourism is the Catlins region, east of Invercargill. This is a rugged, forested region with spectacular coastal scenery. Much of it is protected within the conservation estate.

This unique area supports populations of yellow-eyed penguins, Hooker's sea lions and Hector's dolphins. Another key feature is the Curio Bay fossil forest, nearly 160 million years old.

Outdoor activities include mountain biking, hiking, tramping and climbing, sailing, kayaking, hunting, horse trekking and much more.

I recommend a drive along the coast towards Tuatapere beside the Waiau River, via Riverton, Colac Bay and Te Waewae Bay. Riverton is an interesting fishing port beside the Jacobs River estuary and the small coastal settlements of Colac Bay and Orepuki are uniquely Southland.

Te Waewae Bay is far enough to the west to be out of Stewart Island's wind shadow. It's a wild and windswept stretch of coast notable for the way its seaside beach houses — cribs in southern parlance — are tucked in behind the dunes for shelter, facing away from the sea. There are no sea views from the lounge in this part of the world! Stunted and tortured trees, their tops bent over and flattened by gales, are a reminder that wind is a constant companion along the coast, but a walk along an empty Southland beach is an experience everyone should enjoy at least once in their lives.

See www.venturesouthland.co.nz, www.tourism.net.nz/region/southland and www.visit.southlandnz.com.

Accommodation

Like most parts of New Zealand, Southland offers a wide selection of accommodation, catering to all budgets. It's particularly well endowed with self-catering motels and the like — ideal for the independent traveller — but there are also luxury options and more specialised sports, eco- and nature lodges. There are plenty of home and farmstay options, most outside the towns, and Gore is well serviced with fisher's accommodation.

Camping is popular but the summer season is shorter in Southland than anywhere else in New Zealand except Stewart Island so it's not surprising that most campgrounds offer comfortable cabins.

Most of the accommodation is clustered around Invercargill but there are places to stay close to most of the region's main attractions, including the Catlins. See www.tourism.net.nz or www.visit.southlandnz.com.

Boat ramps

Close to Invercargill there are two boat ramps at Bluff, two at Awarua Bay inside Bluff Harbour, and at Riverton, Colac Bay, Waituna, Fortrose, Oreti River and Kawakaputa Bay. Boats can also be launched over the beach at Monkey Island and Bluecliffs Beach.

Index